GREEN LANTERN
THE MOVIE PREQUELS

GREEN LANTERN
THE MOVIE PREQUELS

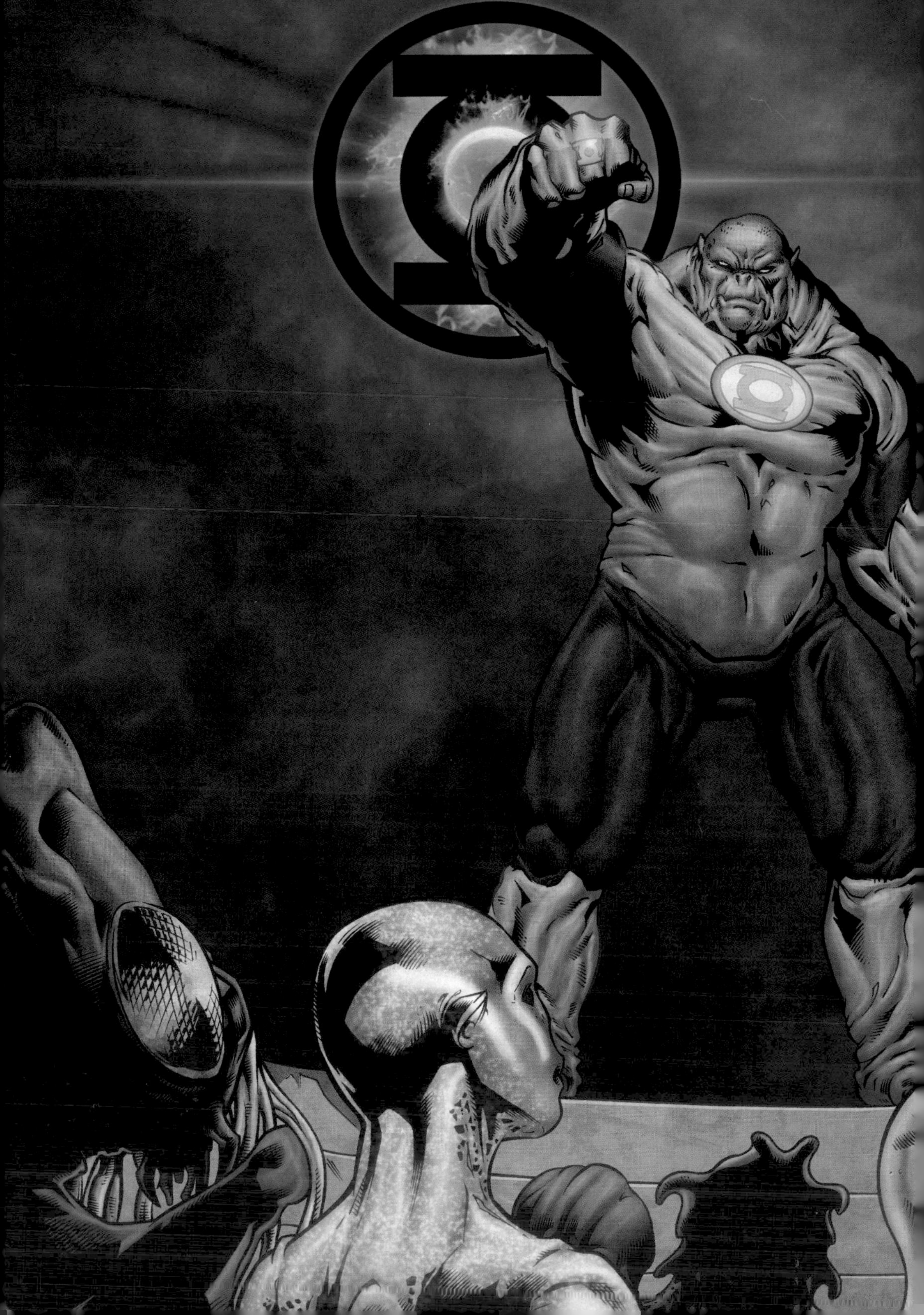

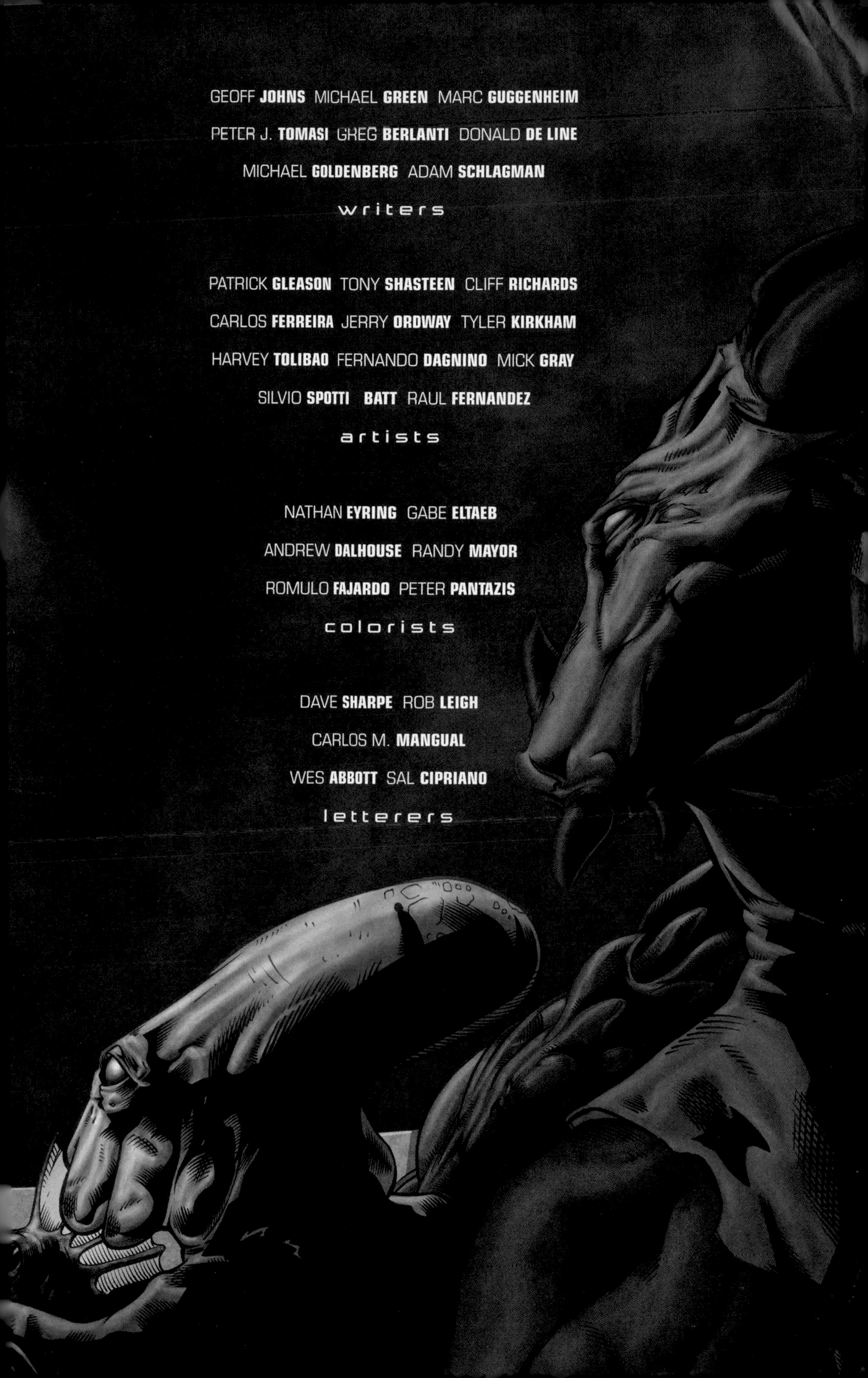

GEOFF **JOHNS** MICHAEL **GREEN** MARC **GUGGENHEIM**

PETER J. **TOMASI** GREG **BERLANTI** DONALD **DE LINE**

MICHAEL **GOLDENBERG** ADAM **SCHLAGMAN**

writers

PATRICK **GLEASON** TONY **SHASTEEN** CLIFF **RICHARDS**

CARLOS **FERREIRA** JERRY **ORDWAY** TYLER **KIRKHAM**

HARVEY **TOLIBAO** FERNANDO **DAGNINO** MICK **GRAY**

SILVIO **SPOTTI** **BATT** RAUL **FERNANDEZ**

artists

NATHAN **EYRING** GABE **ELTAEB**

ANDREW **DALHOUSE** RANDY **MAYOR**

ROMULO **FAJARDO** PETER **PANTAZIS**

colorists

DAVE **SHARPE** ROB **LEIGH**

CARLOS M. **MANGUAL**

WES **ABBOTT** SAL **CIPRIANO**

letterers

EDDIE BERGANZA EDITOR – ORIGINAL SERIES
SEAN MACKIEWICZ ASSISTANT EDITOR – ORIGINAL SERIES
IAN SATTLER DIRECTOR EDITORIAL, SPECIAL PROJECTS AND ARCHIVAL EDITIONS
ROBBIN BROSTERMAN DESIGN DIRECTOR – BOOKS
ROBBIE BIEDERMAN PUBLICATION DESIGN

EDDIE BERGANZA EXECUTIVE EDITOR
BOB HARRAS VP – EDITOR IN CHIEF

DIANE NELSON PRESIDENT
DAN DIDIO AND **JIM LEE** CO-PUBLISHERS
GEOFF JOHNS CHIEF CREATIVE OFFICER
JOHN ROOD EXECUTIVE VP – SALES, MARKETING AND BUSINESS DEVELOPMENT
AMY GENKINS SENIOR VP – BUSINESS AND LEGAL AFFAIRS
NAIRI GARDINER SENIOR VP – FINANCE
JEFF BOISON VP – PUBLISHING OPERATIONS
MARK CHIARELLO VP – ART DIRECTION AND DESIGN
JOHN CUNNINGHAM VP – MARKETING
TERRI CUNNINGHAM VP – TALENT RELATIONS AND SERVICES
ALISON GILL SENIOR VP – MANUFACTURING AND OPERATIONS
DAVID HYDE VP – PUBLICITY
HANK KANALZ SENIOR VP – DIGITAL
JAY KOGAN VP – BUSINESS AND LEGAL AFFAIRS, PUBLISHING
JACK MAHAN VP – BUSINESS AFFAIRS, TALENT
NICK NAPOLITANO VP – MANUFACTURING ADMINISTRATION
SUE POHJA VP – BOOK SALES
COURTNEY SIMMONS SENIOR VP – PUBLICITY
BOB WAYNE SENIOR VP – SALES

GREEN LANTERN – THE MOVIE PREQUELS

DC COMICS, 1700 BROADWAY, NEW YORK, NY 10019. A WARNER BROS. ENTERTAINMENT COMPANY
PRINTED BY RR DONNELLEY, SALEM, VA, USA. 9/9/11. FIRST PRINTING.
ISBN: 978-1-4012-3313-6

SUSTAINABLE
FORESTRY
INITIATIVE
Certified Chain of Custody
Promoting Sustainable
Forest Management
www.sfiprogram.org

Fiber used in this product line meets the
sourcing requirements of the SFI program.
www.sfiprogram.org SGS-SFI/COC-US10/81072

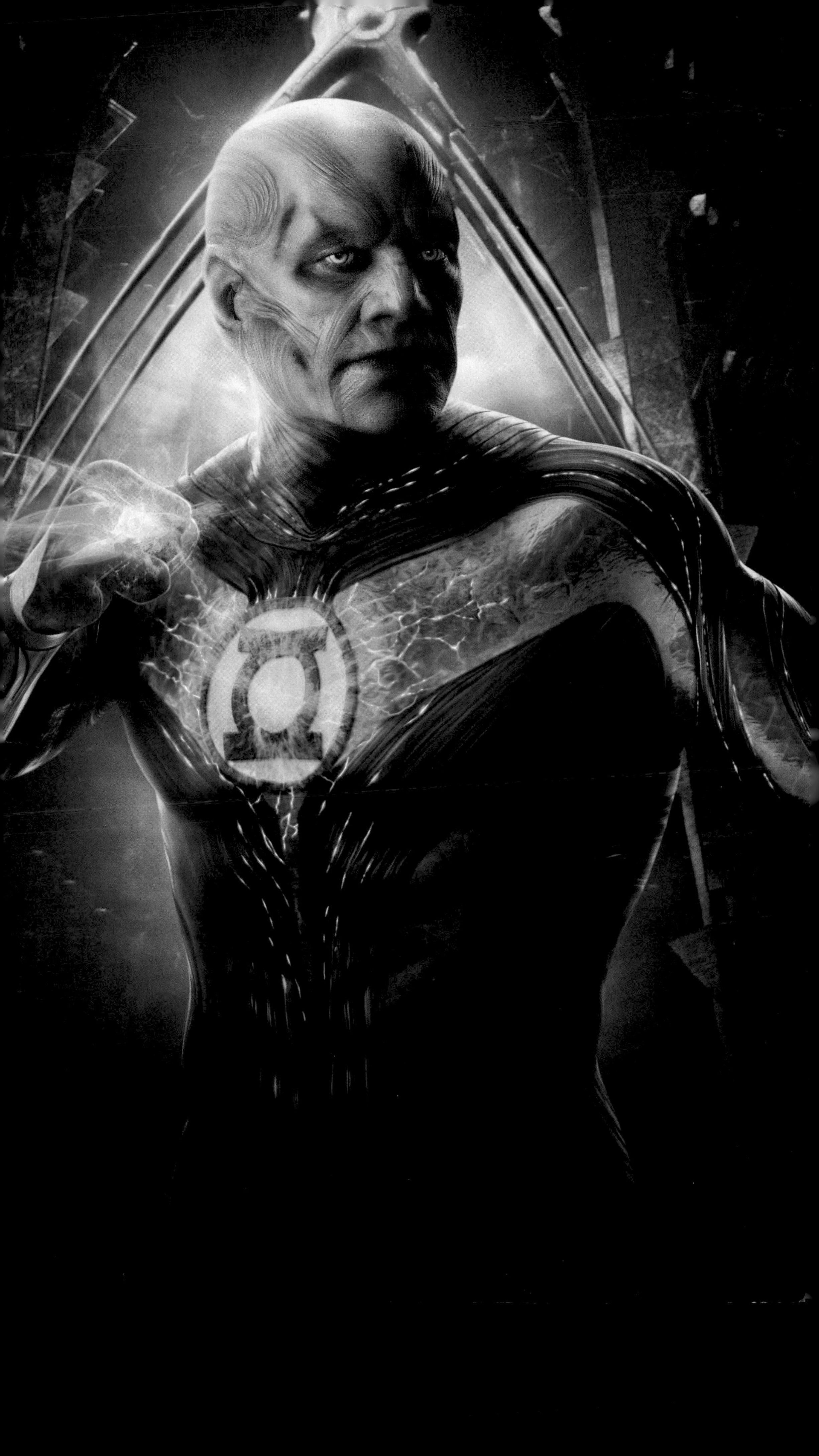

A SMALL, UNREMARKABLE PLANET

MICHAEL **GREEN** writer

PATRICK **GLEASON** & TONY **SHASTEEN** pencillers

MICK **GRAY** & TONY **SHASTEEN** inkers

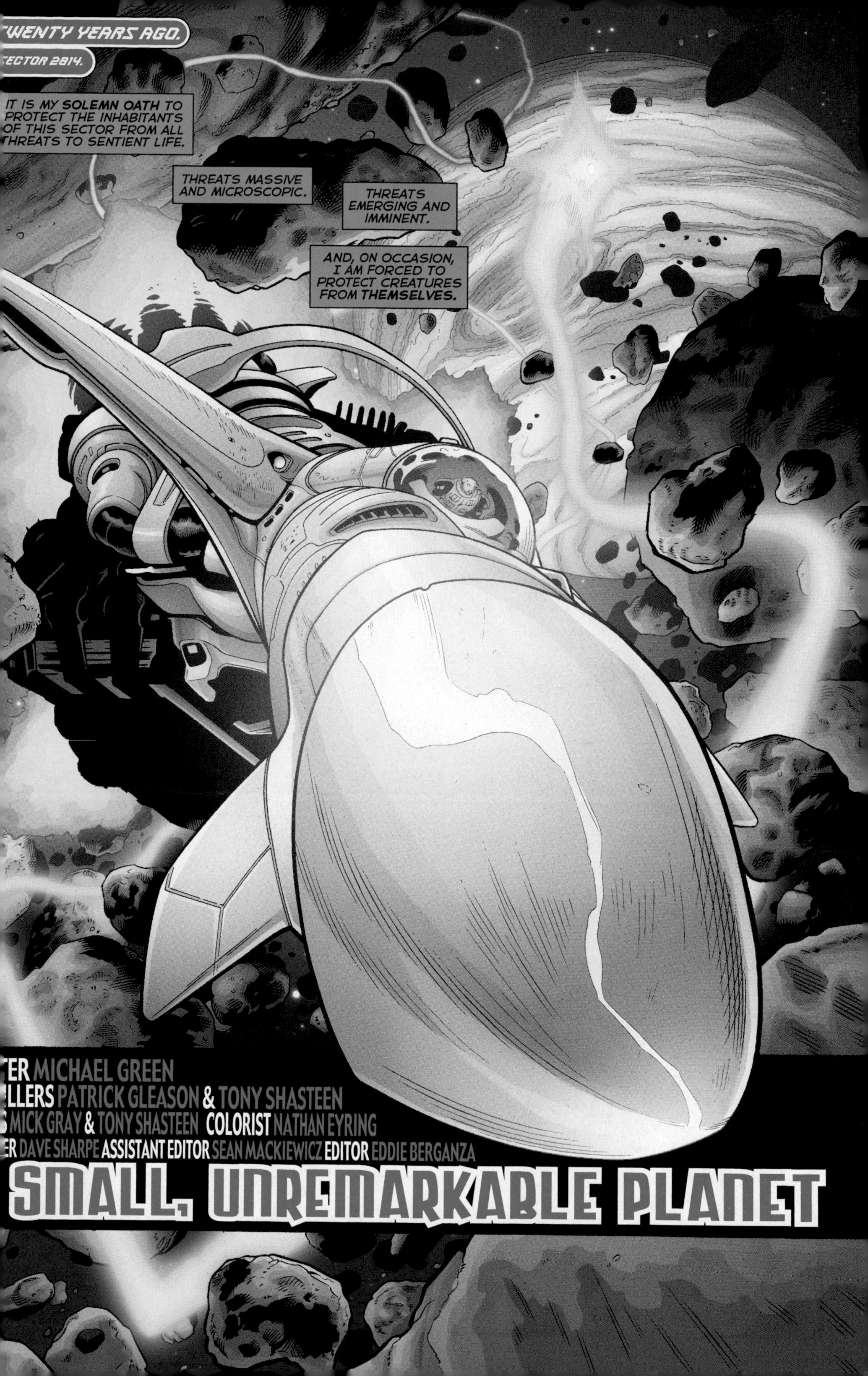
TWENTY YEARS AGO.
SECTOR 2814.
IT IS MY SOLEMN OATH TO PROTECT THE INHABITANTS OF THIS SECTOR FROM ALL THREATS TO SENTIENT LIFE.
THREATS MASSIVE AND MICROSCOPIC.
THREATS EMERGING AND IMMINENT.
AND, ON OCCASION, I AM FORCED TO PROTECT CREATURES FROM THEMSELVES.
ER MICHAEL GREEN
LLERS PATRICK GLEASON & TONY SHASTEEN
MICK GRAY & TONY SHASTEEN COLORIST NATHAN EYRING
ER DAVE SHARPE ASSISTANT EDITOR SEAN MACKIEWICZ EDITOR EDDIE BERGANZA
SMALL, UNREMARKABLE PLANET

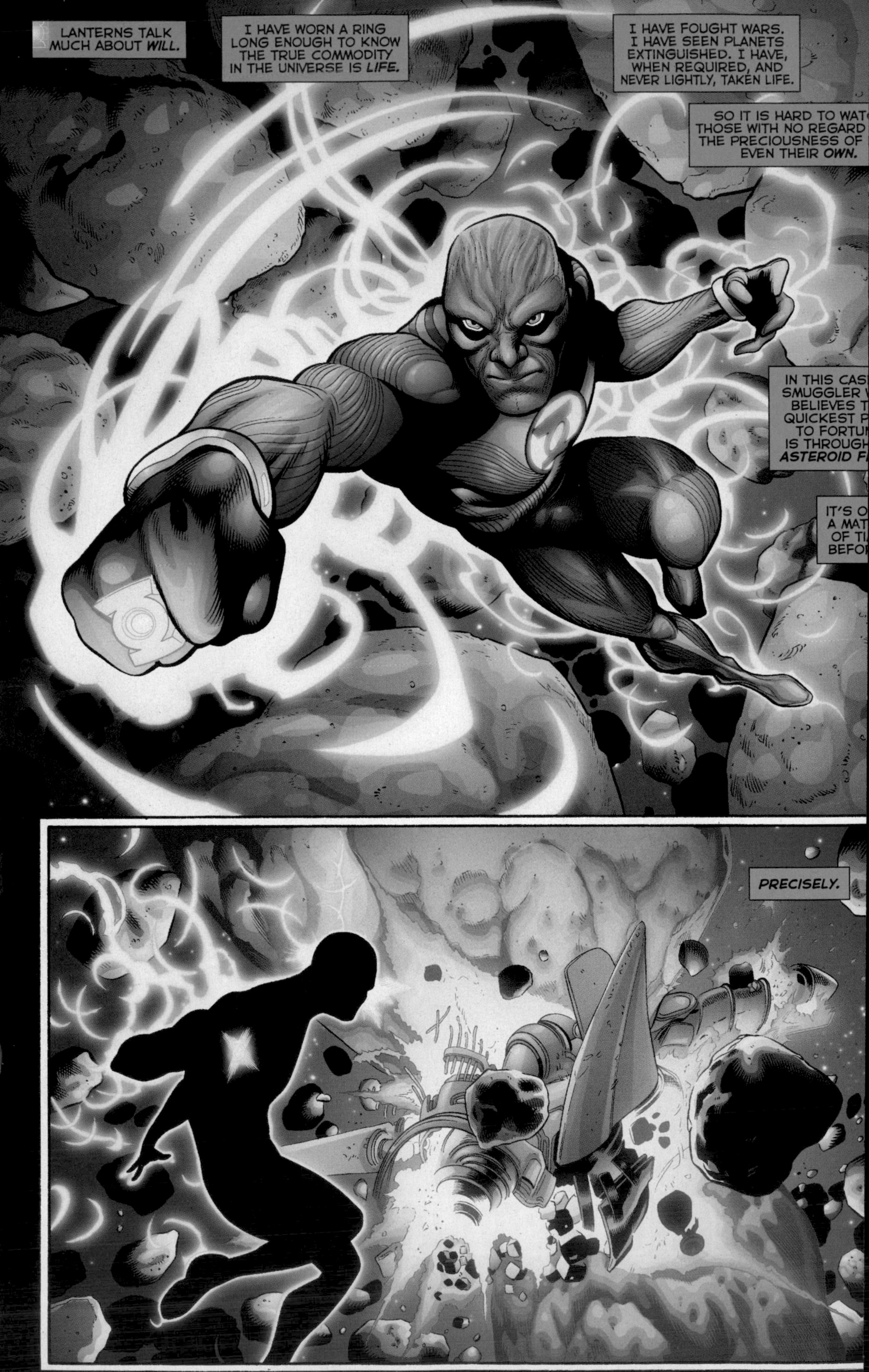
LANTERNS TALK MUCH ABOUT *WILL.*
I HAVE WORN A RING LONG ENOUGH TO KNOW THE TRUE COMMODITY IN THE UNIVERSE IS *LIFE.*
I HAVE FOUGHT WARS. I HAVE SEEN PLANETS EXTINGUISHED. I HAVE, WHEN REQUIRED, AND NEVER LIGHTLY, TAKEN LIFE.
SO IT IS HARD TO WATC
THOSE WITH NO REGARD
THE PRECIOUSNESS OF
EVEN THEIR *OWN.*
IN THIS CAS
SMUGGLER W
BELIEVES T
QUICKEST P
TO FORTUN
IS THROUGH
ASTEROID F
IT'S O
A MAT
OF TI
BEFOR
PRECISELY.

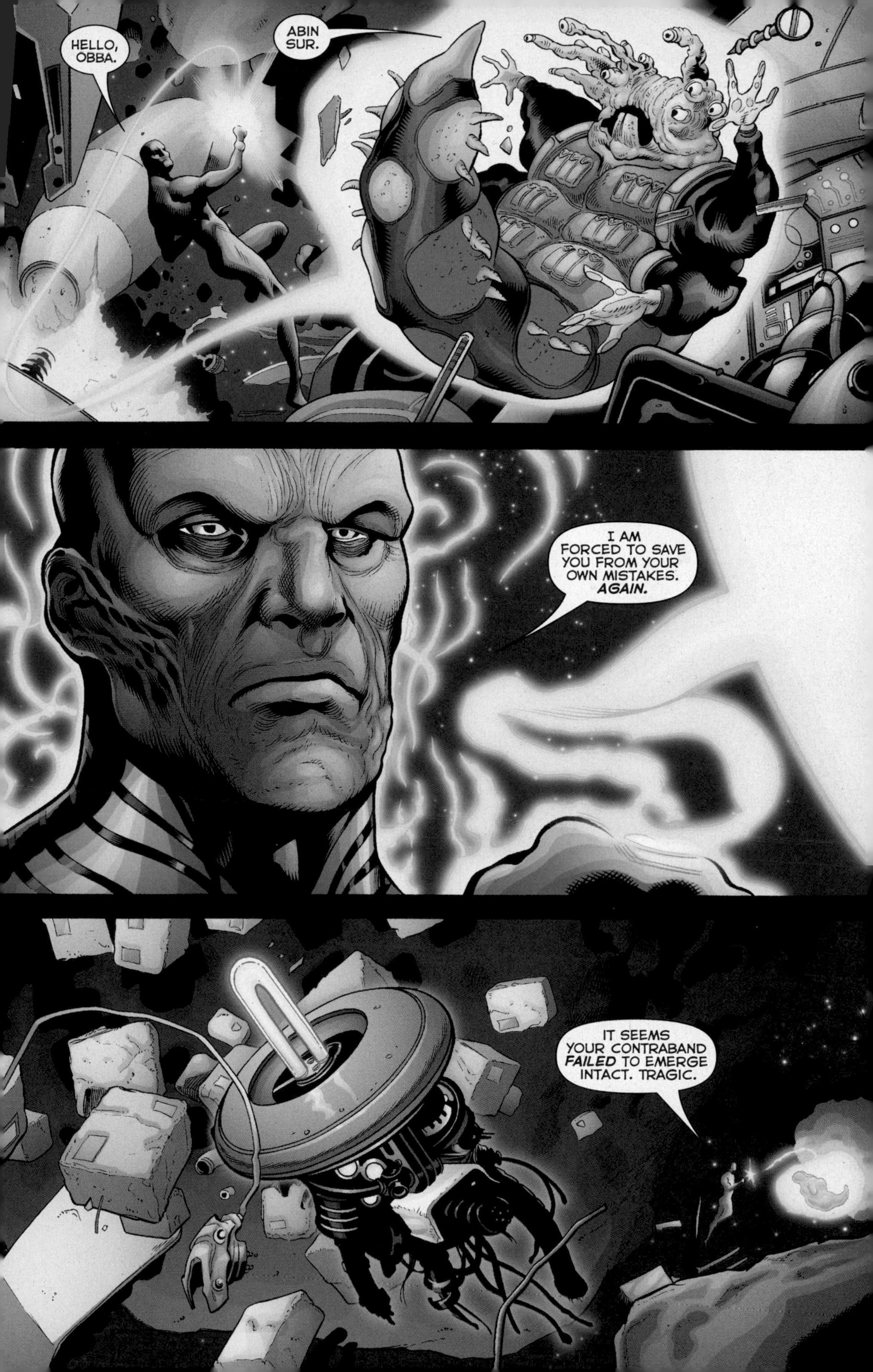
HELLO, OBBA.
ABIN SUR.
I AM FORCED TO SAVE YOU FROM YOUR OWN MISTAKES. AGAIN.
IT SEEMS YOUR CONTRABAND FAILED TO EMERGE INTACT. TRAGIC.

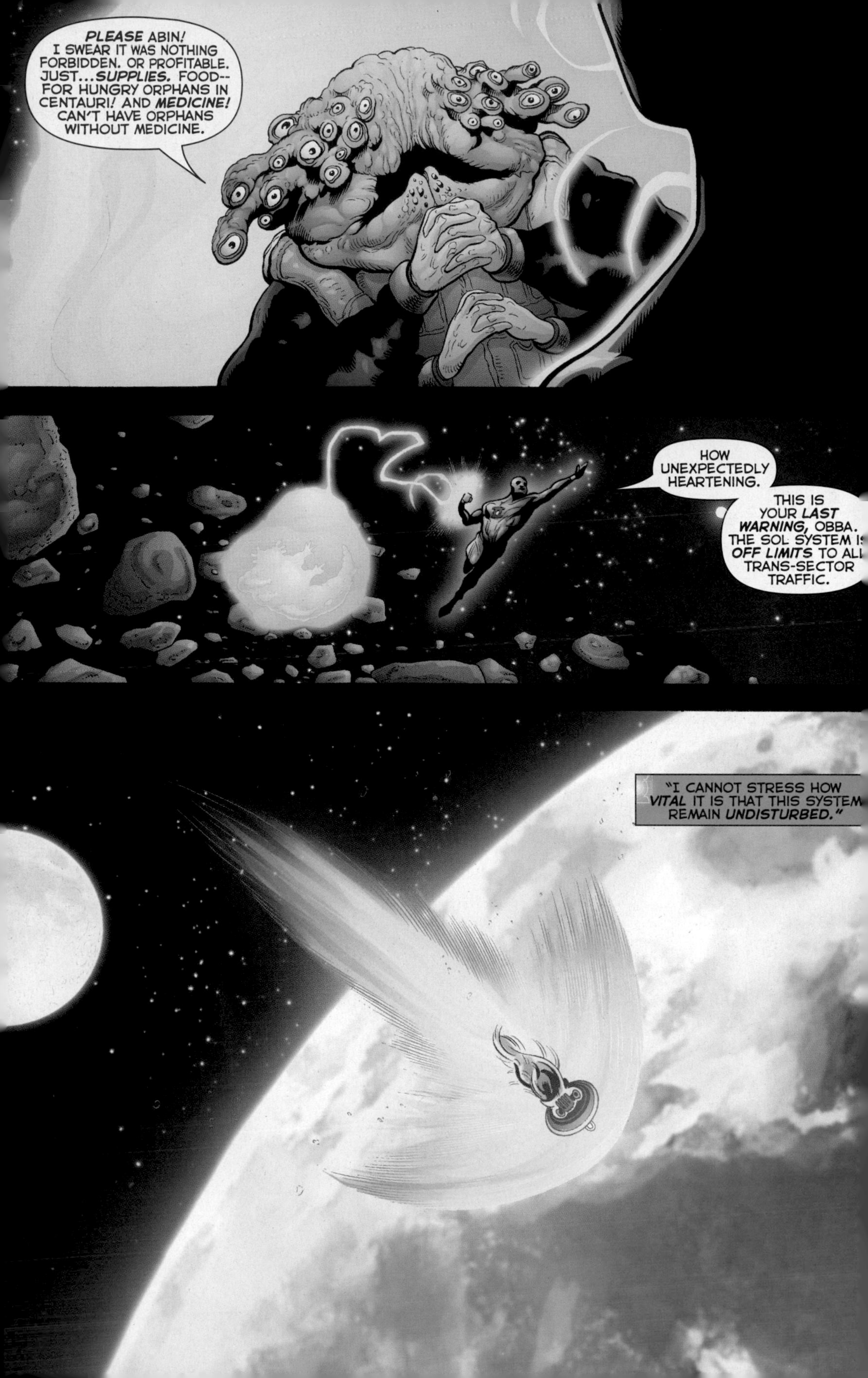
PLEASE ABIN! I SWEAR IT WAS NOTHING FORBIDDEN. OR PROFITABLE. JUST...SUPPLIES. FOOD--FOR HUNGRY ORPHANS IN CENTAURI! AND MEDICINE! CAN'T HAVE ORPHANS WITHOUT MEDICINE.
HOW UNEXPECTEDLY HEARTENING.
THIS IS YOUR LAST WARNING, OBBA. THE SOL SYSTEM IS OFF LIMITS TO ALL TRANS-SECTOR TRAFFIC.
"I CANNOT STRESS HOW VITAL IT IS THAT THIS SYSTEM REMAIN UNDISTURBED."

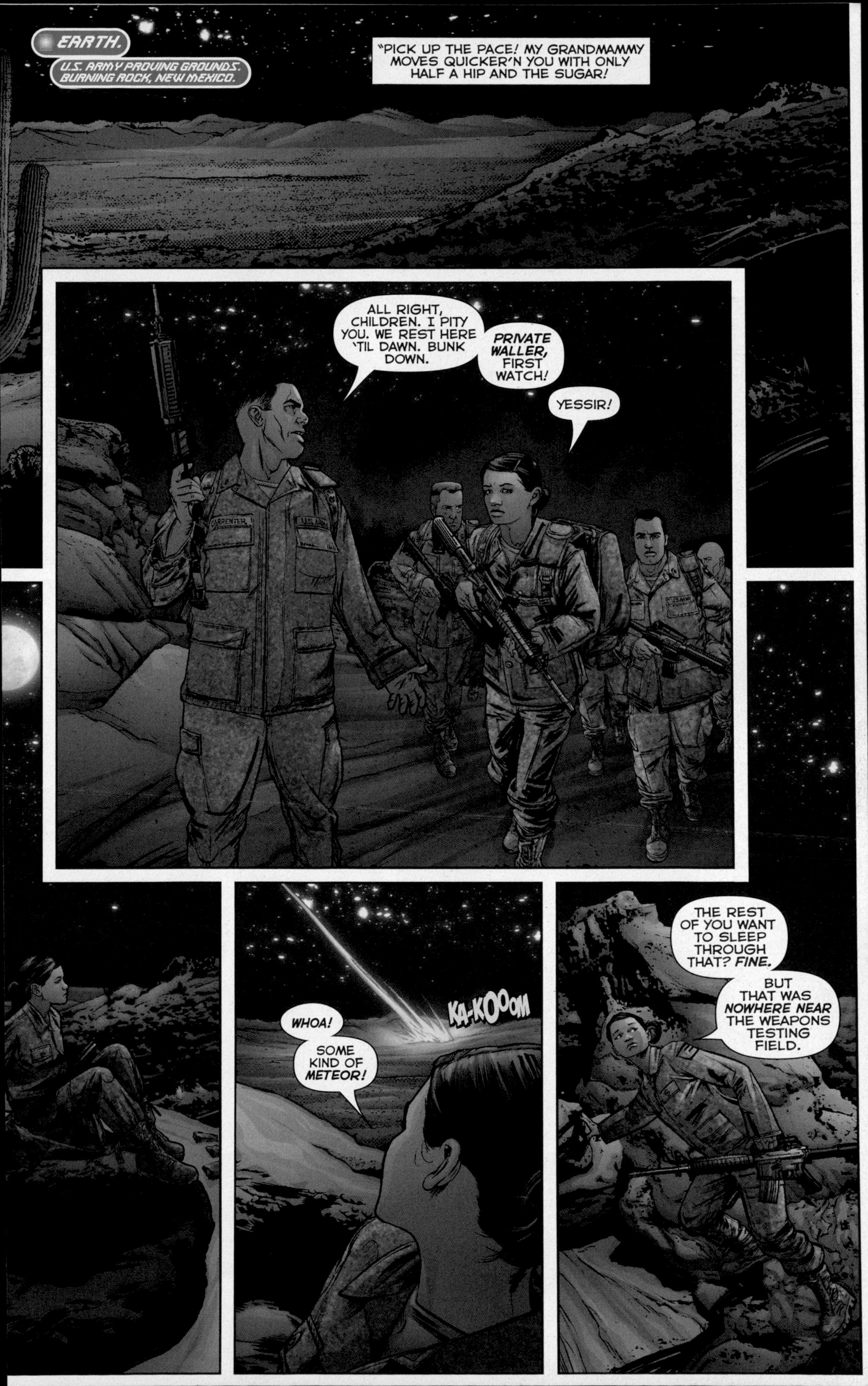
EARTH.
U.S. ARMY PROVING GROUNDS. BURNING ROCK, NEW MEXICO.
"PICK UP THE PACE! MY GRANDMAMMY MOVES QUICKER'N YOU WITH ONLY HALF A HIP AND THE SUGAR!
ALL RIGHT, CHILDREN. I PITY YOU. WE REST HERE 'TIL DAWN. BUNK DOWN.
PRIVATE WALLER, FIRST WATCH!
YESSIR!
CARPENTER
U.S. ARMY
WHOA!
SOME KIND OF METEOR!
KA-KOOOM
THE REST OF YOU WANT TO SLEEP THROUGH THAT? FINE.
BUT THAT WAS NOWHERE NEAR THE WEAPONS TESTING FIELD.

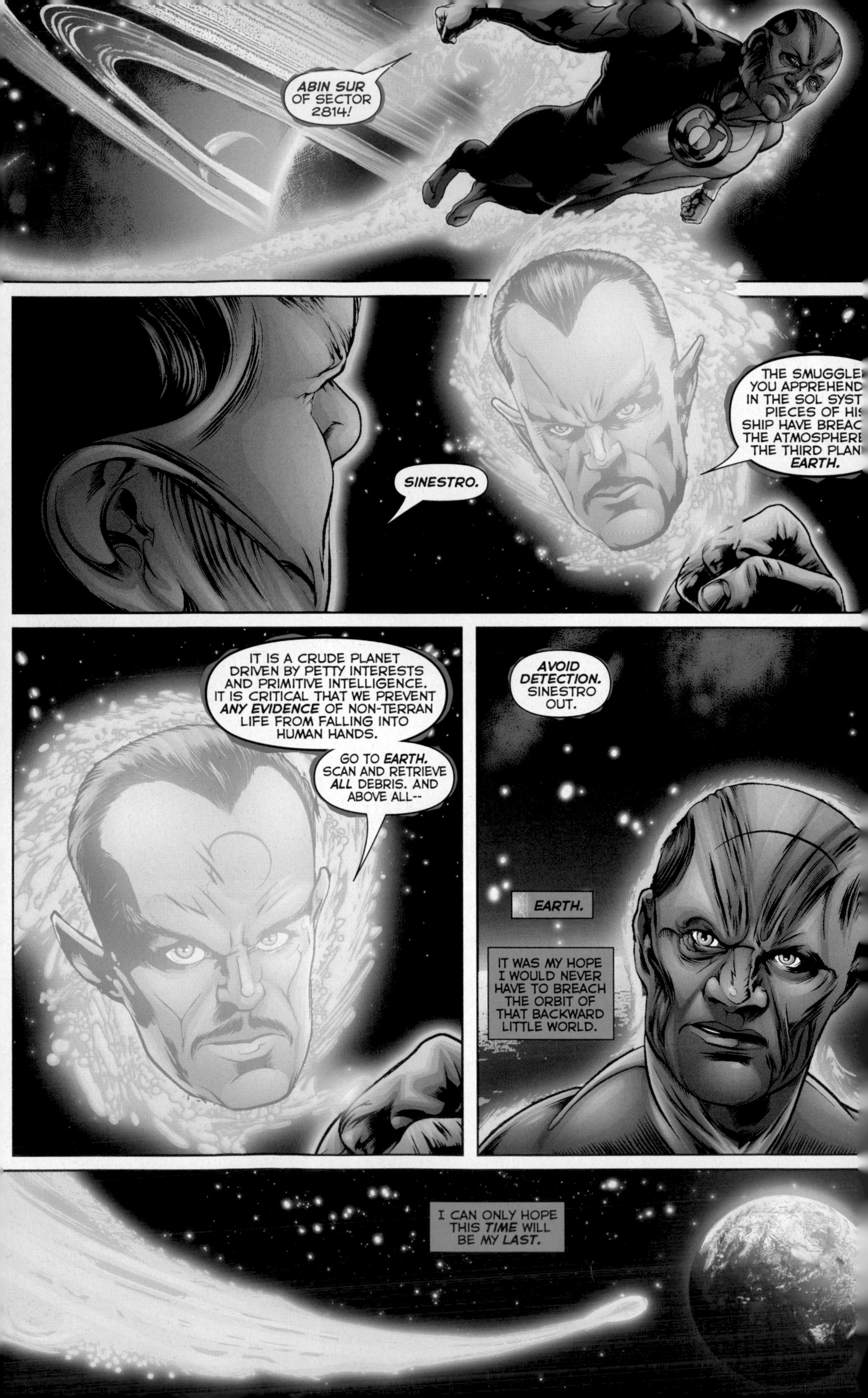
ABIN SUR OF SECTOR 2814!
SINESTRO.
THE SMUGGLE YOU APPREHEND IN THE SOL SYST PIECES OF HIS SHIP HAVE BREAC THE ATMOSPHERE THE THIRD PLAN EARTH.
IT IS A CRUDE PLANET DRIVEN BY PETTY INTERESTS AND PRIMITIVE INTELLIGENCE. IT IS CRITICAL THAT WE PREVENT ANY EVIDENCE OF NON-TERRAN LIFE FROM FALLING INTO HUMAN HANDS.
GO TO EARTH. SCAN AND RETRIEVE ALL DEBRIS. AND ABOVE ALL--
AVOID DETECTION. SINESTRO OUT.
EARTH.
IT WAS MY HOPE I WOULD NEVER HAVE TO BREACH THE ORBIT OF THAT BACKWARD LITTLE WORLD.
I CAN ONLY HOPE THIS TIME WILL BE MY LAST.

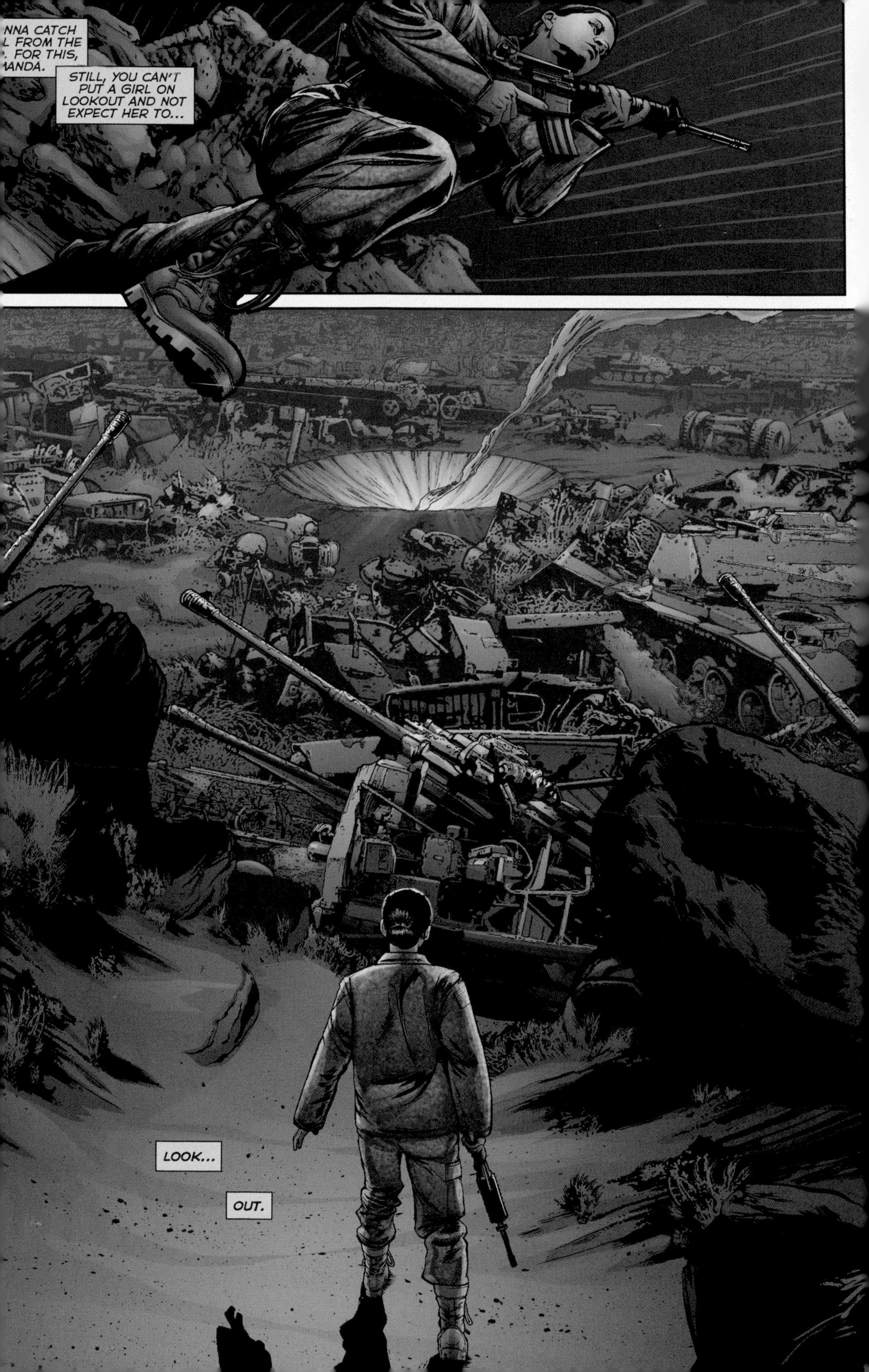
NNA CATCH
L FROM THE
. FOR THIS,
MANDA.
STILL, YOU CAN'T PUT A GIRL ON LOOKOUT AND NOT EXPECT HER TO...
LOOK...
OUT.

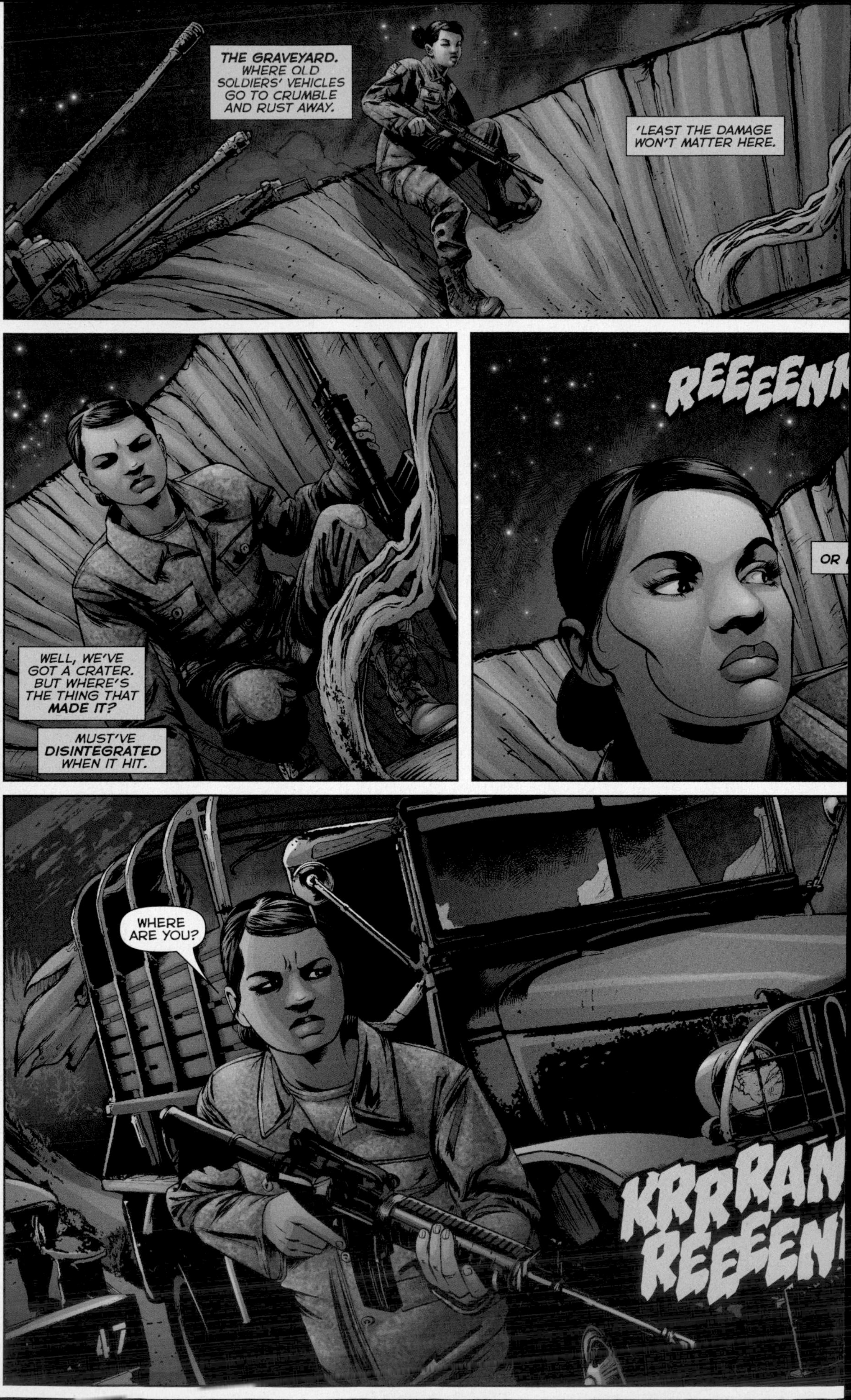

THE GRAVEYARD. WHERE OLD SOLDIERS' VEHICLES GO TO CRUMBLE AND RUST AWAY.
'LEAST THE DAMAGE WON'T MATTER HERE.
WELL, WE'VE GOT A CRATER. BUT WHERE'S THE THING THAT MADE IT?
MUST'VE DISINTEGRATED WHEN IT HIT.
REEEEEN
OR
WHERE ARE YOU?
KRRRAN
REEEEN
47

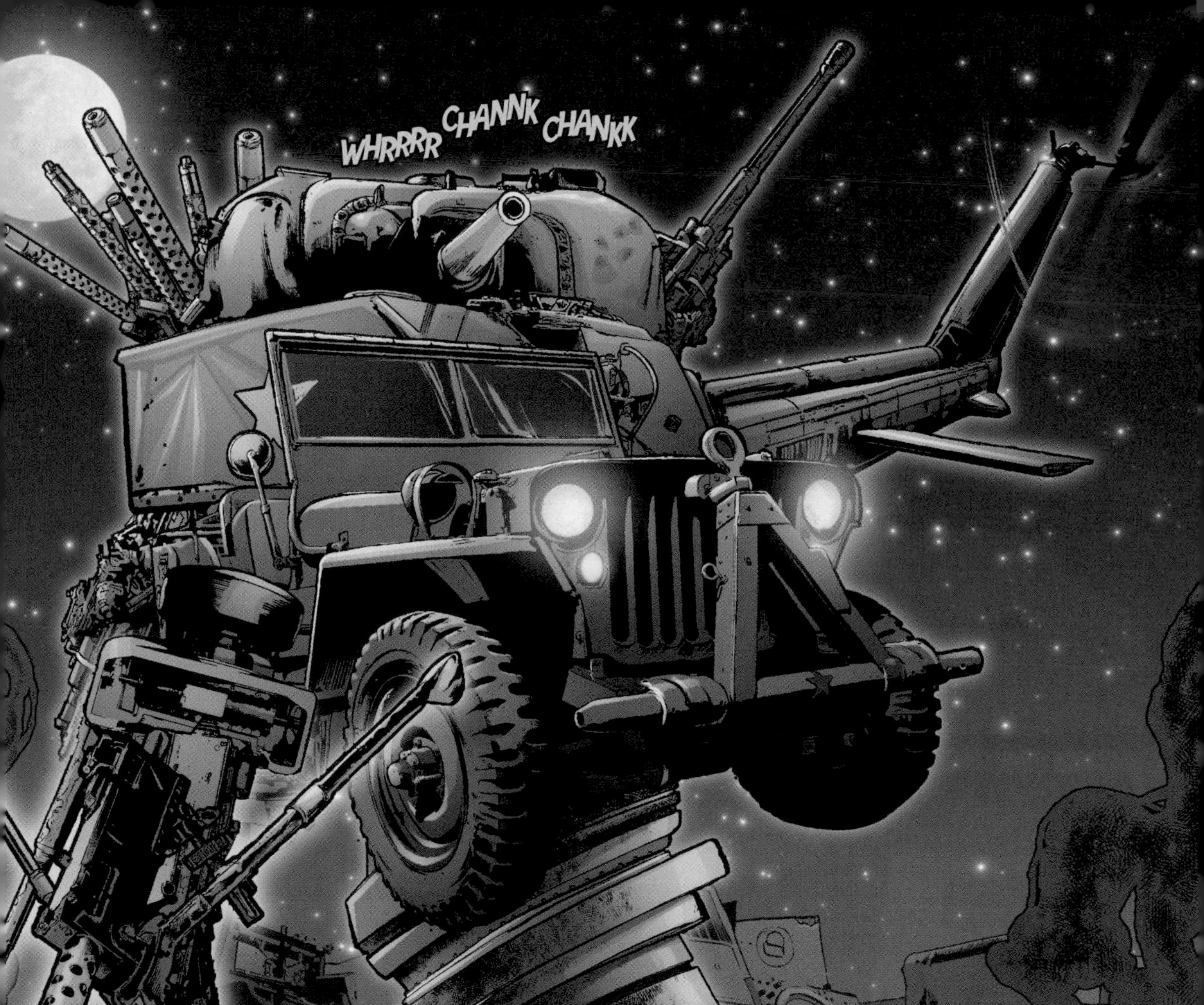
WHRRRR CHANNK CHANKK
OKAAAY...

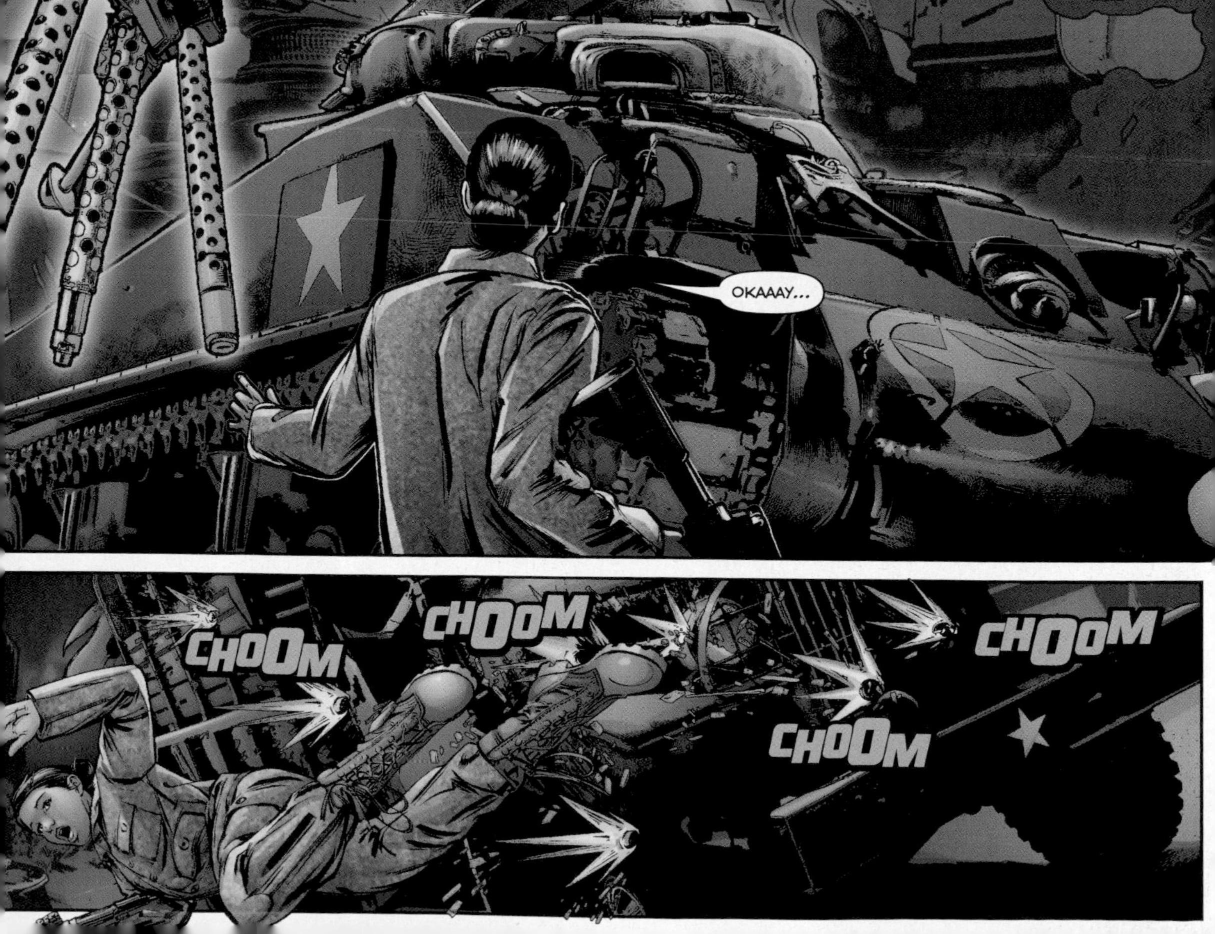
CHOOM
CHOOM
CHOOM
CHOOM

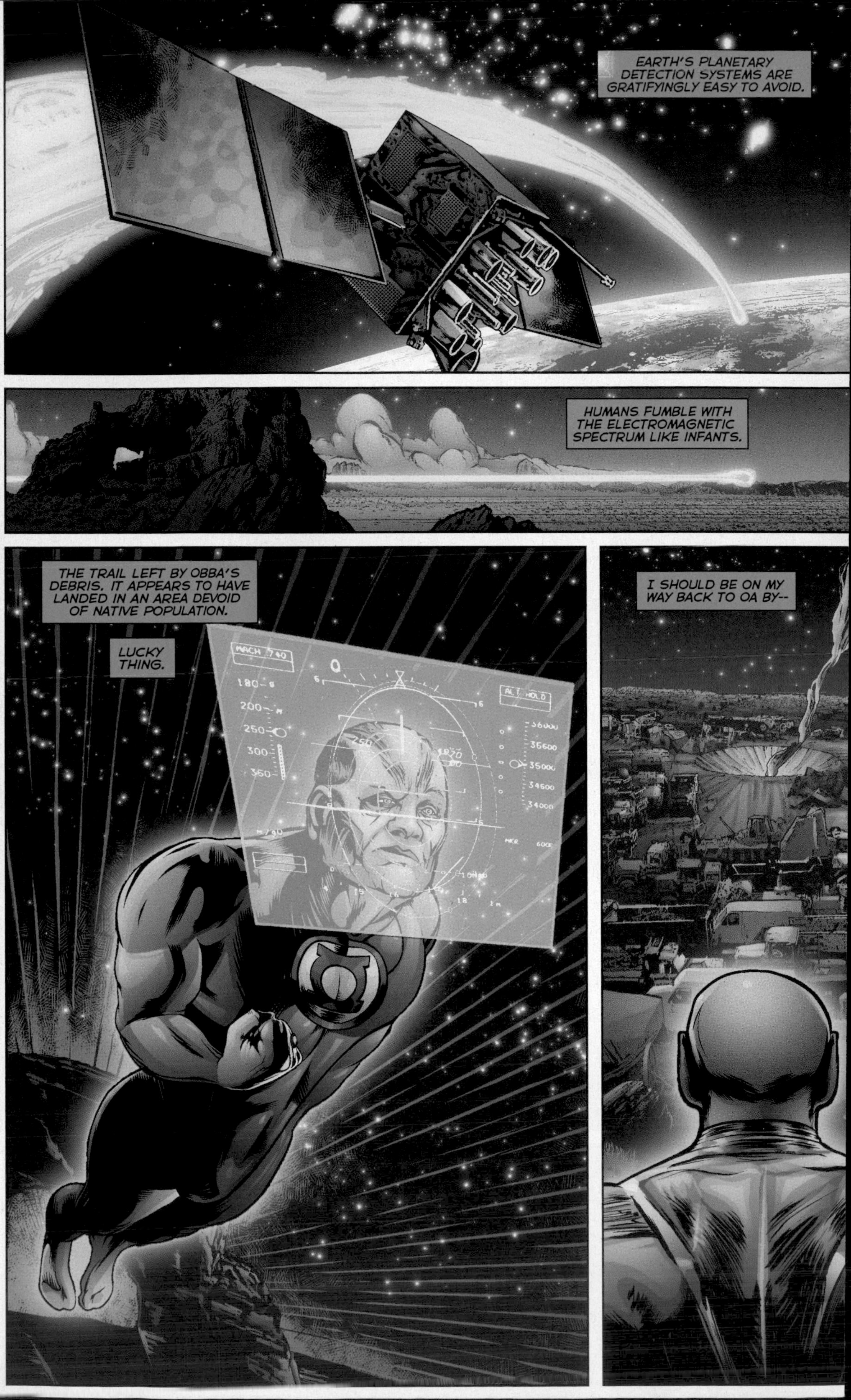
EARTH'S PLANETARY DETECTION SYSTEMS ARE GRATIFYINGLY EASY TO AVOID.
HUMANS FUMBLE WITH THE ELECTROMAGNETIC SPECTRUM LIKE INFANTS.
THE TRAIL LEFT BY OBBA'S DEBRIS. IT APPEARS TO HAVE LANDED IN AN AREA DEVOID OF NATIVE POPULATION.
LUCKY THING.
I SHOULD BE ON MY WAY BACK TO OA BY--

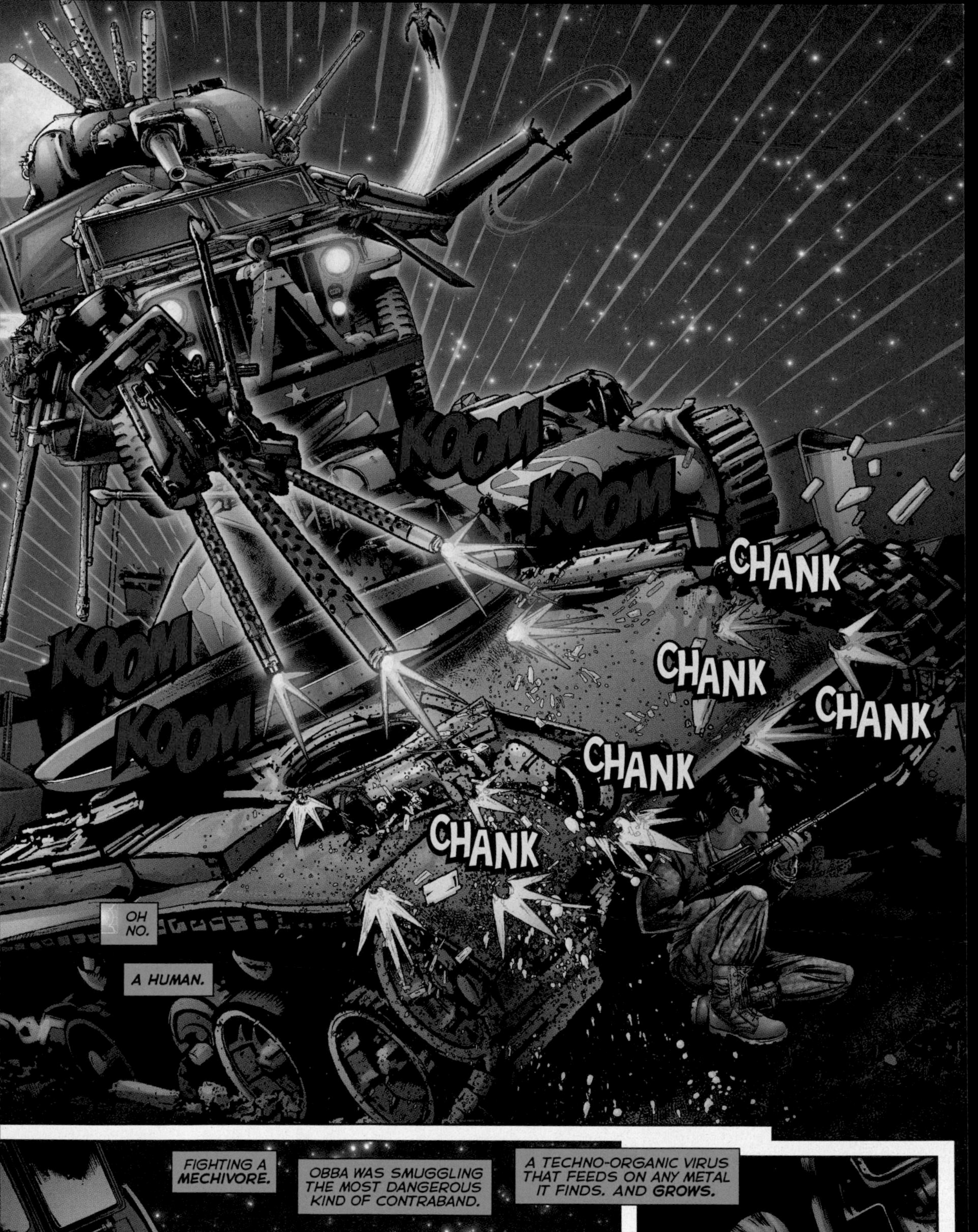
KOOM
KOOM
KOOM
KOOM
CHANK
CHANK
CHANK
CHANK
CHANK
OH NO.
A HUMAN.

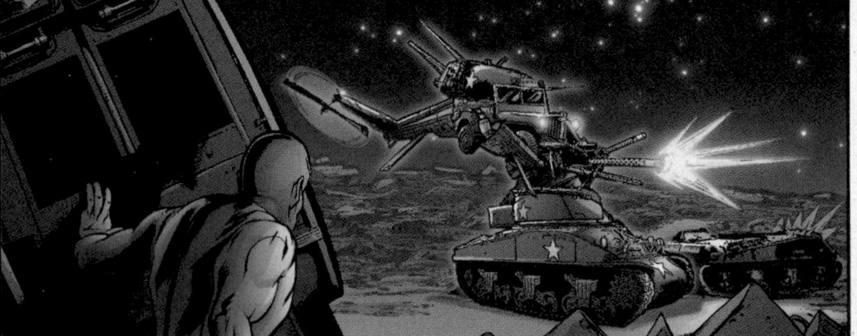
FIGHTING A MECHIVORE.
OBBA WAS SMUGGLING THE MOST DANGEROUS KIND OF CONTRABAND.
A TECHNO-ORGANIC VIRUS THAT FEEDS ON ANY METAL IT FINDS. AND GROWS.

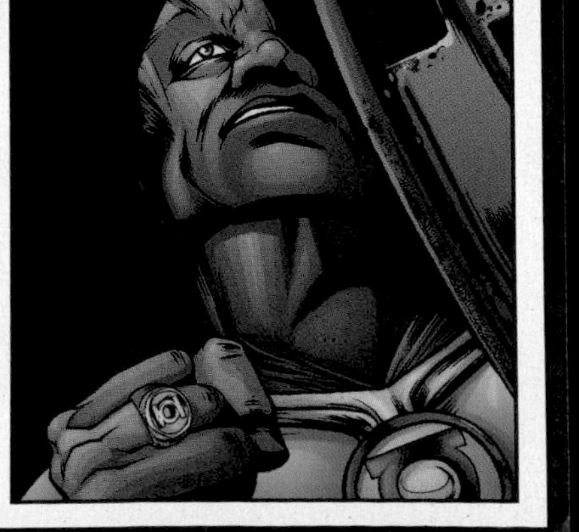

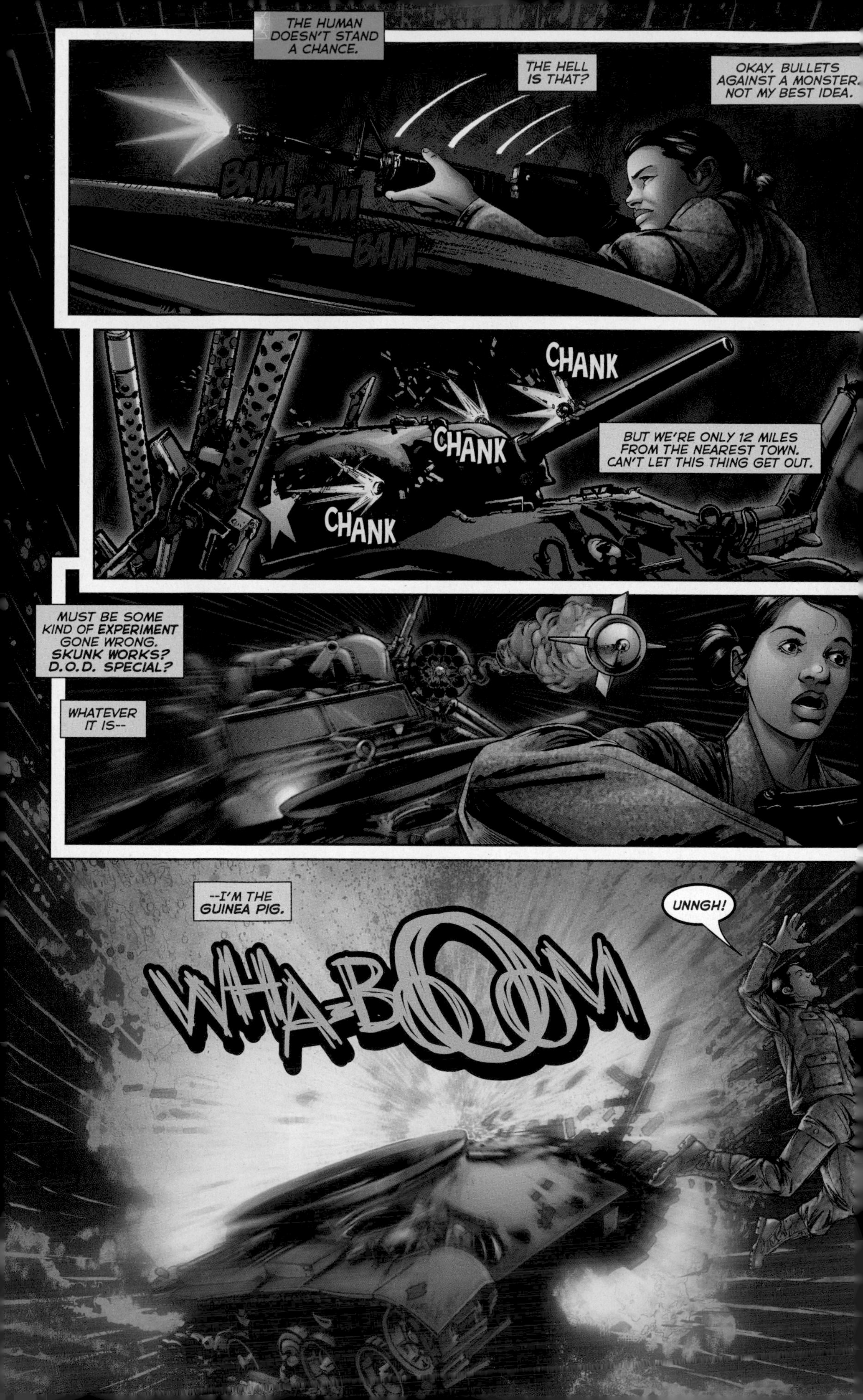
THE HUMAN DOESN'T STAND A CHANCE.
THE HELL IS THAT?
OKAY. BULLETS AGAINST A MONSTER. NOT MY BEST IDEA.
BAM
BAM
BAM
CHANK
CHANK
CHANK
BUT WE'RE ONLY 12 MILES FROM THE NEAREST TOWN. CAN'T LET THIS THING GET OUT.
MUST BE SOME KIND OF EXPERIMENT GONE WRONG. SKUNK WORKS? D.O.D. SPECIAL?
WHATEVER IT IS--
--I'M THE GUINEA PIG.
UNNGH!
WHA-BOOM

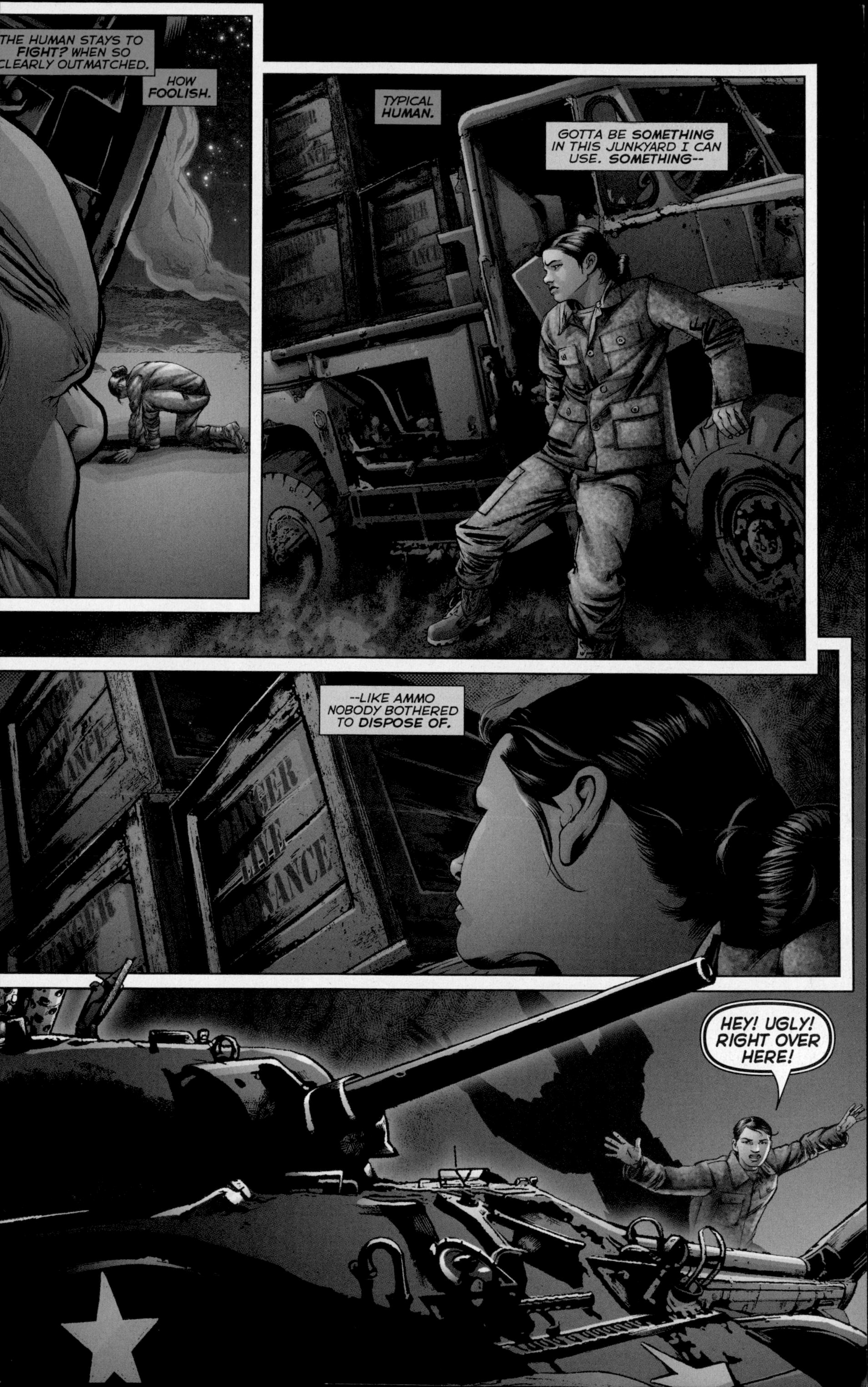
THE HUMAN STAYS TO FIGHT? WHEN SO CLEARLY OUTMATCHED.
HOW FOOLISH.
TYPICAL HUMAN.
GOTTA BE SOMETHING IN THIS JUNKYARD I CAN USE. SOMETHING--
--LIKE AMMO NOBODY BOTHERED TO DISPOSE OF.
HEY! UGLY! RIGHT OVER HERE!

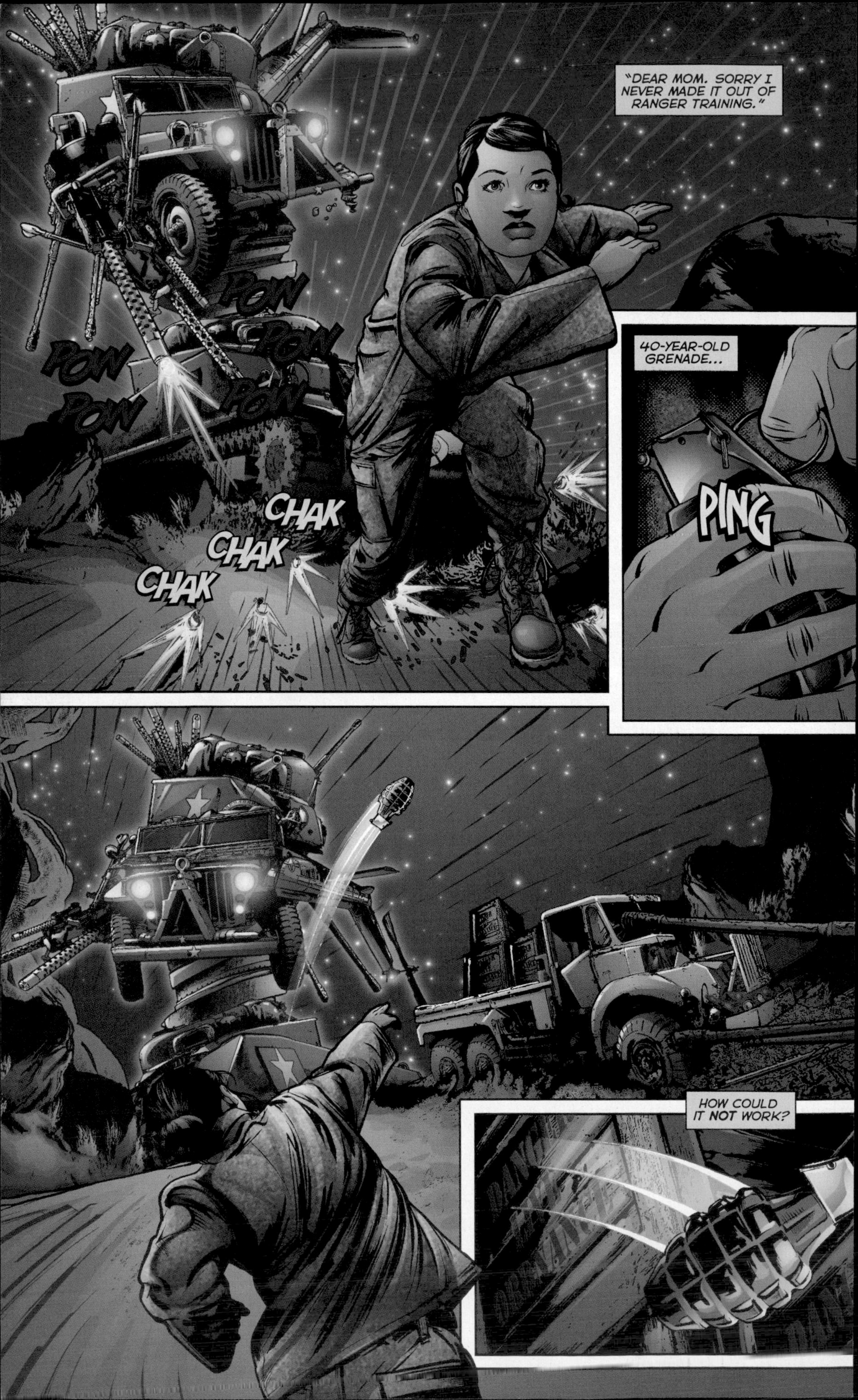
"DEAR MOM. SORRY I NEVER MADE IT OUT OF RANGER TRAINING."
POW
POW
POW
POW
POW
CHAK
CHAK
CHAK
40-YEAR-OLD GRENADE...
PING
HOW COULD IT NOT WORK?

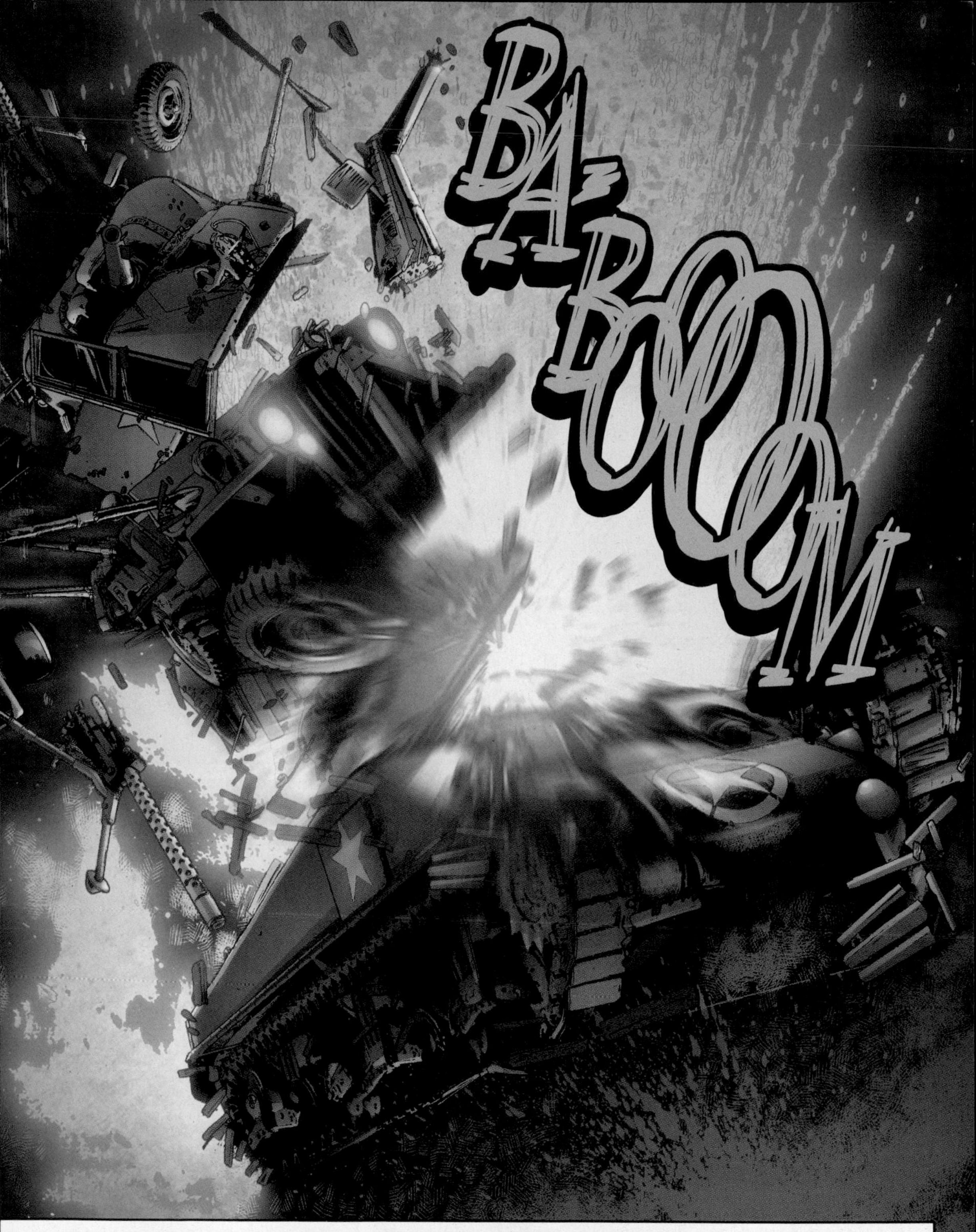
BA-BA-BOOOOM

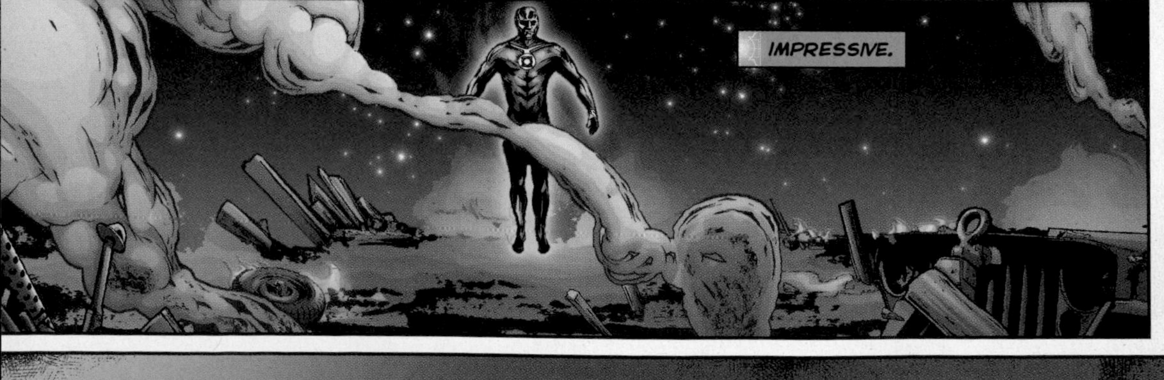
IMPRESSIVE.

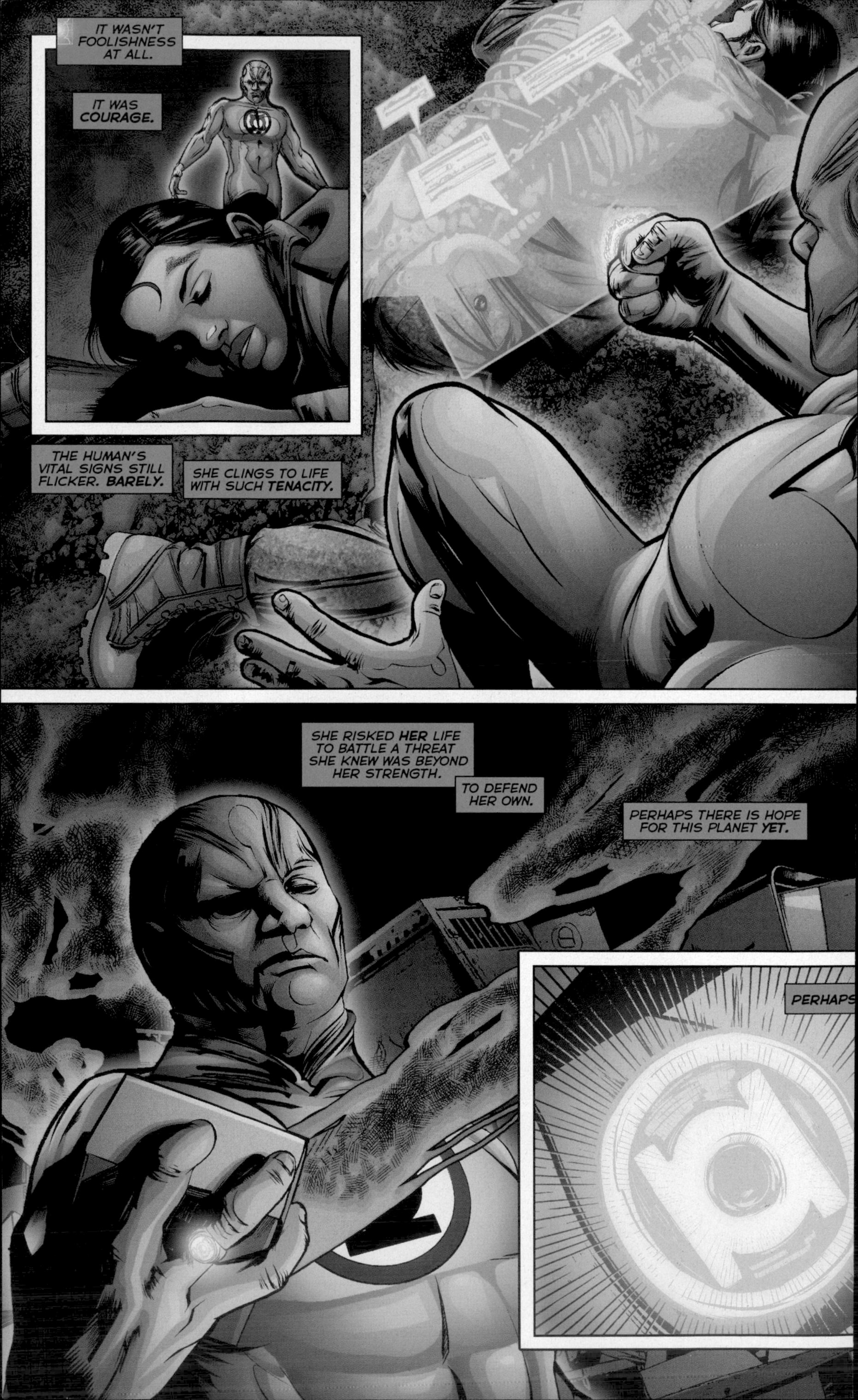
IT WASN'T FOOLISHNESS AT ALL.
IT WAS COURAGE.
THE HUMAN'S VITAL SIGNS STILL FLICKER. BARELY.
SHE CLINGS TO LIFE WITH SUCH TENACITY.
SHE RISKED HER LIFE TO BATTLE A THREAT SHE KNEW WAS BEYOND HER STRENGTH.
TO DEFEND HER OWN.
PERHAPS THERE IS HOPE FOR THIS PLANET YET.
PERHAPS

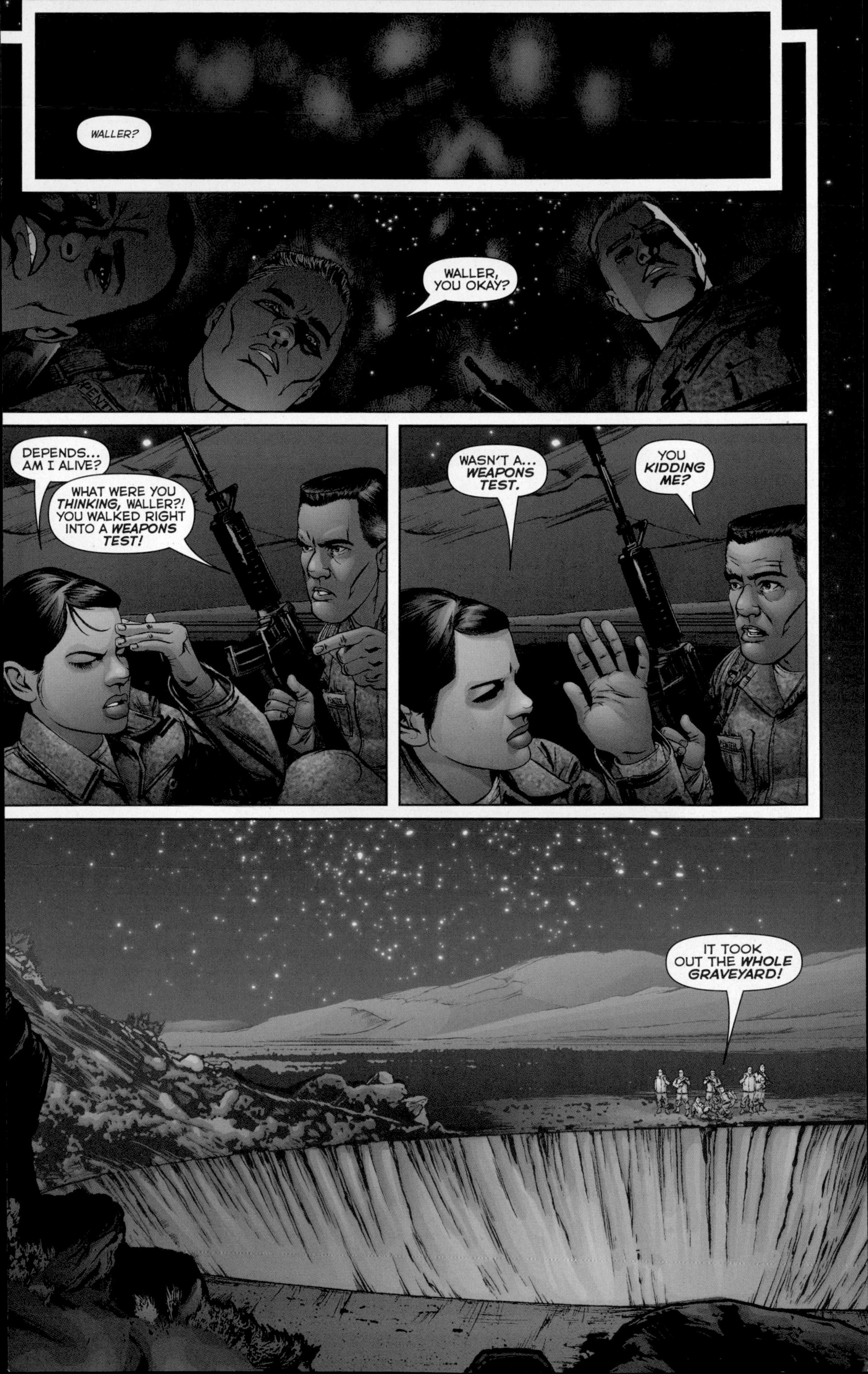
WALLER?
WALLER, YOU OKAY?
DEPENDS... AM I ALIVE?
WHAT WERE YOU THINKING, WALLER?! YOU WALKED RIGHT INTO A WEAPONS TEST!
WASN'T A... WEAPONS TEST.
YOU KIDDING ME?
IT TOOK OUT THE WHOLE GRAVEYARD!

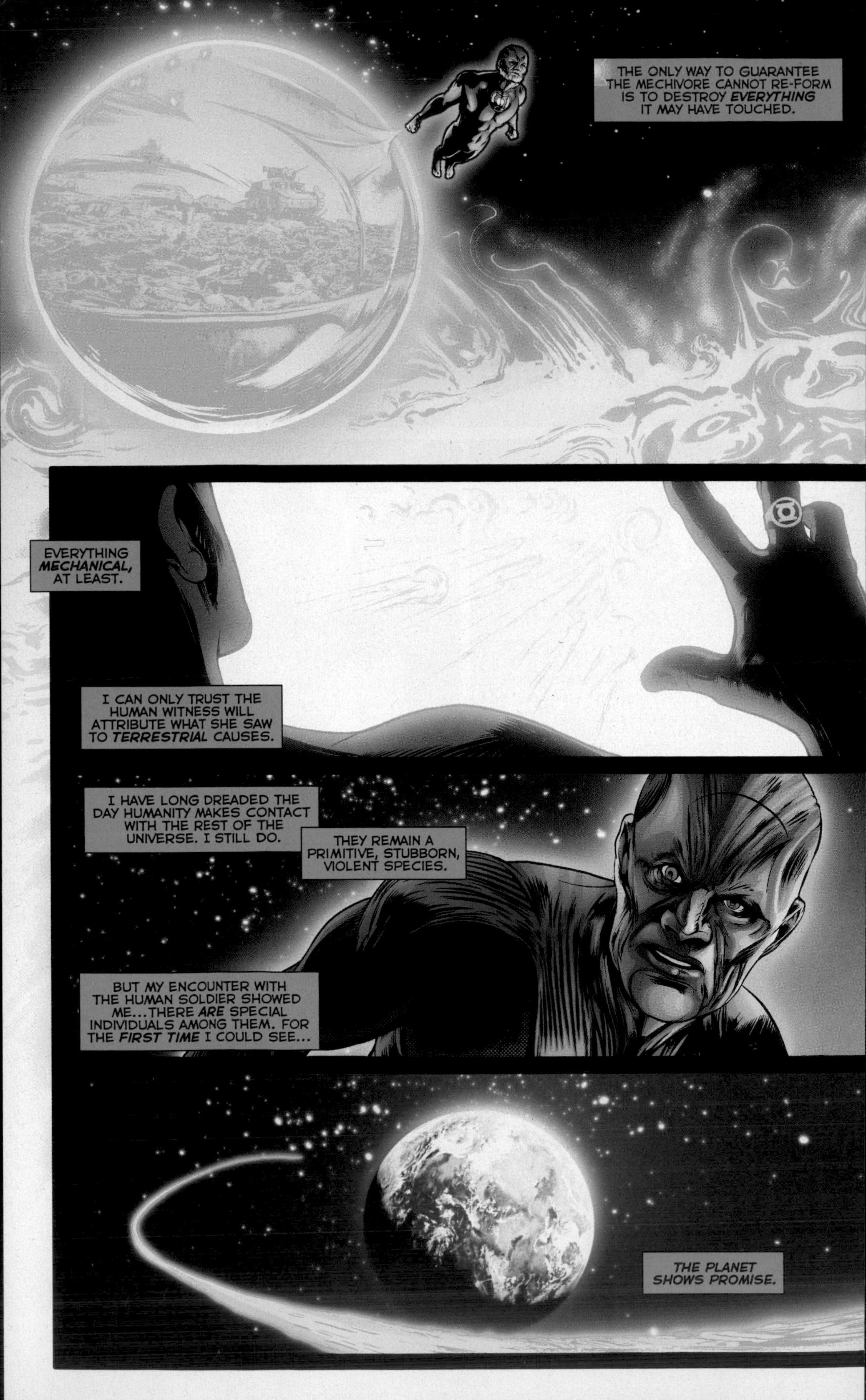
THE ONLY WAY TO GUARANTEE THE MECHIVORE CANNOT RE-FORM IS TO DESTROY *EVERYTHING* IT MAY HAVE TOUCHED.
EVERYTHING *MECHANICAL,* AT LEAST.
I CAN ONLY TRUST THE HUMAN WITNESS WILL ATTRIBUTE WHAT SHE SAW TO *TERRESTRIAL* CAUSES.
I HAVE LONG DREADED THE DAY HUMANITY MAKES CONTACT WITH THE REST OF THE UNIVERSE. I STILL DO.
THEY REMAIN A PRIMITIVE, STUBBORN, VIOLENT SPECIES.
BUT MY ENCOUNTER WITH THE HUMAN SOLDIER SHOWED ME...THERE *ARE* SPECIAL INDIVIDUALS AMONG THEM. FOR THE *FIRST TIME* I COULD SEE...
THE PLANET SHOWS PROMISE.

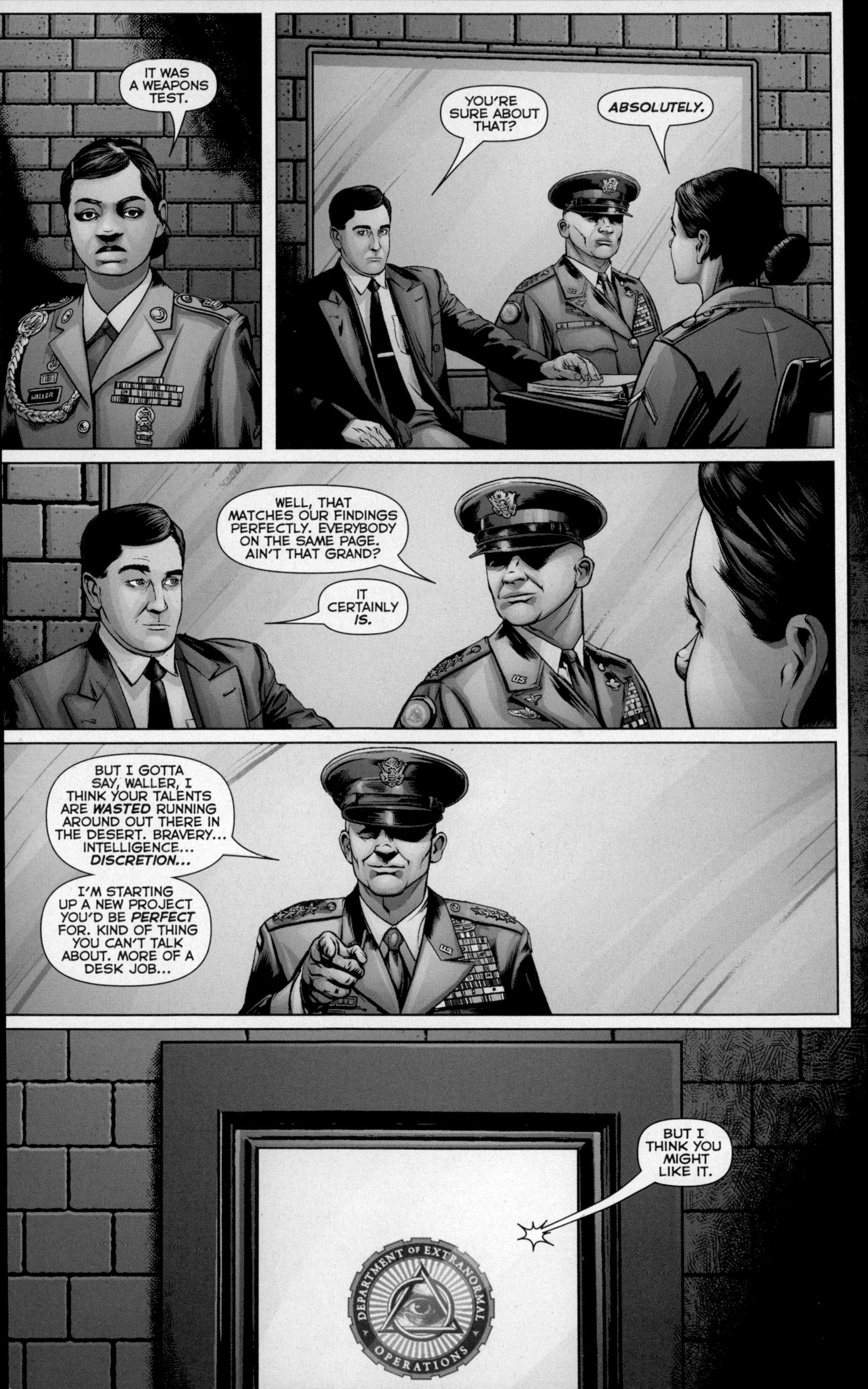
IT WAS A WEAPONS TEST.
YOU'RE SURE ABOUT THAT?
ABSOLUTELY.
WALLER
WELL, THAT MATCHES OUR FINDINGS PERFECTLY. EVERYBODY ON THE SAME PAGE. AIN'T THAT GRAND?
IT CERTAINLY IS.
BUT I GOTTA SAY, WALLER, I THINK YOUR TALENTS ARE WASTED RUNNING AROUND OUT THERE IN THE DESERT. BRAVERY... INTELLIGENCE... DISCRETION...
I'M STARTING UP A NEW PROJECT YOU'D BE PERFECT FOR. KIND OF THING YOU CAN'T TALK ABOUT. MORE OF A DESK JOB...
BUT I THINK YOU MIGHT LIKE IT.
DEPARTMENT OF EXTRANORMAL OPERATIONS

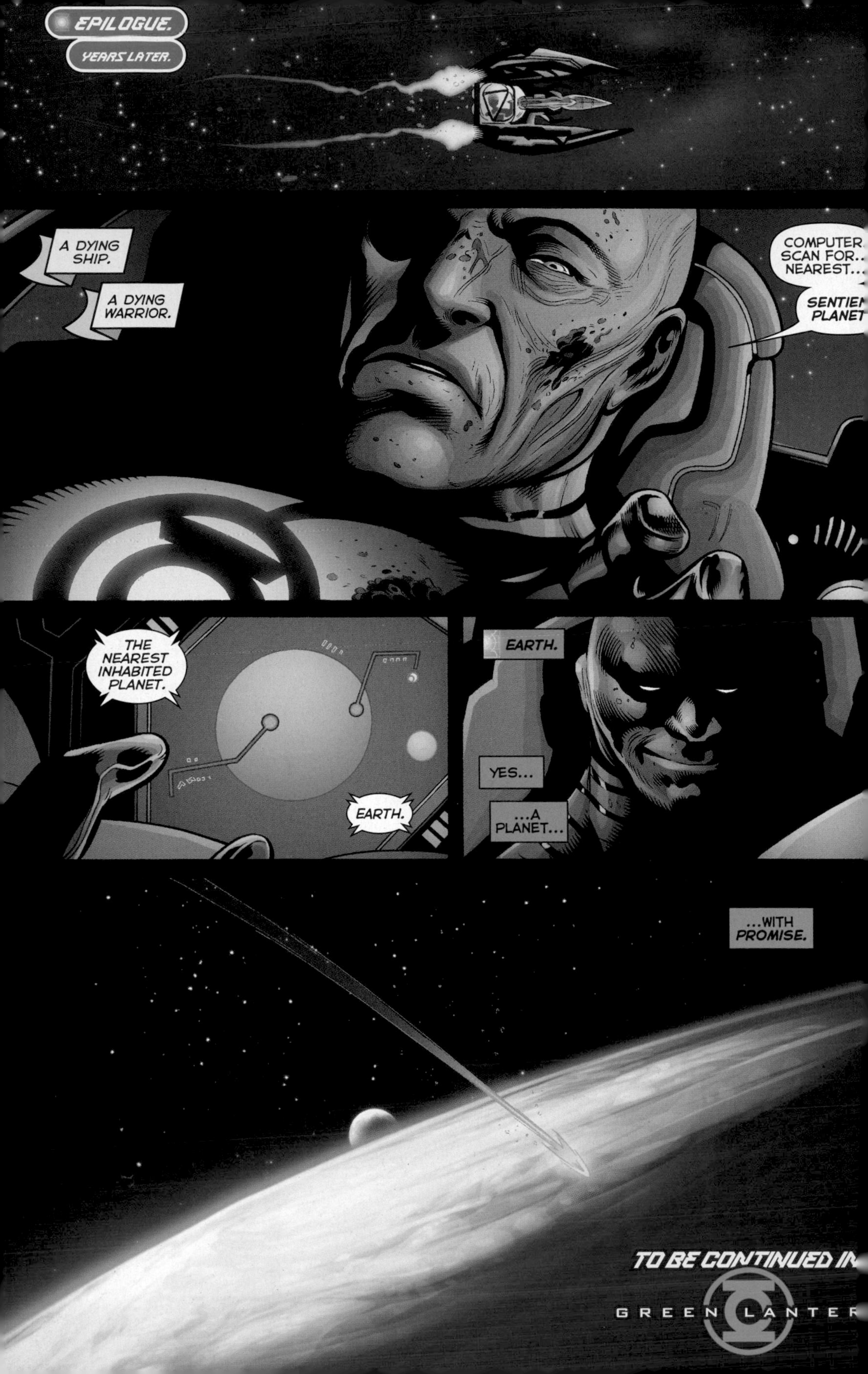
EPILOGUE.
YEARS LATER.
A DYING SHIP.
A DYING WARRIOR.
COMPUTER SCAN FOR... NEAREST...
SENTIENT PLANET
THE NEAREST INHABITED PLANET.
EARTH.
EARTH.
YES...
...A PLANET...
...WITH PROMISE.
TO BE CONTINUED IN
GREEN LANTERN

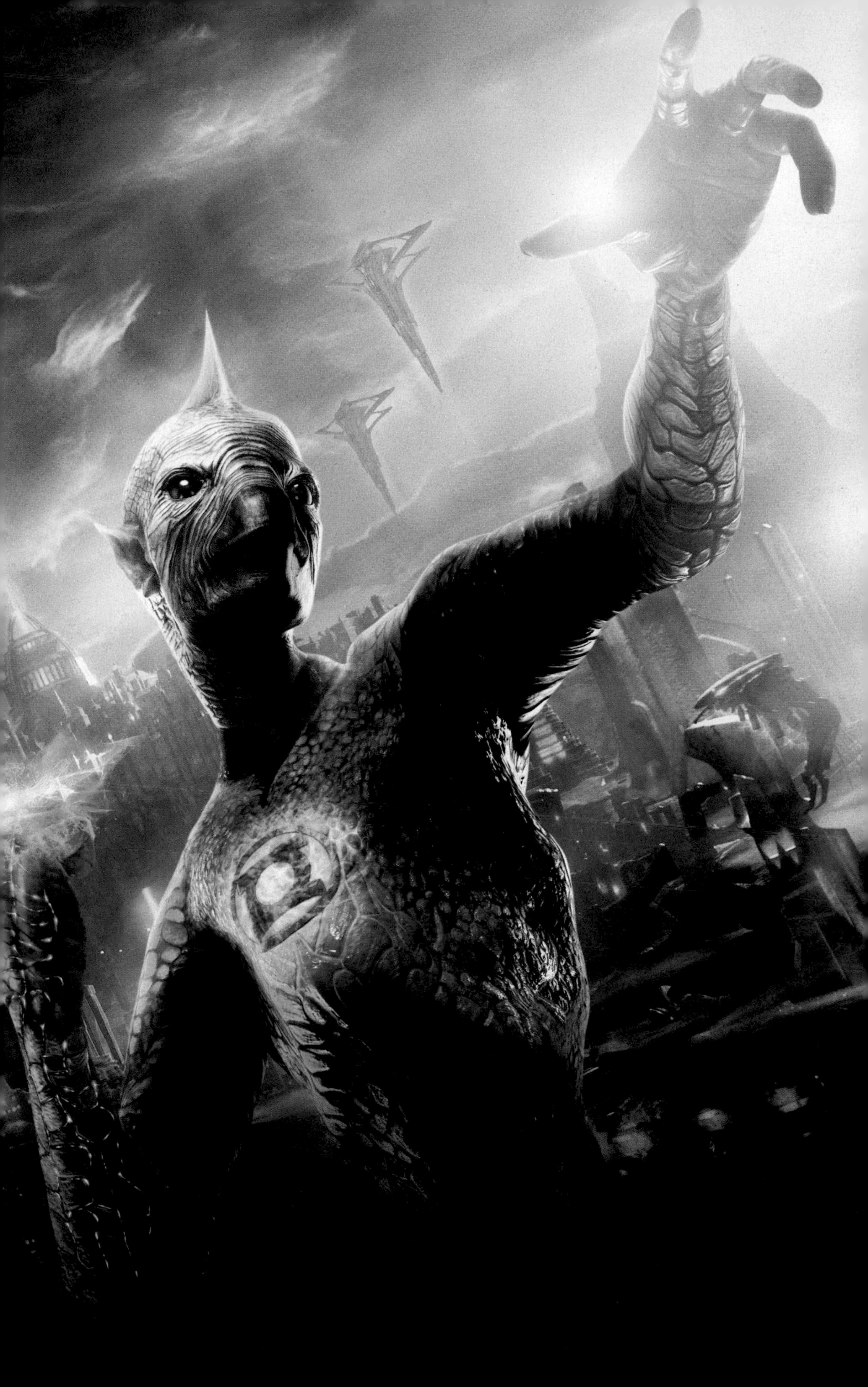

FORBIDDEN PLANET

MARC **GUGGENHEIM** writer

CLIFF **RICHARDS** artist

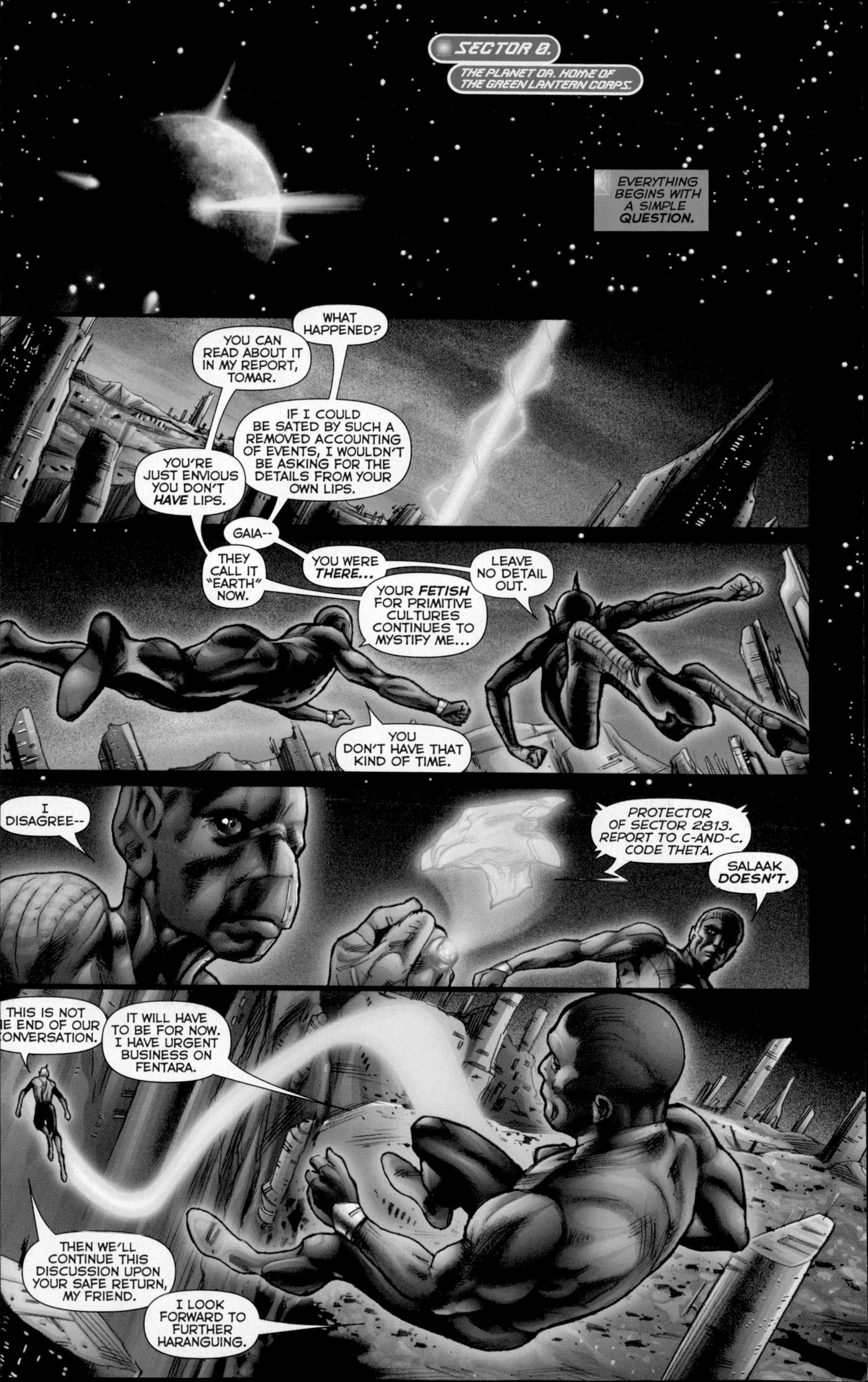
SECTOR 0.
THE PLANET OA. HOME OF THE GREEN LANTERN CORPS.
EVERYTHING BEGINS WITH A SIMPLE QUESTION.
WHAT HAPPENED?
YOU CAN READ ABOUT IT IN MY REPORT, TOMAR.
IF I COULD BE SATED BY SUCH A REMOVED ACCOUNTING OF EVENTS, I WOULDN'T BE ASKING FOR THE DETAILS FROM YOUR OWN LIPS.
YOU'RE JUST ENVIOUS YOU DON'T HAVE LIPS.
GAIA--
THEY CALL IT "EARTH" NOW.
YOU WERE THERE...
LEAVE NO DETAIL OUT.
YOUR FETISH FOR PRIMITIVE CULTURES CONTINUES TO MYSTIFY ME...
YOU DON'T HAVE THAT KIND OF TIME.
I DISAGREE--
PROTECTOR OF SECTOR 2813. REPORT TO C-AND-C. CODE THETA.
SALAAK DOESN'T.
THIS IS NOT THE END OF OUR CONVERSATION.
IT WILL HAVE TO BE FOR NOW. I HAVE URGENT BUSINESS ON FENTARA.
THEN WE'LL CONTINUE THIS DISCUSSION UPON YOUR SAFE RETURN, MY FRIEND.
I LOOK FORWARD TO FURTHER HARANGUING.

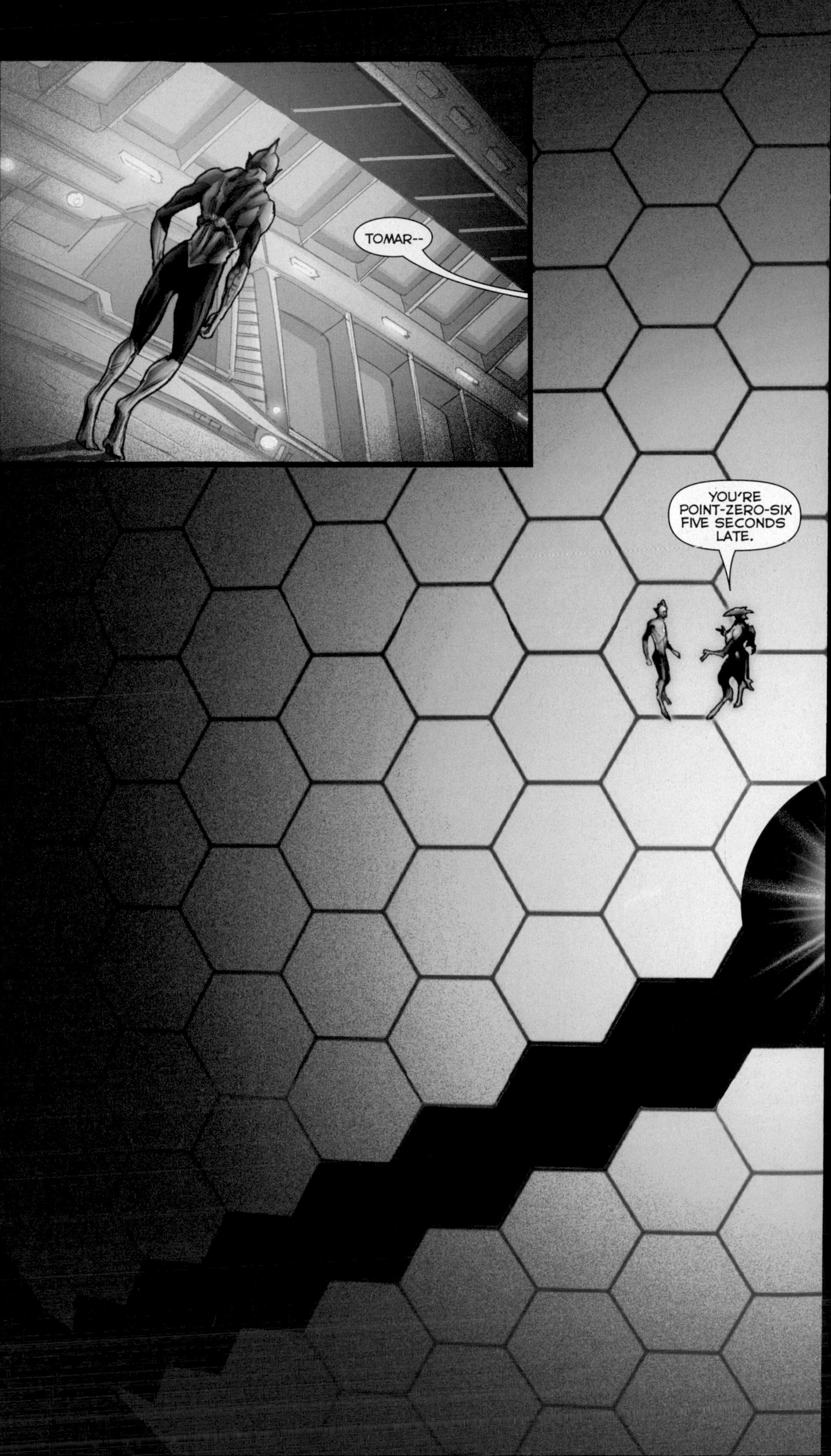
TOMAR--
YOU'RE POINT-ZERO-SIX FIVE SECONDS LATE.

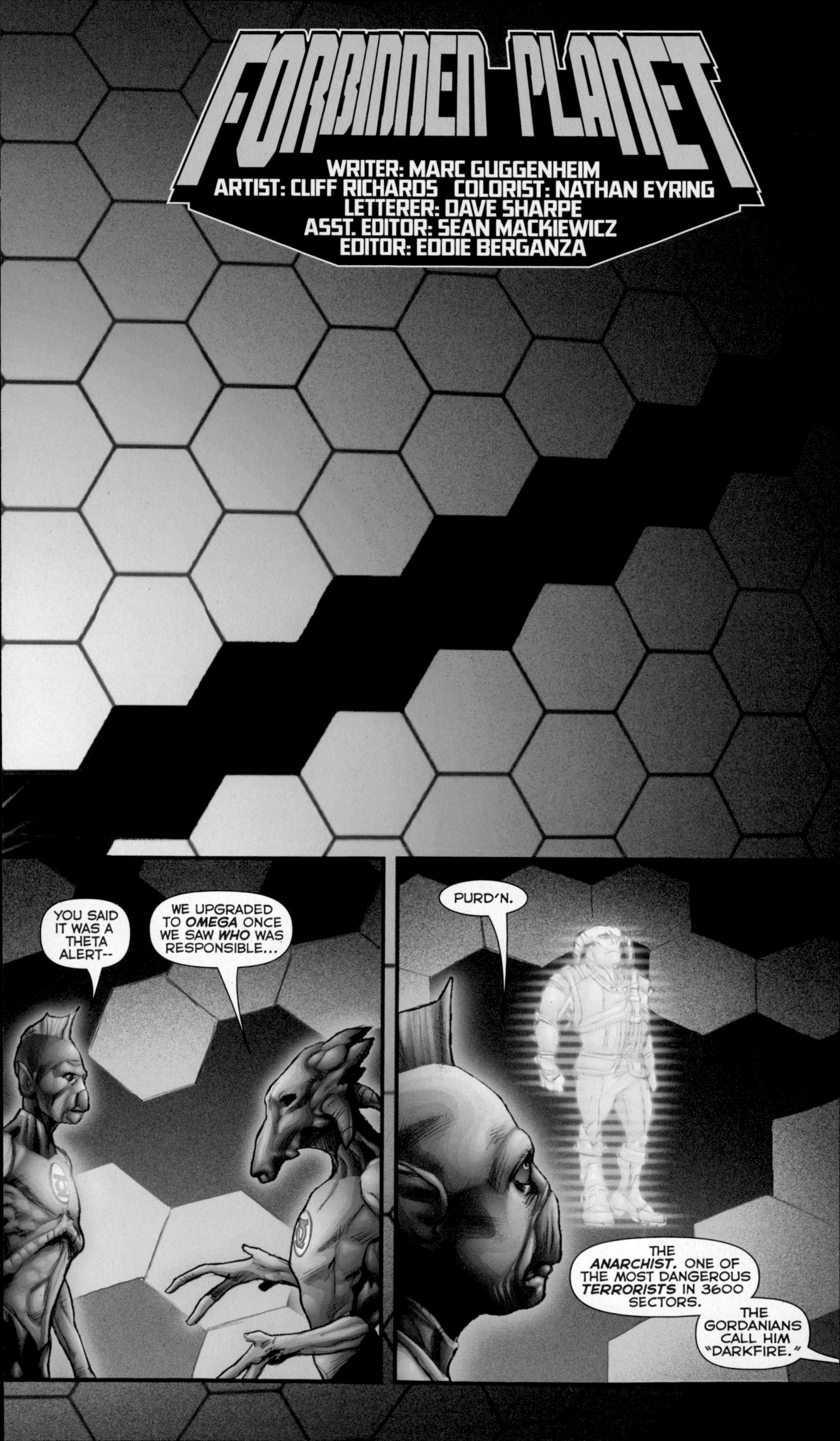
FORBIDDEN PLANET
WRITER: MARC GUGGENHEIM
ARTIST: CLIFF RICHARDS COLORIST: NATHAN EYRING
LETTERER: DAVE SHARPE
ASST. EDITOR: SEAN MACKIEWICZ
EDITOR: EDDIE BERGANZA
YOU SAID IT WAS A THETA ALERT--
WE UPGRADED TO *OMEGA* ONCE WE SAW *WHO* WAS RESPONSIBLE...
PURD'N.
THE *ANARCHIST.* ONE OF THE MOST DANGEROUS *TERRORISTS* IN 3600 SECTORS.
THE GORDANIANS CALL HIM "DARKFIRE."

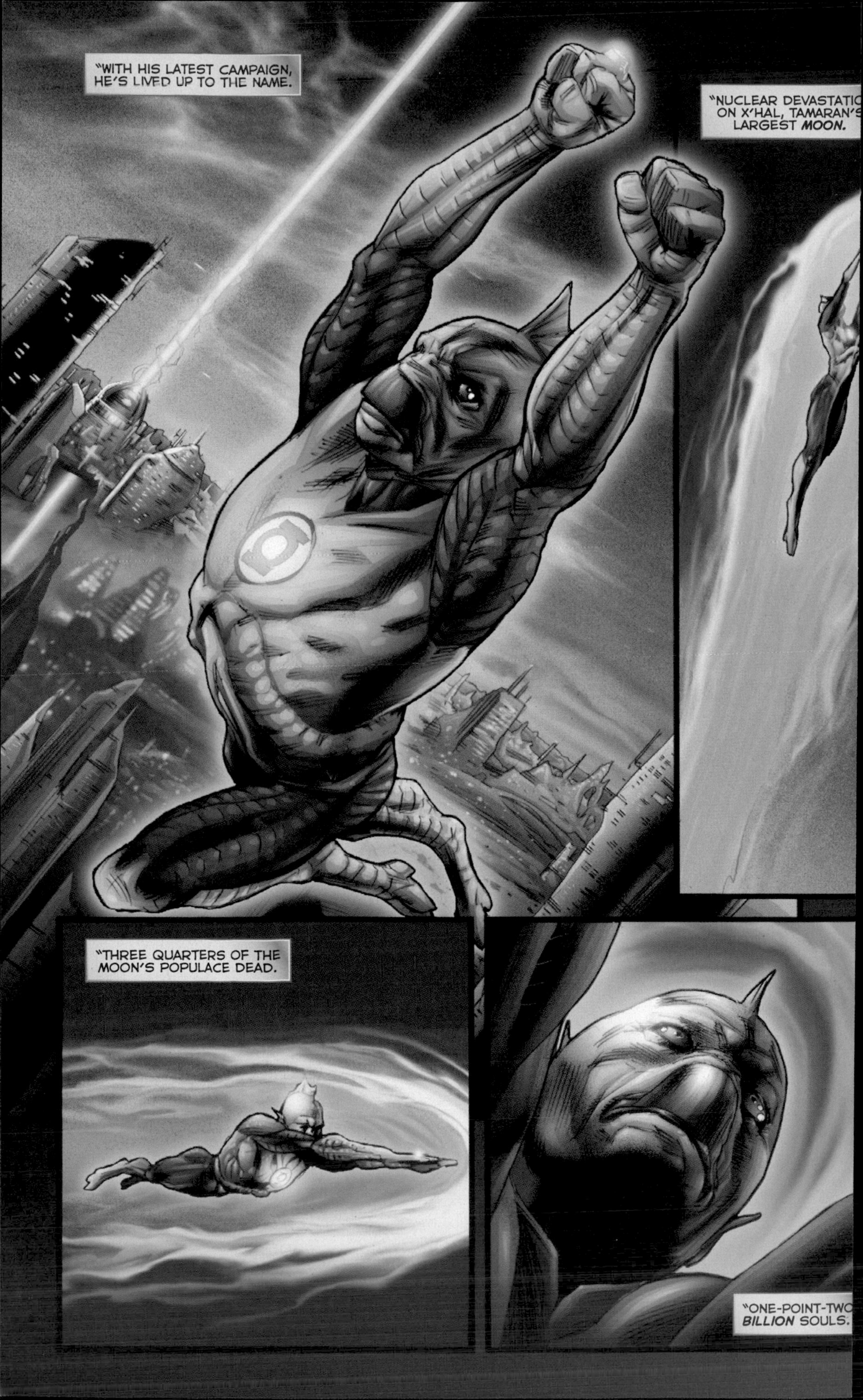
"WITH HIS LATEST CAMPAIGN, HE'S LIVED UP TO THE NAME.
"NUCLEAR DEVASTATIC ON X'HAL, TAMARAN'S LARGEST MOON.
"THREE QUARTERS OF THE MOON'S POPULACE DEAD.
"ONE-POINT-TWO BILLION SOULS.

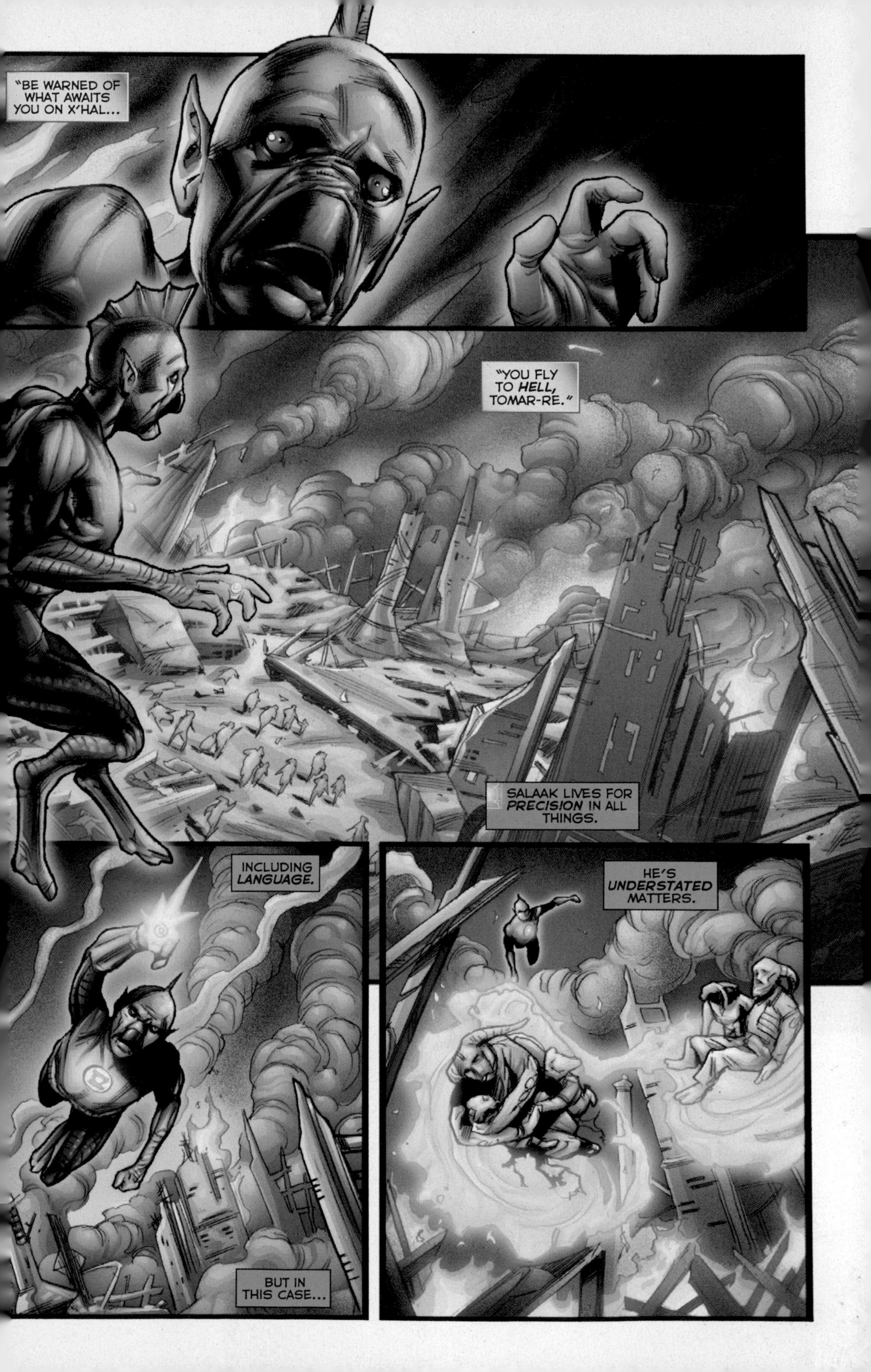
"BE WARNED OF WHAT AWAITS YOU ON X'HAL...
"YOU FLY TO HELL, TOMAR-RE."
SALAAK LIVES FOR PRECISION IN ALL THINGS.
INCLUDING LANGUAGE.
BUT IN THIS CASE...
HE'S UNDERSTATED MATTERS.

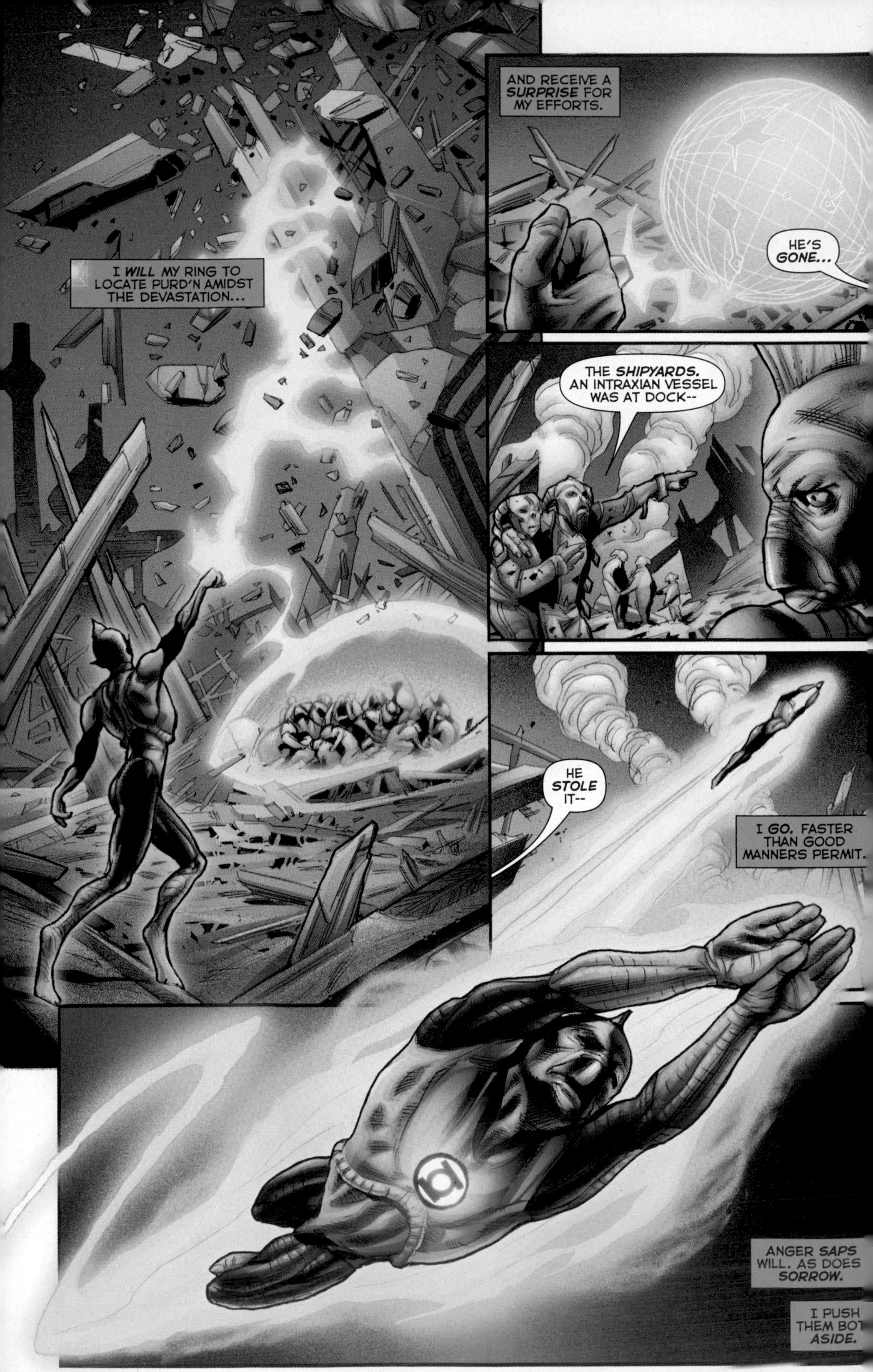
I WILL MY RING TO LOCATE PURD'N AMIDST THE DEVASTATION...
AND RECEIVE A SURPRISE FOR MY EFFORTS.
HE'S GONE...
THE SHIPYARDS. AN INTRAXIAN VESSEL WAS AT DOCK--
HE STOLE IT--
I GO. FASTER THAN GOOD MANNERS PERMIT.
ANGER SAPS WILL. AS DOES SORROW.
I PUSH THEM BOT ASIDE.

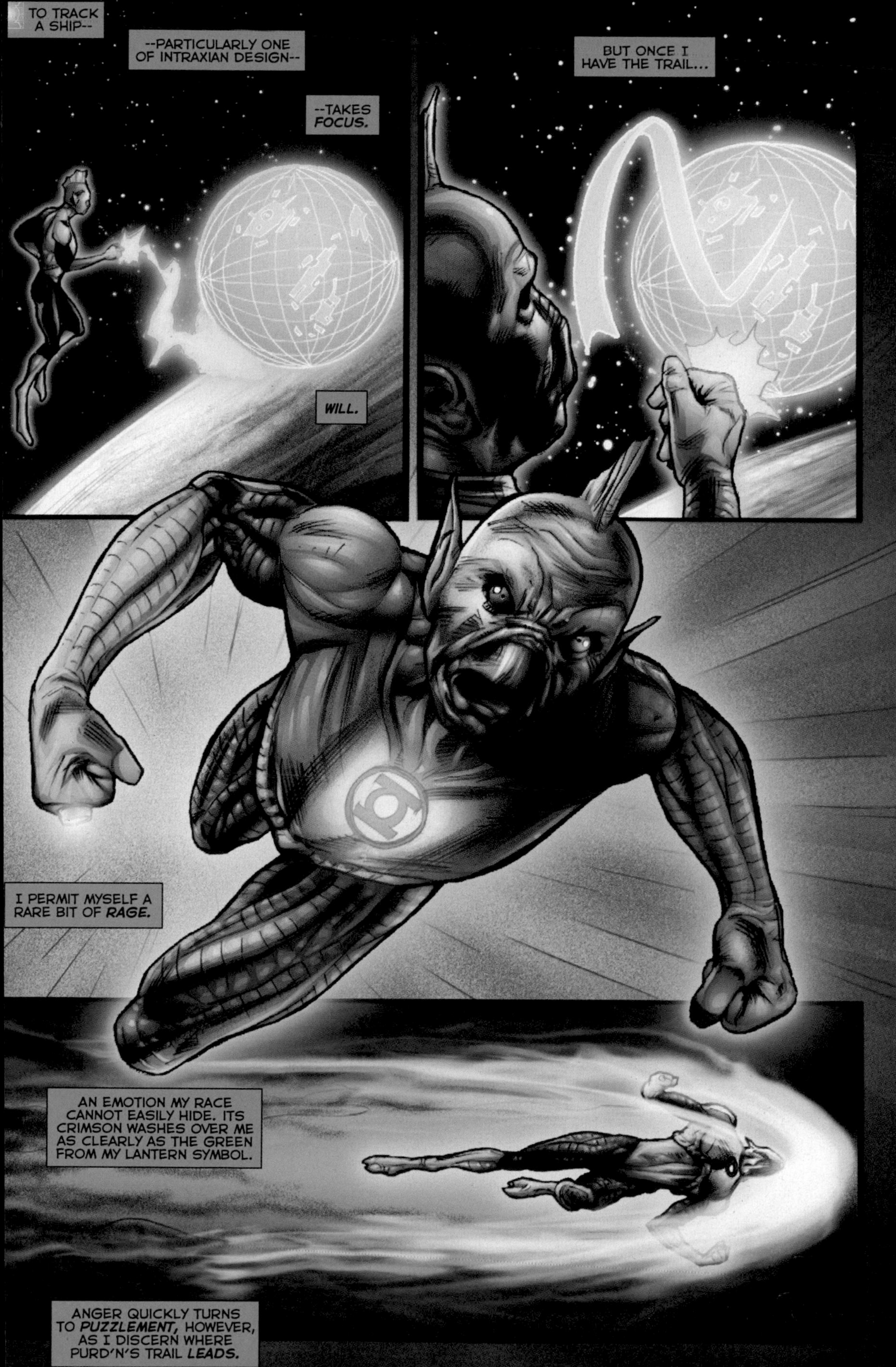
TO TRACK A SHIP--
--PARTICULARLY ONE OF INTRAXIAN DESIGN--
--TAKES *FOCUS.*
WILL.
BUT ONCE I HAVE THE TRAIL...
I PERMIT MYSELF A RARE BIT OF *RAGE.*
AN EMOTION MY RACE CANNOT EASILY HIDE. ITS CRIMSON WASHES OVER ME AS CLEARLY AS THE GREEN FROM MY LANTERN SYMBOL.
ANGER QUICKLY TURNS TO *PUZZLEMENT,* HOWEVER, AS I DISCERN WHERE PURD'N'S TRAIL *LEADS.*

THE LOST
SECTOR.

MY RING
PROTESTS.

THE PROHIBITION
IS THE WILL OF
THE *GUARDIANS.*

THOUGH AS IS
TYPICAL WHERE
THE WILL OF TH[E]
GUARDIANS IS
CONCERNED, T[HE]
PROHIBITION
COMES WITHOU[T]
EXPLANATION.

BUT IT IS A *STANDING
ORDER.* ONE OF THE
MOST INVIOLATE.

I AM A GREEN
LANTERN.

A MEMBER OF THE *HONOR
GUARD* OF THE CORPS.

KEEPER OF THE
BOOK OF OA.

THE WILL OF THE GUARDIANS IS MY
BREATH, THE BLOOD IN MY VEINS.

OF THE 3600
SECTORS IN THE
UNIVERSE, THE
LOST SECTOR IS
THE *ONE* WHERE
NO MEMBER OF
THE GREEN
LANTERN CORPS
IS PERMITTED
TO TREAD.

BUT SAVING *INNOCENTS...*
AVENGING *INJUSTICE...*

THAT IS THE WILL OF
THE GUARDIANS, TOO.

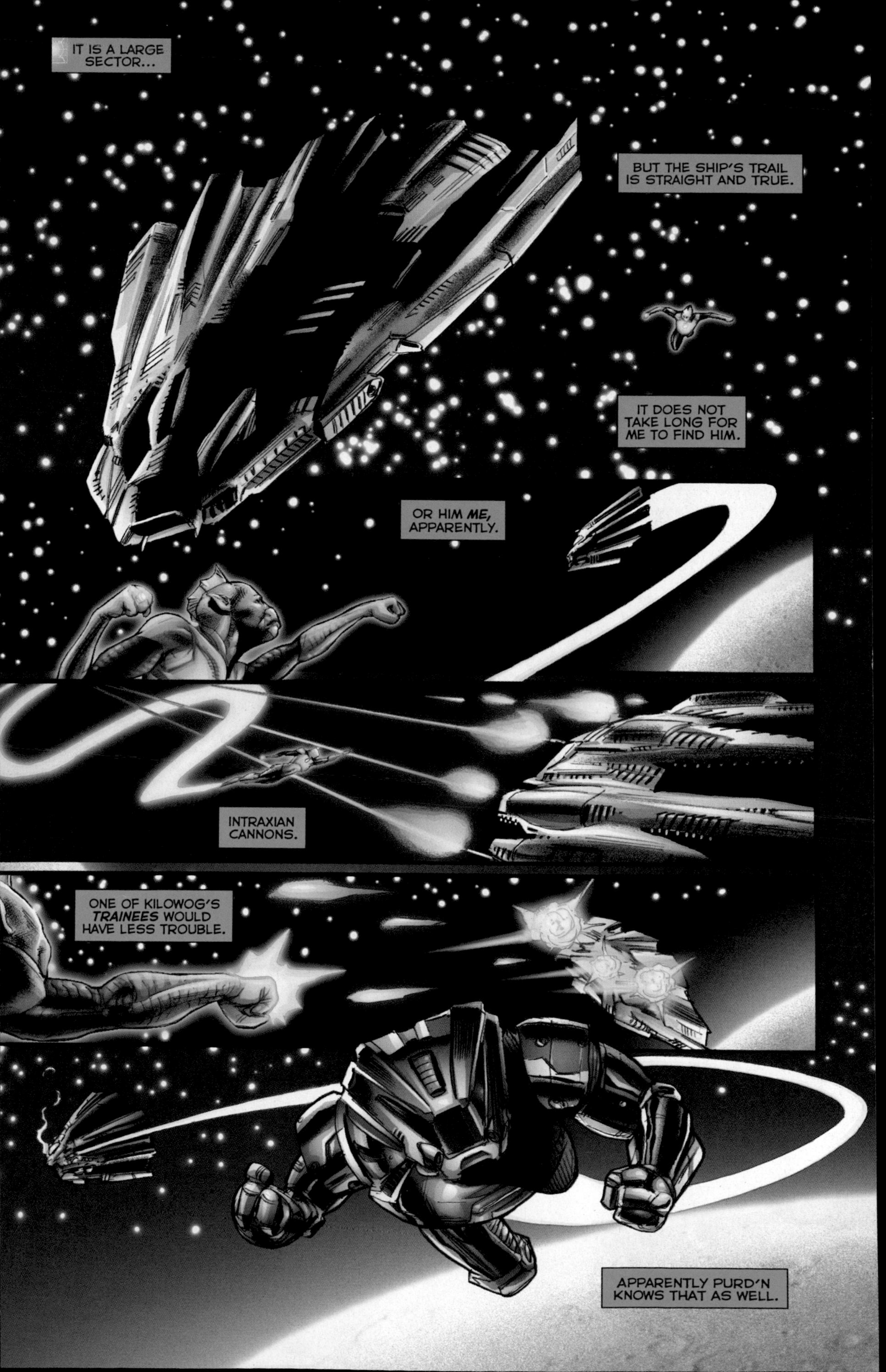
IT IS A LARGE SECTOR...
BUT THE SHIP'S TRAIL IS STRAIGHT AND TRUE.
IT DOES NOT TAKE LONG FOR ME TO FIND HIM.
OR HIM *ME*, APPARENTLY.
INTRAXIAN CANNONS.
ONE OF KILOWOG'S *TRAINEES* WOULD HAVE LESS TROUBLE.
APPARENTLY PURD'N KNOWS THAT AS WELL.

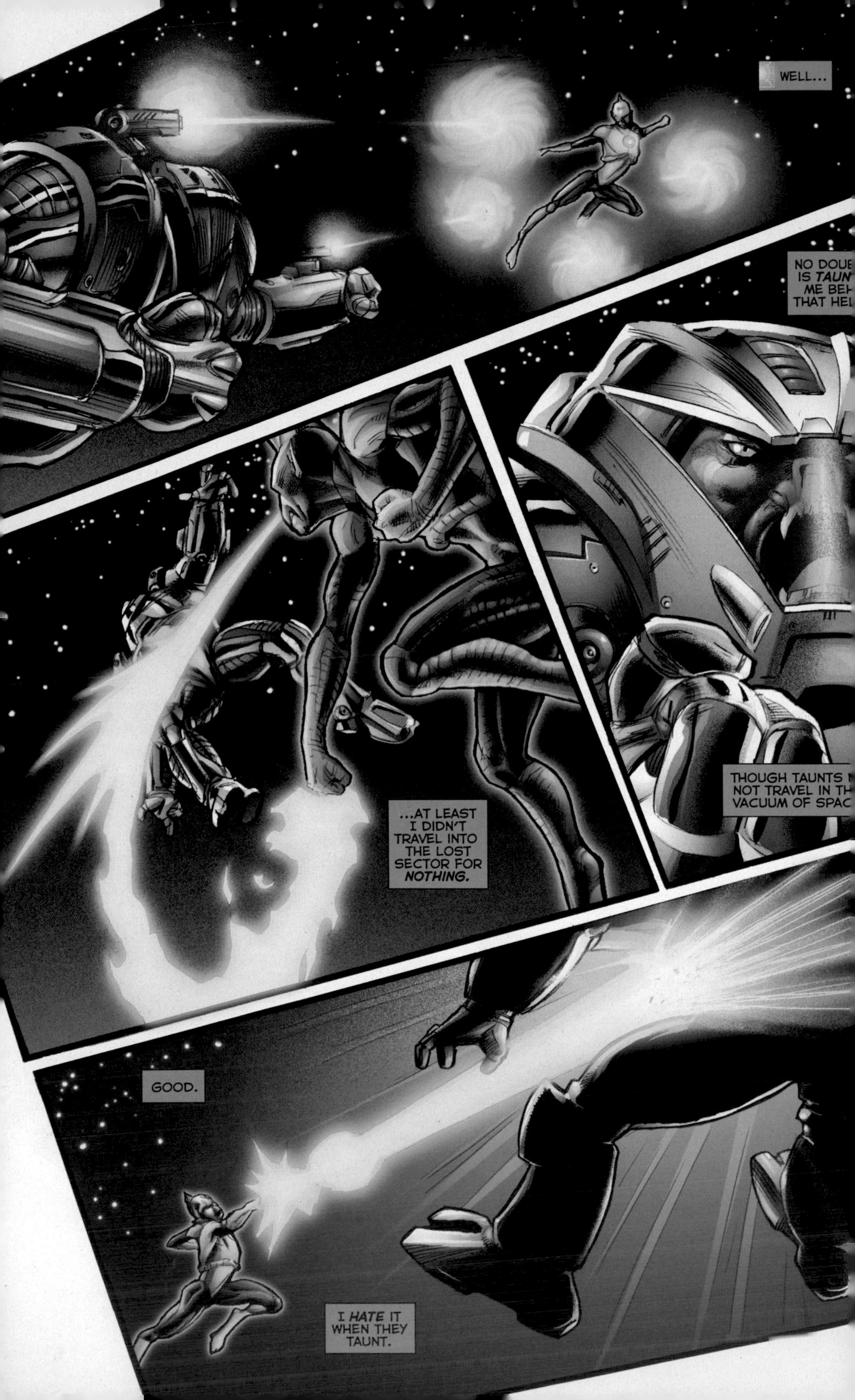

WELL...
NO DOUB
IS TAUN
ME BEH
THAT HE
...AT LEAST I DIDN'T TRAVEL INTO THE LOST SECTOR FOR NOTHING.
THOUGH TAUNTS
NOT TRAVEL IN TH
VACUUM OF SPAC
GOOD.
I HATE IT WHEN THEY TAUNT.

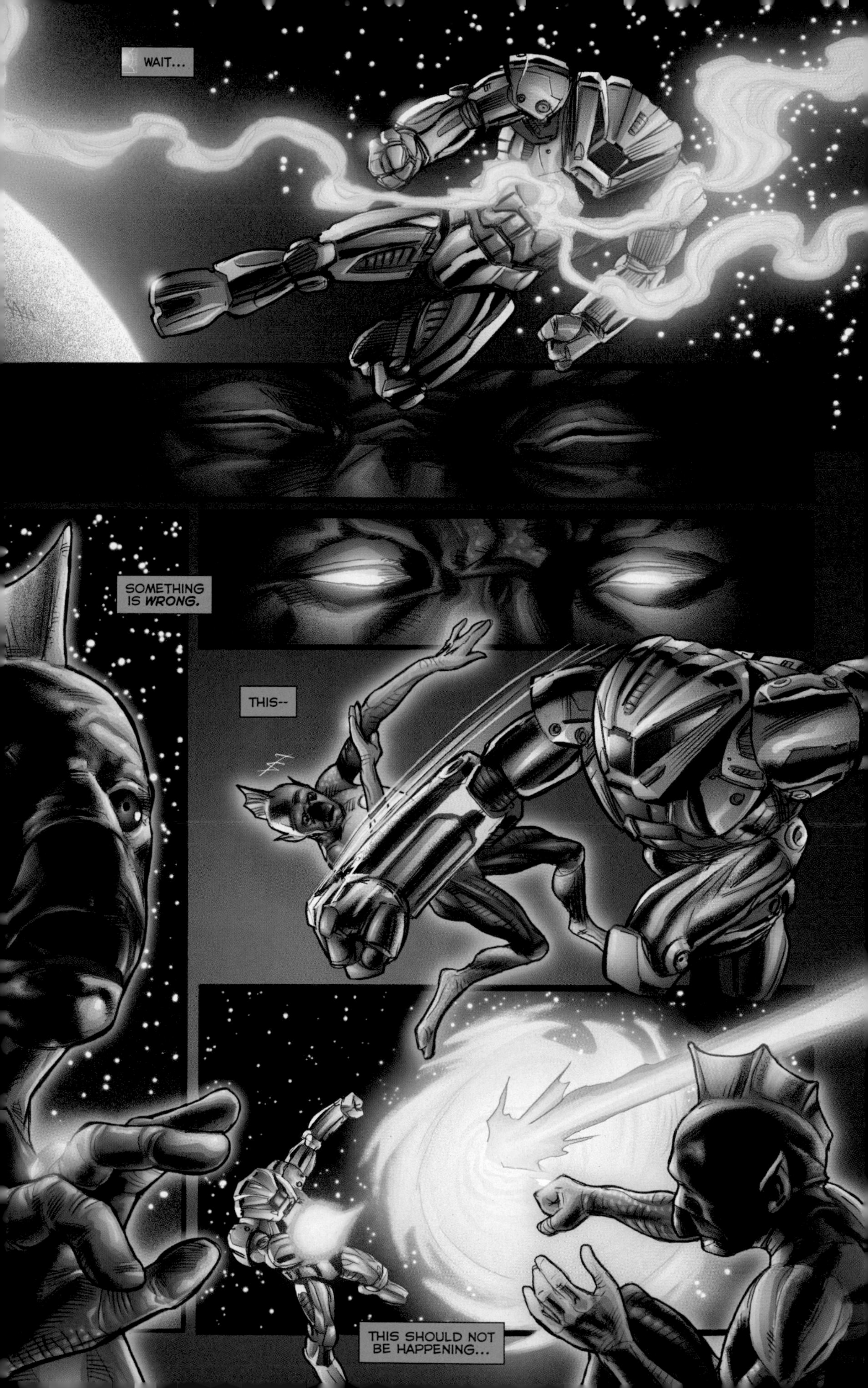
WAIT...
SOMETHING IS *WRONG.*
THIS--
THIS SHOULD NOT BE HAPPENING...

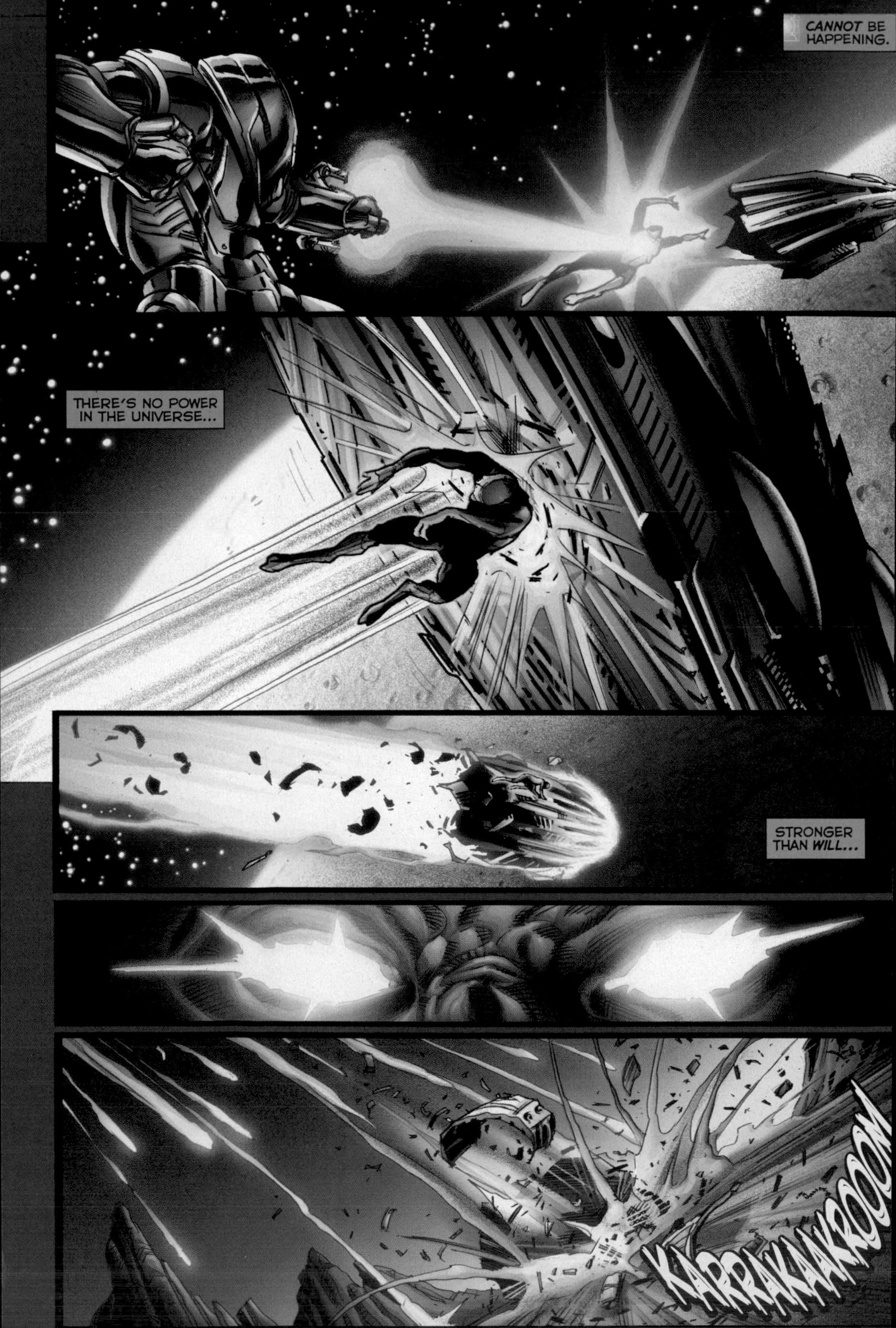
CANNOT BE HAPPENING.
THERE'S NO POWER IN THE UNIVERSE...
STRONGER THAN WILL...
KARRAKAAKROOOM

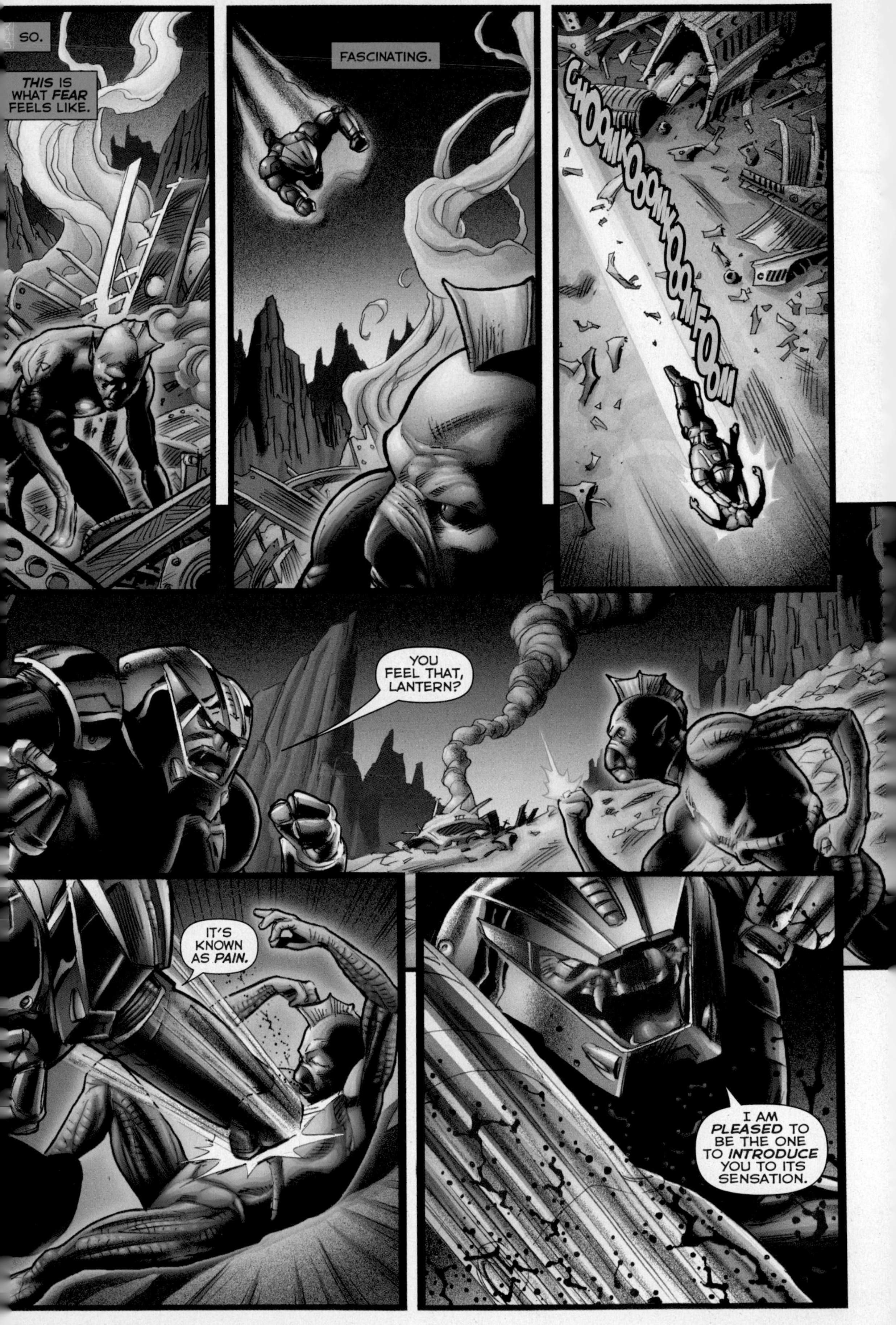
SO.
THIS IS WHAT FEAR FEELS LIKE.
FASCINATING.
CHOOMKOOOMKOOOMFOOOM
YOU FEEL THAT, LANTERN?
IT'S KNOWN AS PAIN.
I AM PLEASED TO BE THE ONE TO INTRODUCE YOU TO ITS SENSATION.

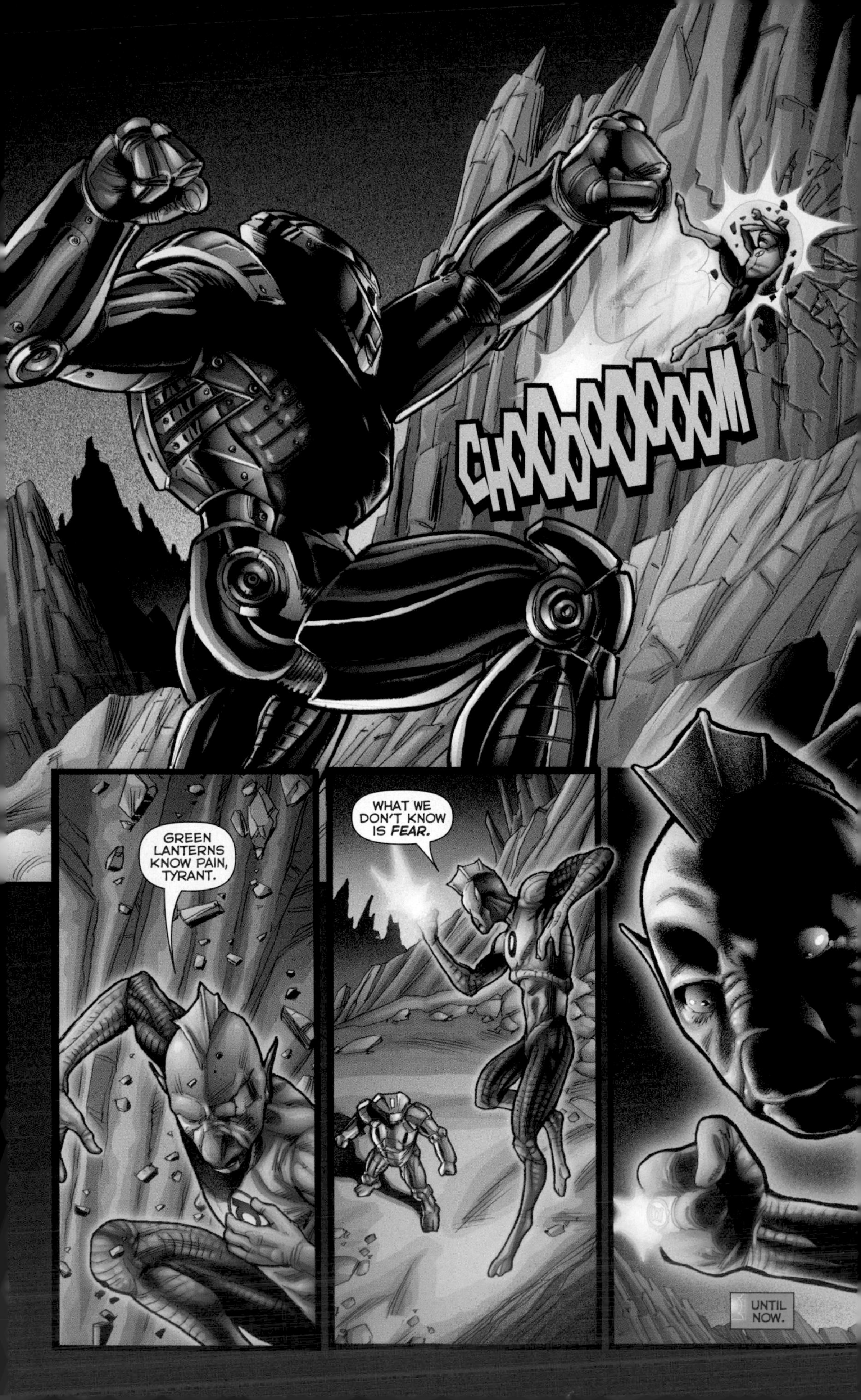
CHOOOOOOOOM
GREEN LANTERNS KNOW PAIN, TYRANT.
WHAT WE DON'T KNOW IS *FEAR.*
UNTIL NOW.

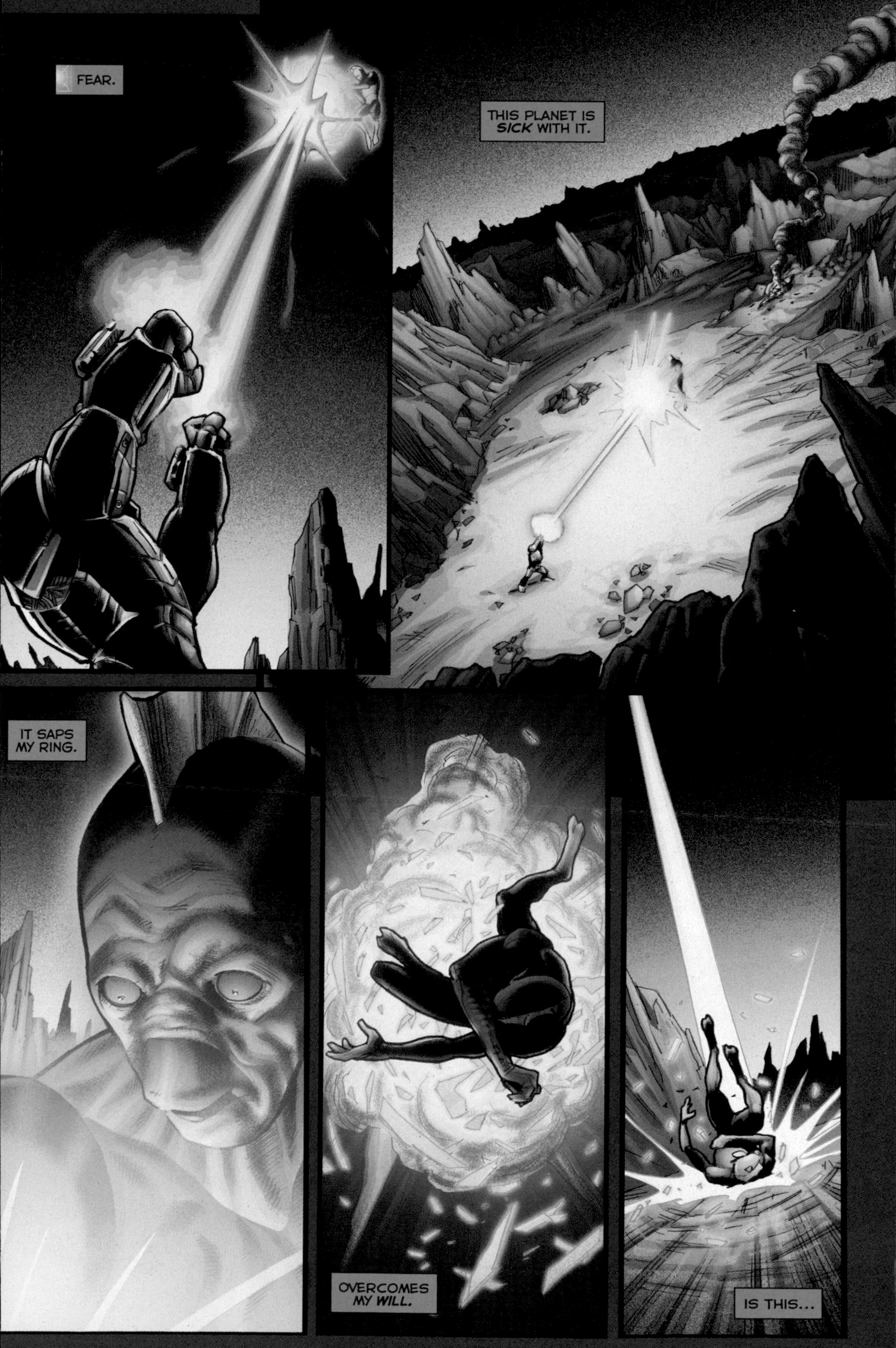
FEAR.
THIS PLANET IS SICK WITH IT.
IT SAPS MY RING.
OVERCOMES MY WILL.
IS THIS...

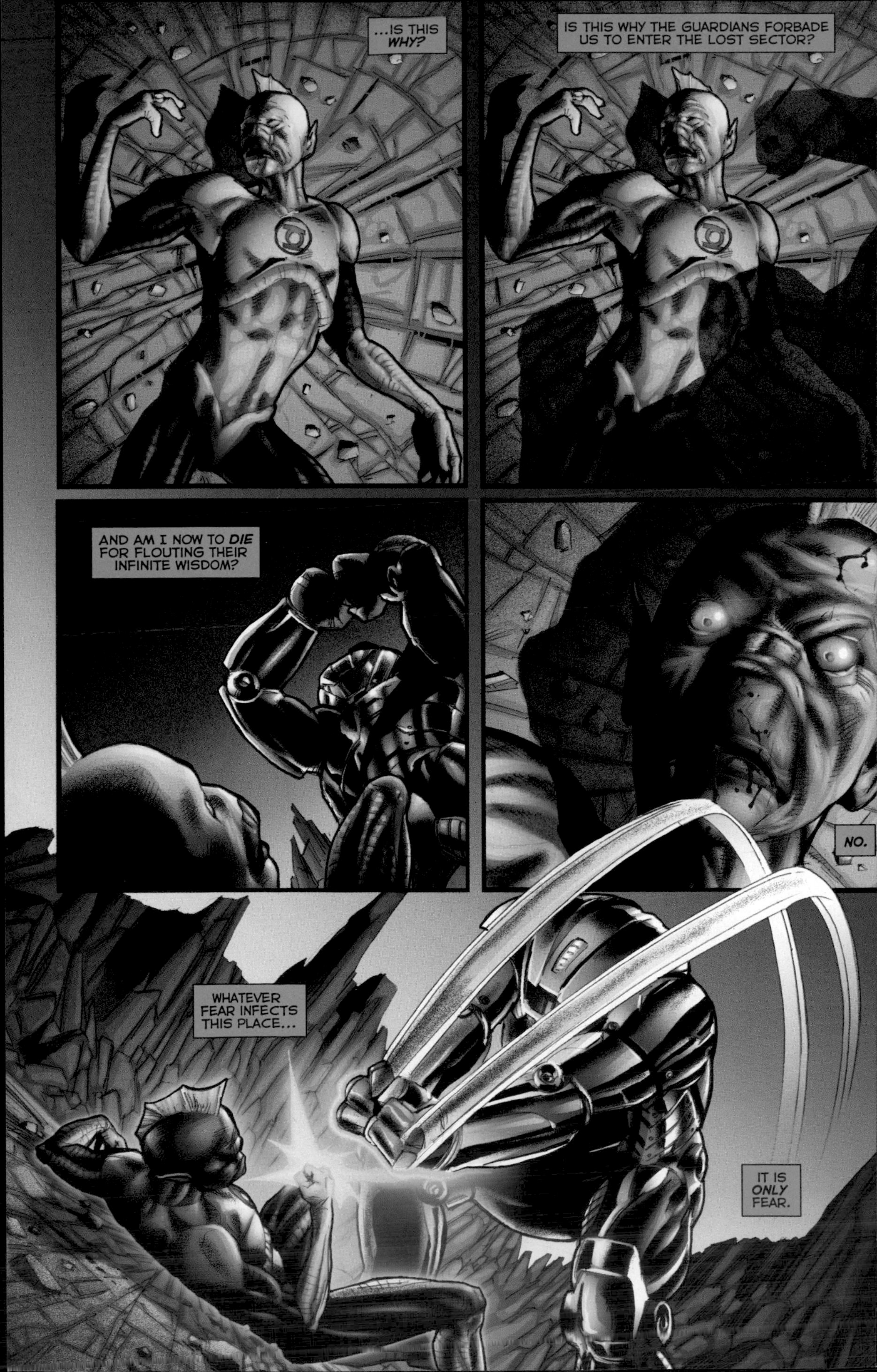
...IS THIS WHY?
IS THIS WHY THE GUARDIANS FORBADE US TO ENTER THE LOST SECTOR?
AND AM I NOW TO DIE FOR FLOUTING THEIR INFINITE WISDOM?
NO.
WHATEVER FEAR INFECTS THIS PLACE...
IT IS ONLY FEAR.

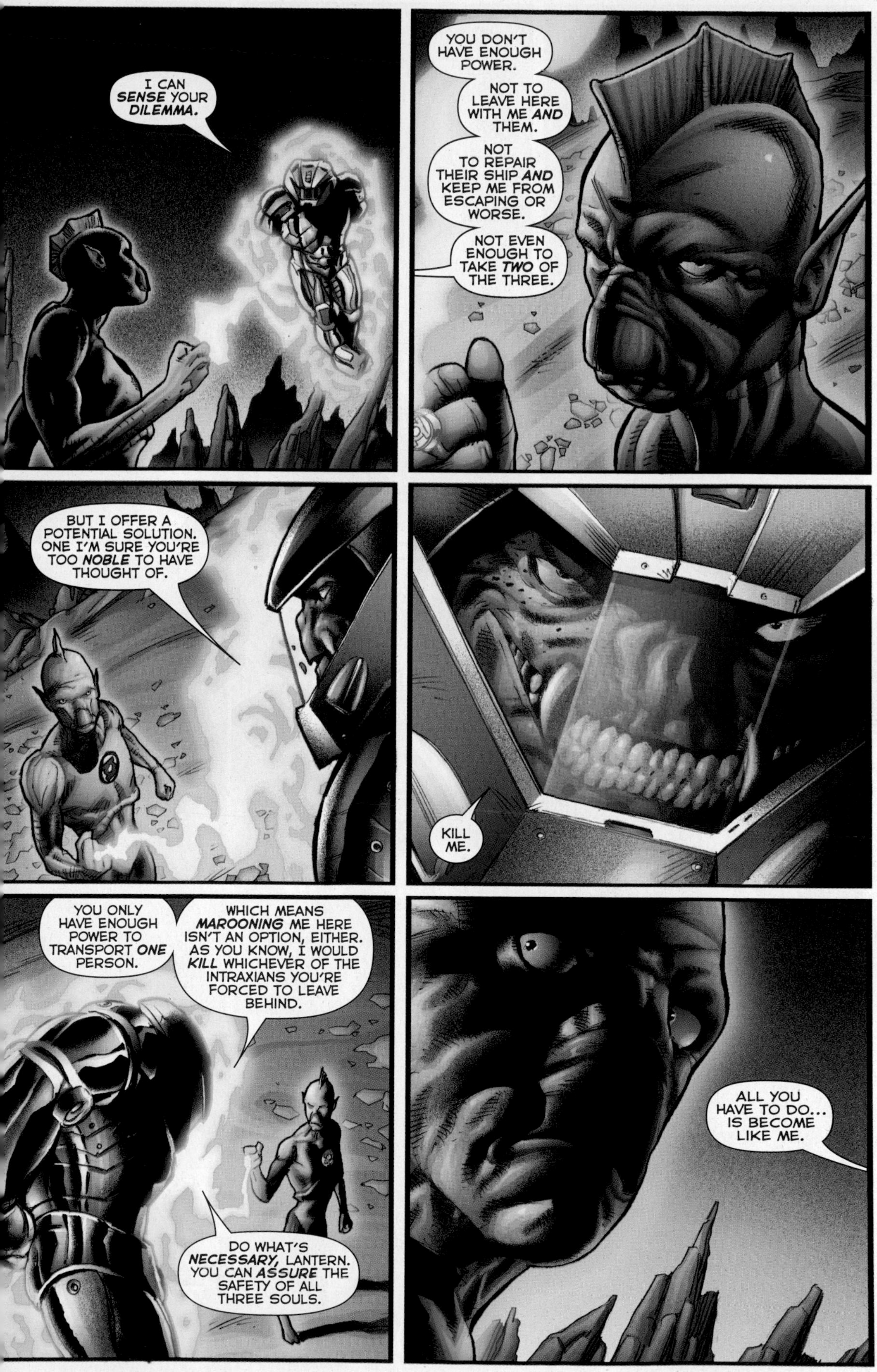
I CAN SENSE YOUR DILEMMA.
YOU DON'T HAVE ENOUGH POWER.
NOT TO LEAVE HERE WITH ME AND THEM.
NOT TO REPAIR THEIR SHIP AND KEEP ME FROM ESCAPING OR WORSE.
NOT EVEN ENOUGH TO TAKE TWO OF THE THREE.
BUT I OFFER A POTENTIAL SOLUTION. ONE I'M SURE YOU'RE TOO NOBLE TO HAVE THOUGHT OF.
KILL ME.
YOU ONLY HAVE ENOUGH POWER TO TRANSPORT ONE PERSON.
WHICH MEANS MAROONING ME HERE ISN'T AN OPTION, EITHER. AS YOU KNOW, I WOULD KILL WHICHEVER OF THE INTRAXIANS YOU'RE FORCED TO LEAVE BEHIND.
DO WHAT'S NECESSARY, LANTERN. YOU CAN ASSURE THE SAFETY OF ALL THREE SOULS.
ALL YOU HAVE TO DO... IS BECOME LIKE ME.

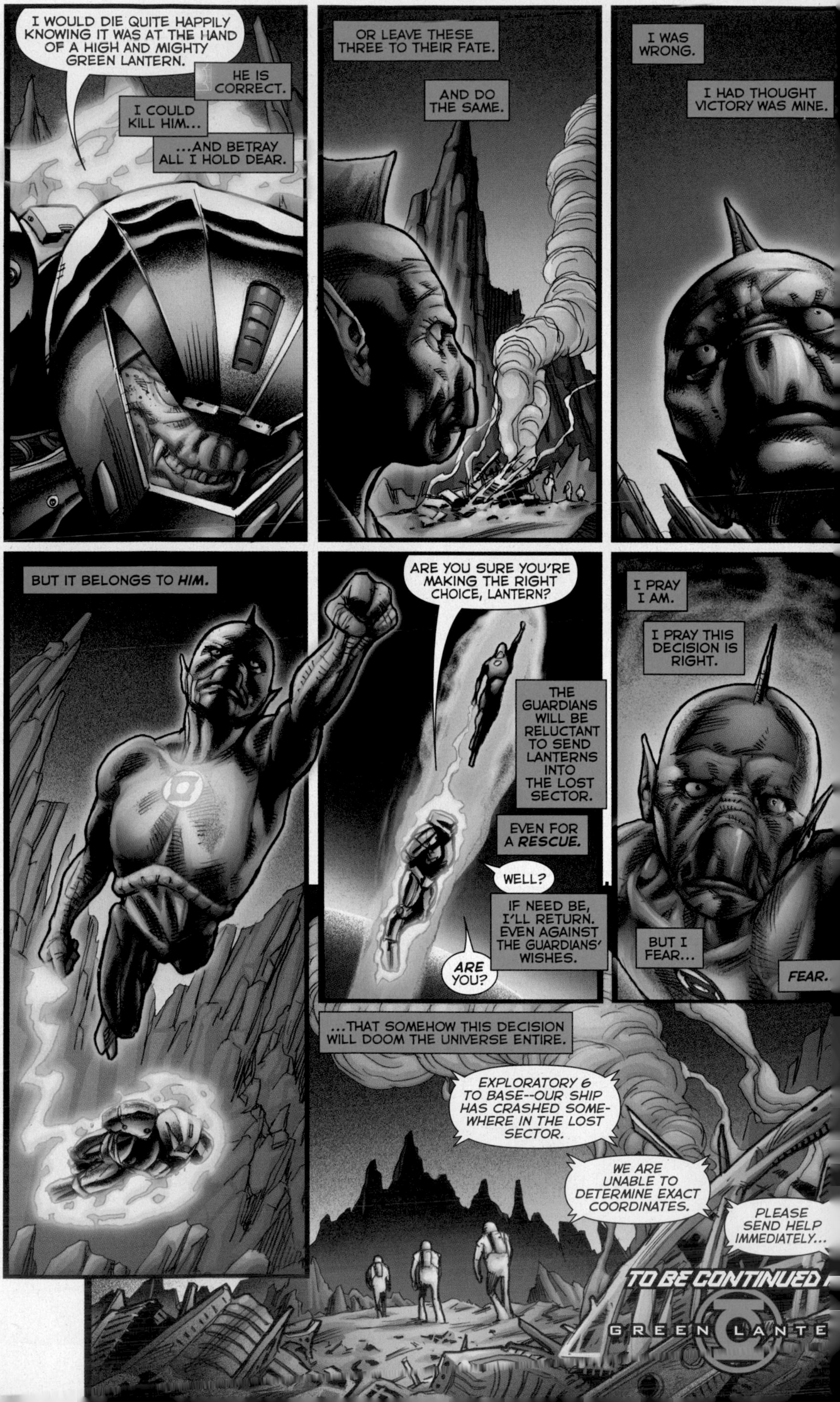
I WOULD DIE QUITE HAPPILY KNOWING IT WAS AT THE HAND OF A HIGH AND MIGHTY GREEN LANTERN.
HE IS CORRECT.
I COULD KILL HIM...
...AND BETRAY ALL I HOLD DEAR.
OR LEAVE THESE THREE TO THEIR FATE.
AND DO THE SAME.
I WAS WRONG.
I HAD THOUGHT VICTORY WAS MINE.
BUT IT BELONGS TO *HIM.*
ARE YOU SURE YOU'RE MAKING THE RIGHT CHOICE, LANTERN?
THE GUARDIANS WILL BE RELUCTANT TO SEND LANTERNS INTO THE LOST SECTOR.
EVEN FOR A *RESCUE.*
WELL?
IF NEED BE, I'LL RETURN. EVEN AGAINST THE GUARDIANS' WISHES.
ARE YOU?
I PRAY I AM.
I PRAY THIS DECISION IS RIGHT.
BUT I FEAR...
FEAR.
...THAT SOMEHOW THIS DECISION WILL DOOM THE UNIVERSE ENTIRE.
EXPLORATORY 6 TO BASE--OUR SHIP HAS CRASHED SOMEWHERE IN THE LOST SECTOR.
WE ARE UNABLE TO DETERMINE EXACT COORDINATES.
PLEASE SEND HELP IMMEDIATELY...
TO BE CONTINUED

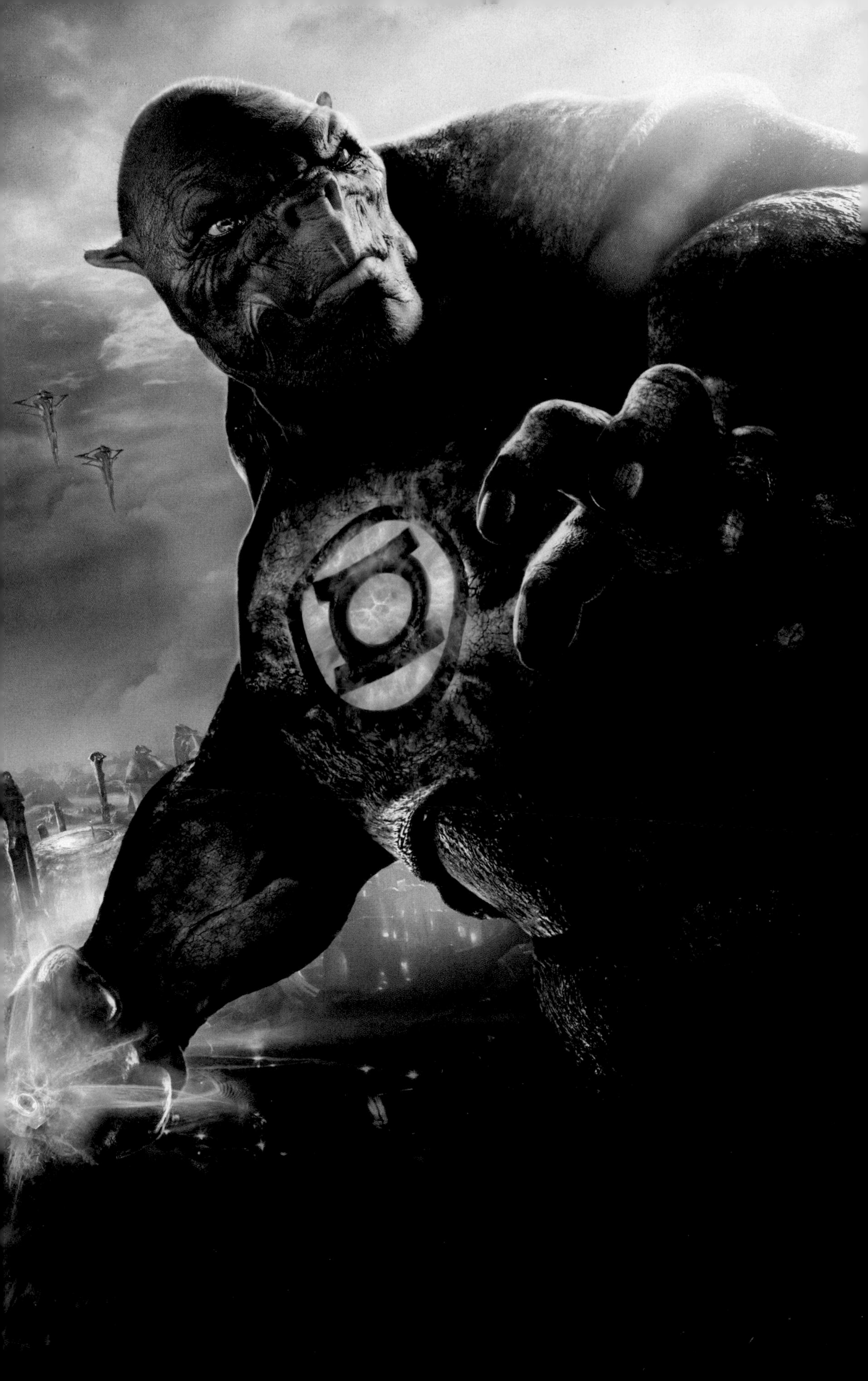

TO BUILD A BETTER LANTERN

PETER J. **TOMASI** writer

CARLOS **FERREIRA** penciller

SILVIO **SPOTTI** inker

Kilowog created by STEVE **ENGLEHART** and JOE **STANTON**

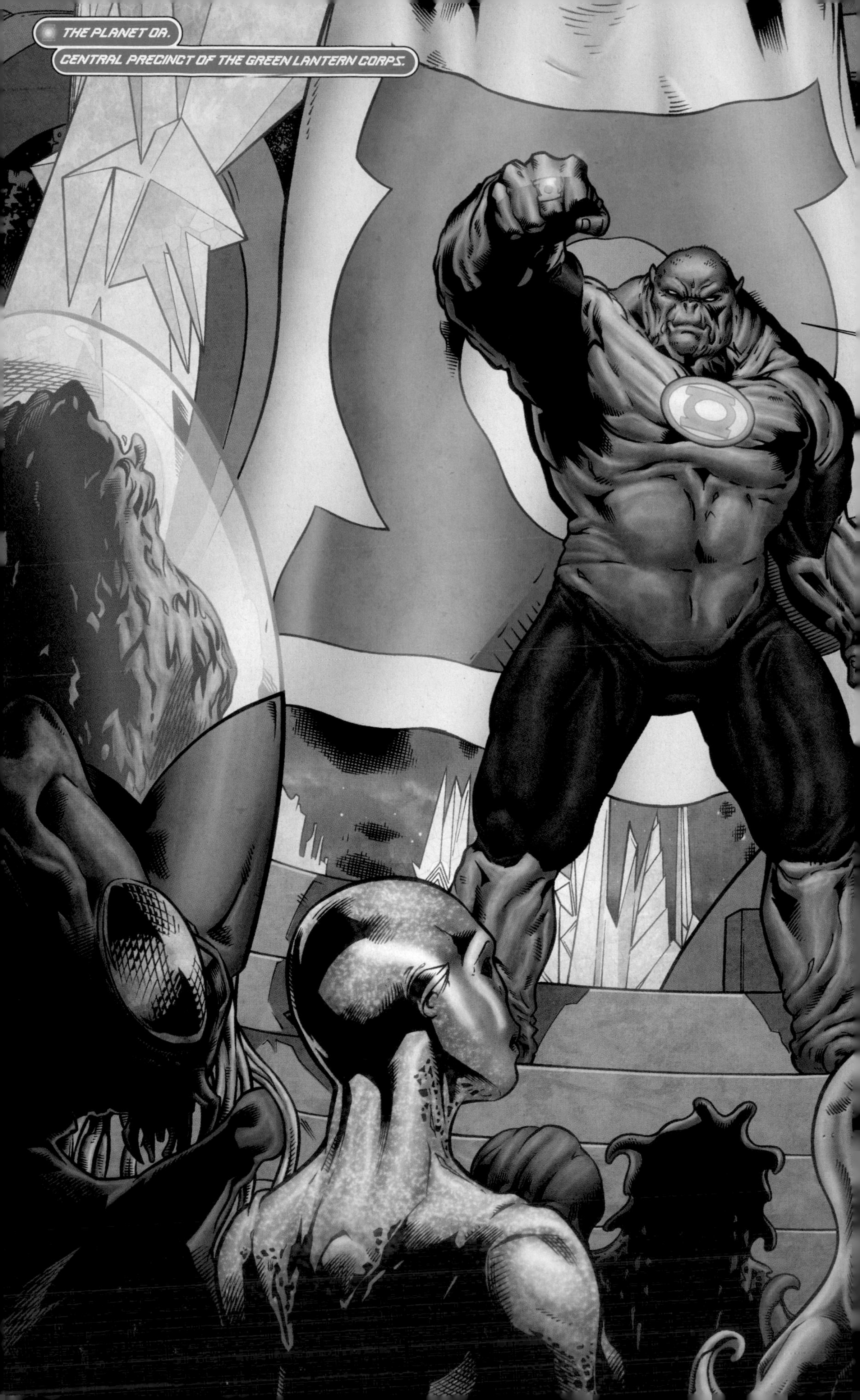
THE PLANET OA.
CENTRAL PRECINCT OF THE GREEN LANTERN CORPS.

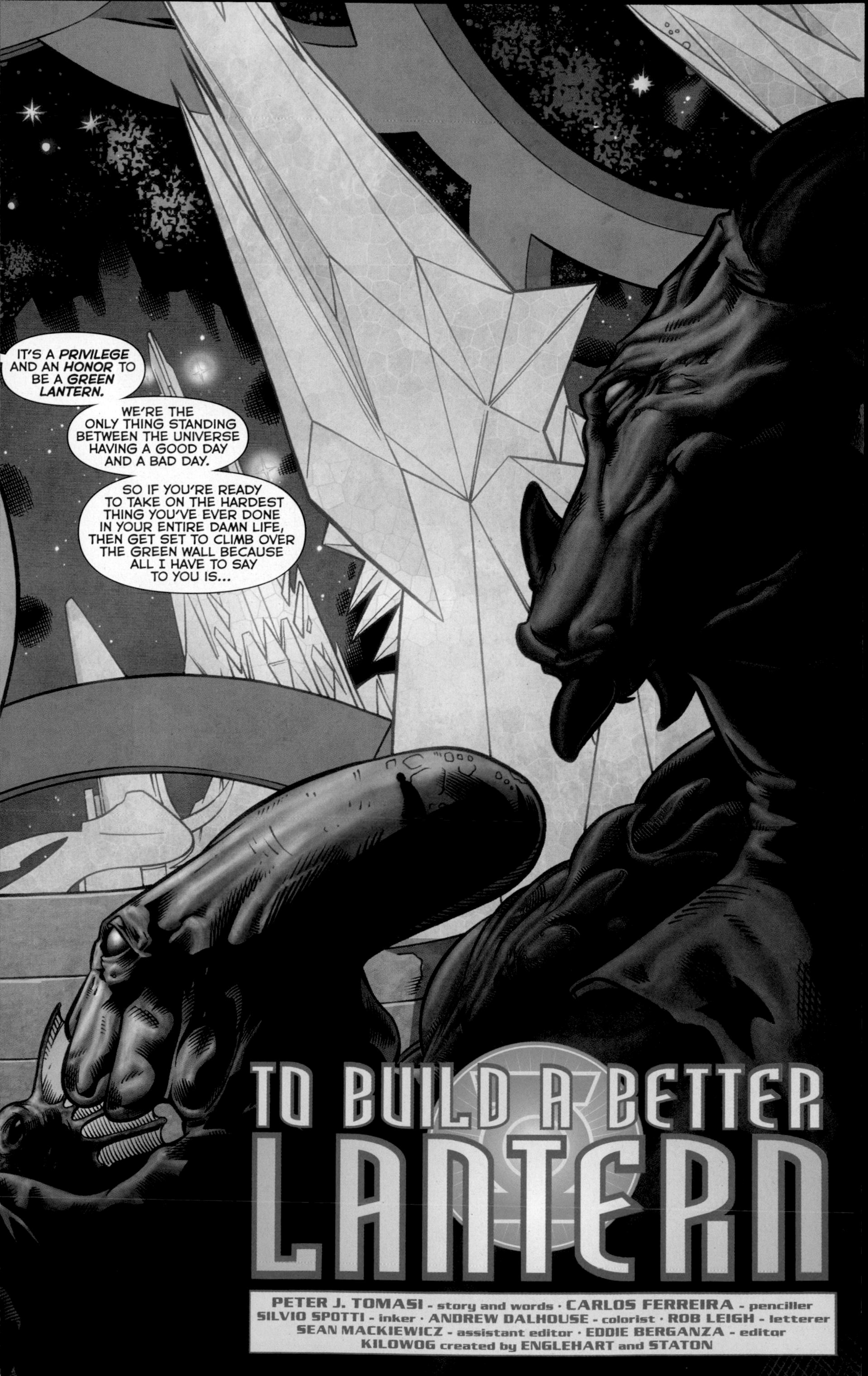
IT'S A *PRIVILEGE* AND AN *HONOR* TO BE A *GREEN LANTERN.*
WE'RE THE ONLY THING STANDING BETWEEN THE UNIVERSE HAVING A GOOD DAY AND A BAD DAY.
SO IF YOU'RE READY TO TAKE ON THE HARDEST THING YOU'VE EVER DONE IN YOUR ENTIRE DAMN LIFE, THEN GET SET TO CLIMB OVER THE GREEN WALL BECAUSE ALL I HAVE TO SAY TO YOU IS...
TO BUILD A BETTER LANTERN
PETER J. TOMASI - story and words · CARLOS FERREIRA - penciller
SILVIO SPOTTI - inker · ANDREW DALHOUSE - colorist · ROB LEIGH - letterer
SEAN MACKIEWICZ - assistant editor · EDDIE BERGANZA - editor
KILOWOG created by ENGLEHART and STATON

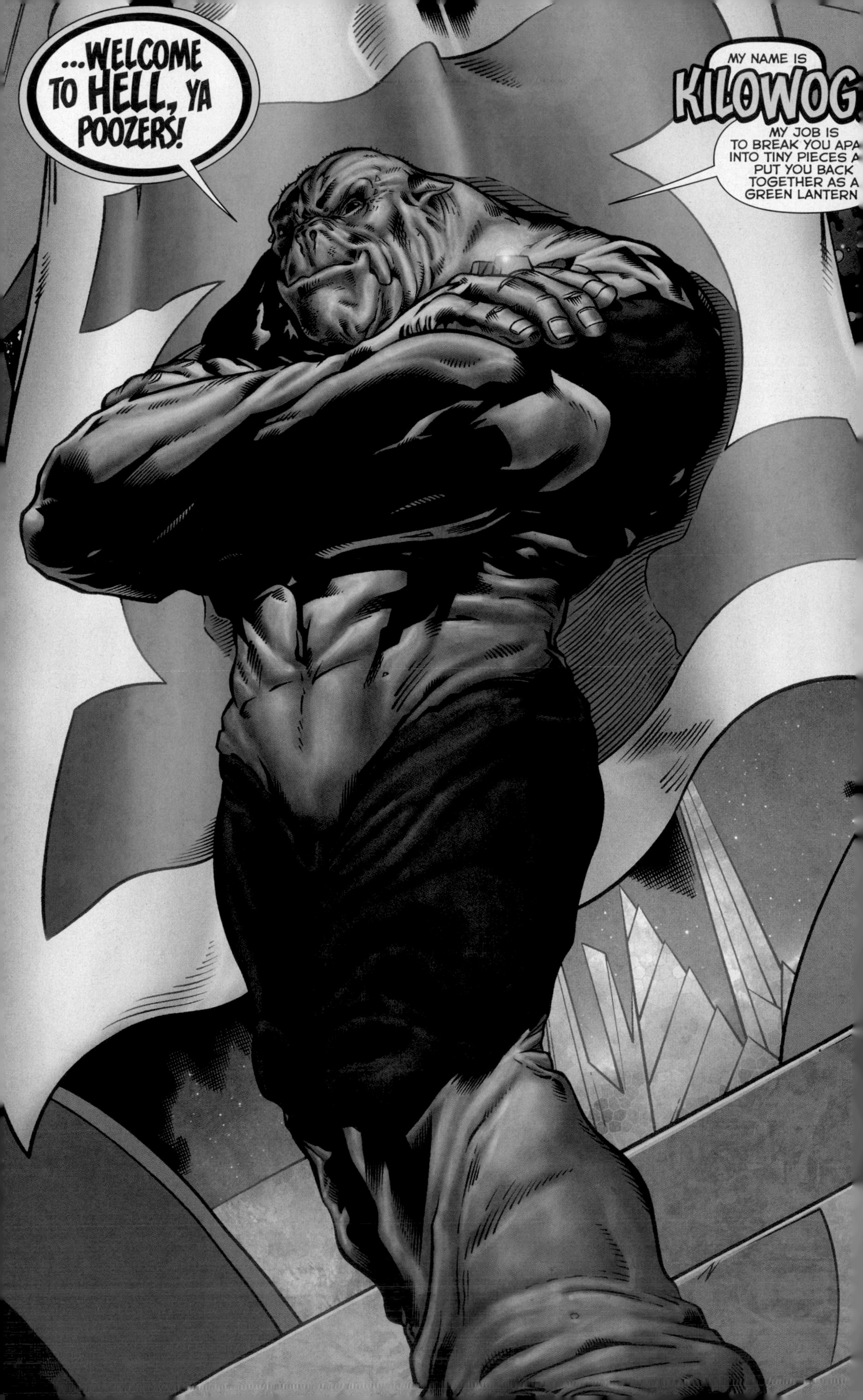
...WELCOME TO HELL, YA POOZERS!
MY NAME IS KILOWOG
MY JOB IS TO BREAK YOU APA INTO TINY PIECES A PUT YOU BACK TOGETHER AS A GREEN LANTERN

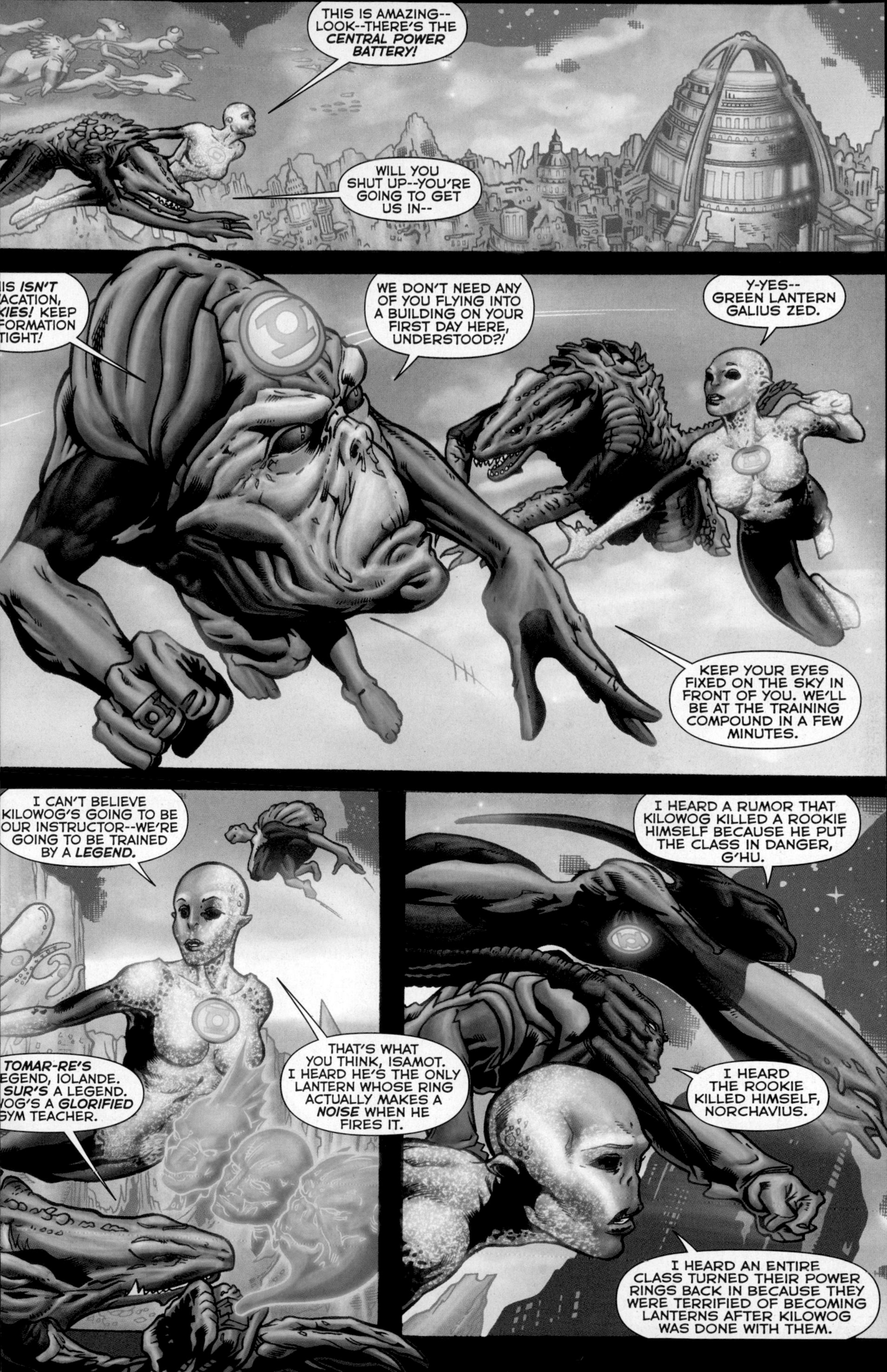
THIS IS AMAZING--LOOK--THERE'S THE *CENTRAL POWER BATTERY!*
WILL YOU SHUT UP--YOU'RE GOING TO GET US IN--
IS *ISN'T* ACATION, KIES! KEEP FORMATION TIGHT!
WE DON'T NEED ANY OF YOU FLYING INTO A BUILDING ON YOUR FIRST DAY HERE, UNDERSTOOD?!
Y-YES--GREEN LANTERN GALIUS ZED.
KEEP YOUR EYES FIXED ON THE SKY IN FRONT OF YOU. WE'LL BE AT THE TRAINING COMPOUND IN A FEW MINUTES.
I CAN'T BELIEVE KILOWOG'S GOING TO BE OUR INSTRUCTOR--WE'RE GOING TO BE TRAINED BY A *LEGEND.*
TOMAR-RE'S EGEND, IOLANDE. *SUR'S* A LEGEND. WOG'S A *GLORIFIED* GYM TEACHER.
THAT'S WHAT YOU THINK, ISAMOT. I HEARD HE'S THE ONLY LANTERN WHOSE RING ACTUALLY MAKES A *NOISE* WHEN HE FIRES IT.
I HEARD A RUMOR THAT KILOWOG KILLED A ROOKIE HIMSELF BECAUSE HE PUT THE CLASS IN DANGER, G'HU.
I HEARD THE ROOKIE KILLED HIMSELF, NORCHAVIUS.
I HEARD AN ENTIRE CLASS TURNED THEIR POWER RINGS BACK IN BECAUSE THEY WERE TERRIFIED OF BECOMING LANTERNS AFTER KILOWOG WAS DONE WITH THEM.

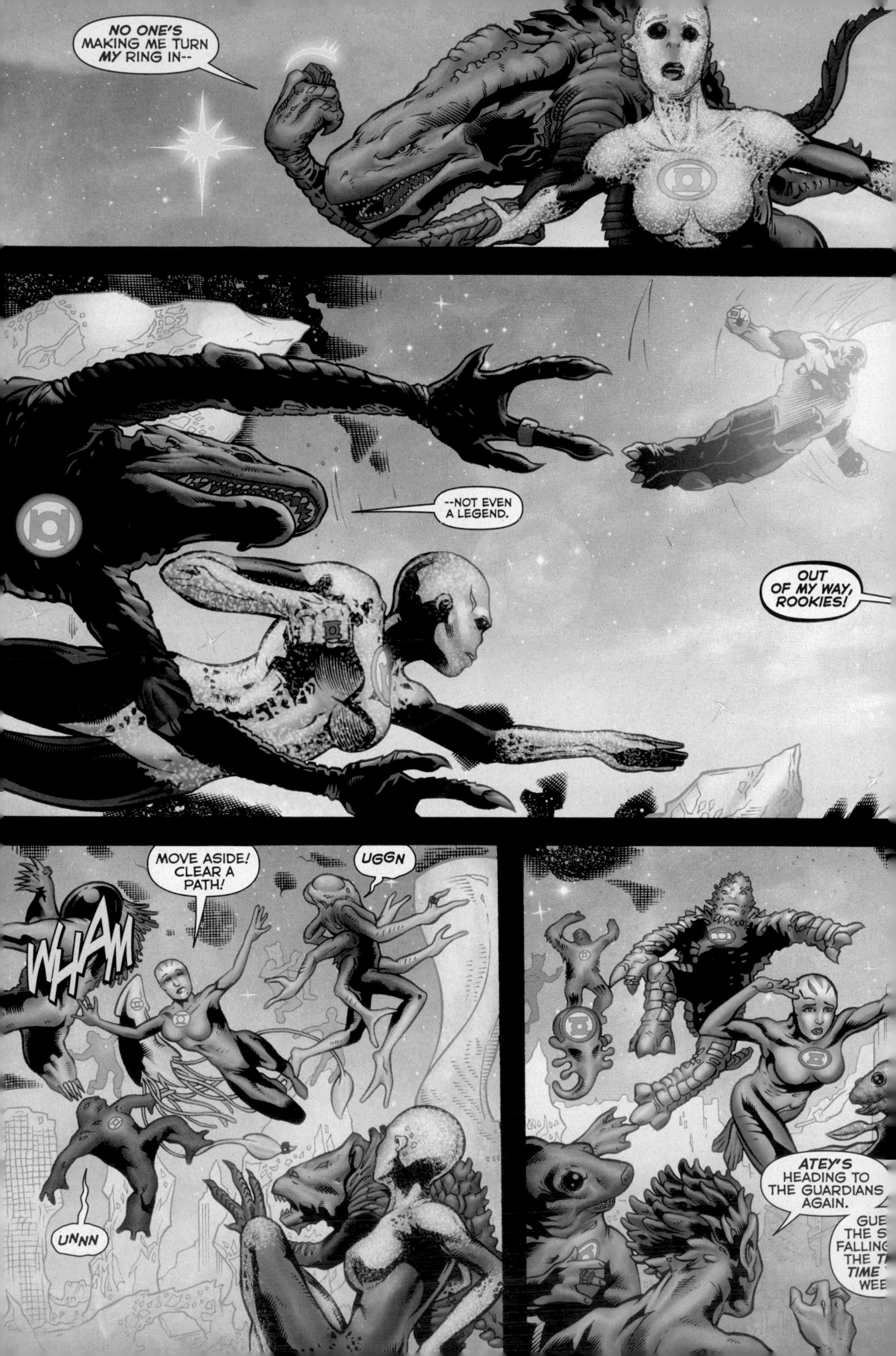

NO ONE'S MAKING ME TURN *MY* RING IN--
--NOT EVEN A LEGEND.
OUT OF MY WAY, ROOKIES!
WHAM
MOVE ASIDE! CLEAR A PATH!
UGGN
UNNN
ATEY'S HEADING TO THE GUARDIANS AGAIN.

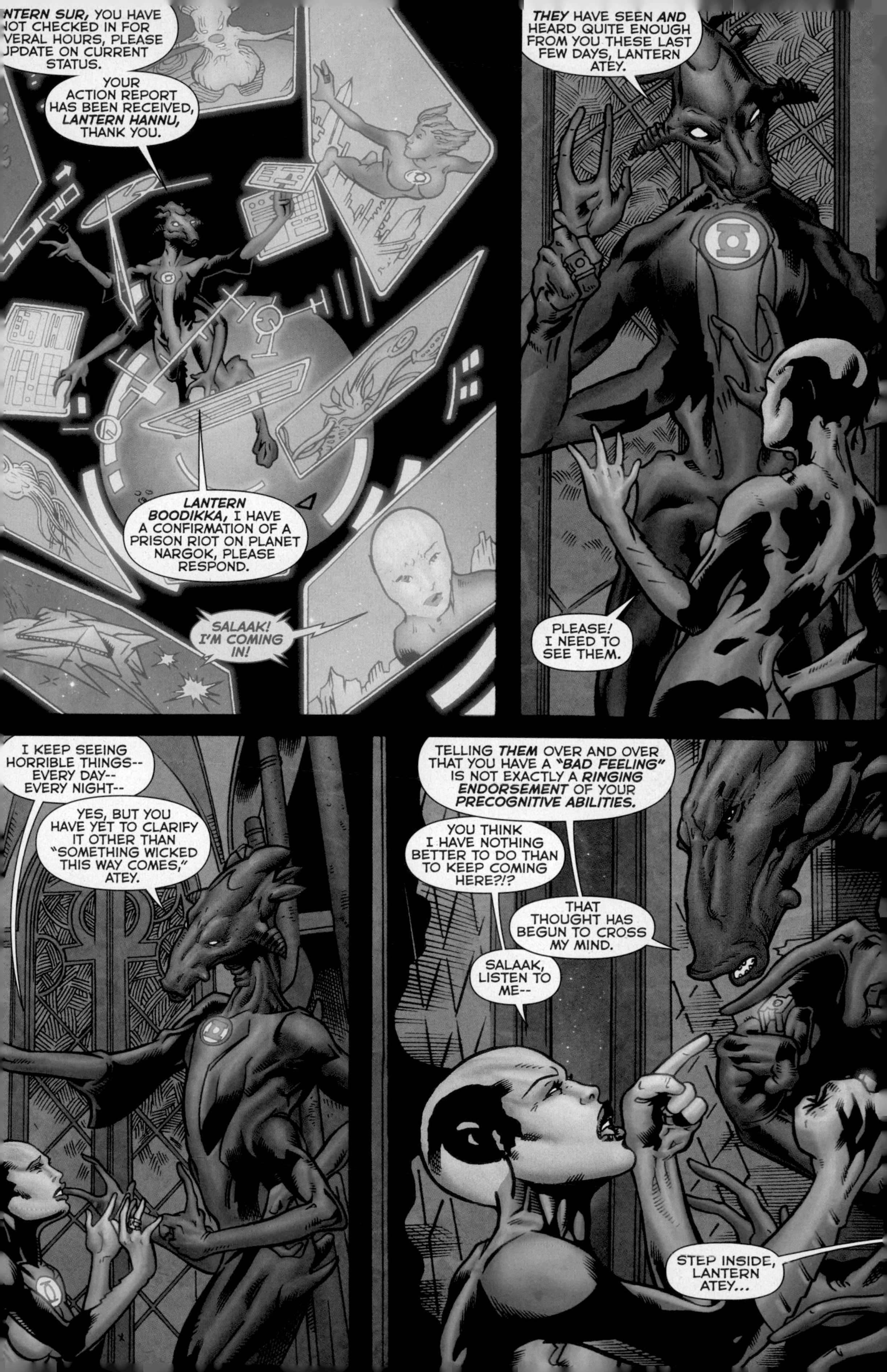
NTERN SUR, YOU HAVE NOT CHECKED IN FOR VERAL HOURS, PLEASE UPDATE ON CURRENT STATUS.
YOUR ACTION REPORT HAS BEEN RECEIVED, LANTERN HANNU, THANK YOU.
LANTERN BOODIKKA, I HAVE A CONFIRMATION OF A PRISON RIOT ON PLANET NARGOK, PLEASE RESPOND.
SALAAK! I'M COMING IN!
THEY HAVE SEEN AND HEARD QUITE ENOUGH FROM YOU THESE LAST FEW DAYS, LANTERN ATEY.
PLEASE! I NEED TO SEE THEM.
I KEEP SEEING HORRIBLE THINGS-- EVERY DAY-- EVERY NIGHT--
YES, BUT YOU HAVE YET TO CLARIFY IT OTHER THAN "SOMETHING WICKED THIS WAY COMES," ATEY.
TELLING THEM OVER AND OVER THAT YOU HAVE A "BAD FEELING" IS NOT EXACTLY A RINGING ENDORSEMENT OF YOUR PRECOGNITIVE ABILITIES.
YOU THINK I HAVE NOTHING BETTER TO DO THAN TO KEEP COMING HERE?!?
THAT THOUGHT HAS BEGUN TO CROSS MY MIND.
SALAAK, LISTEN TO ME--
STEP INSIDE, LANTERN ATEY...

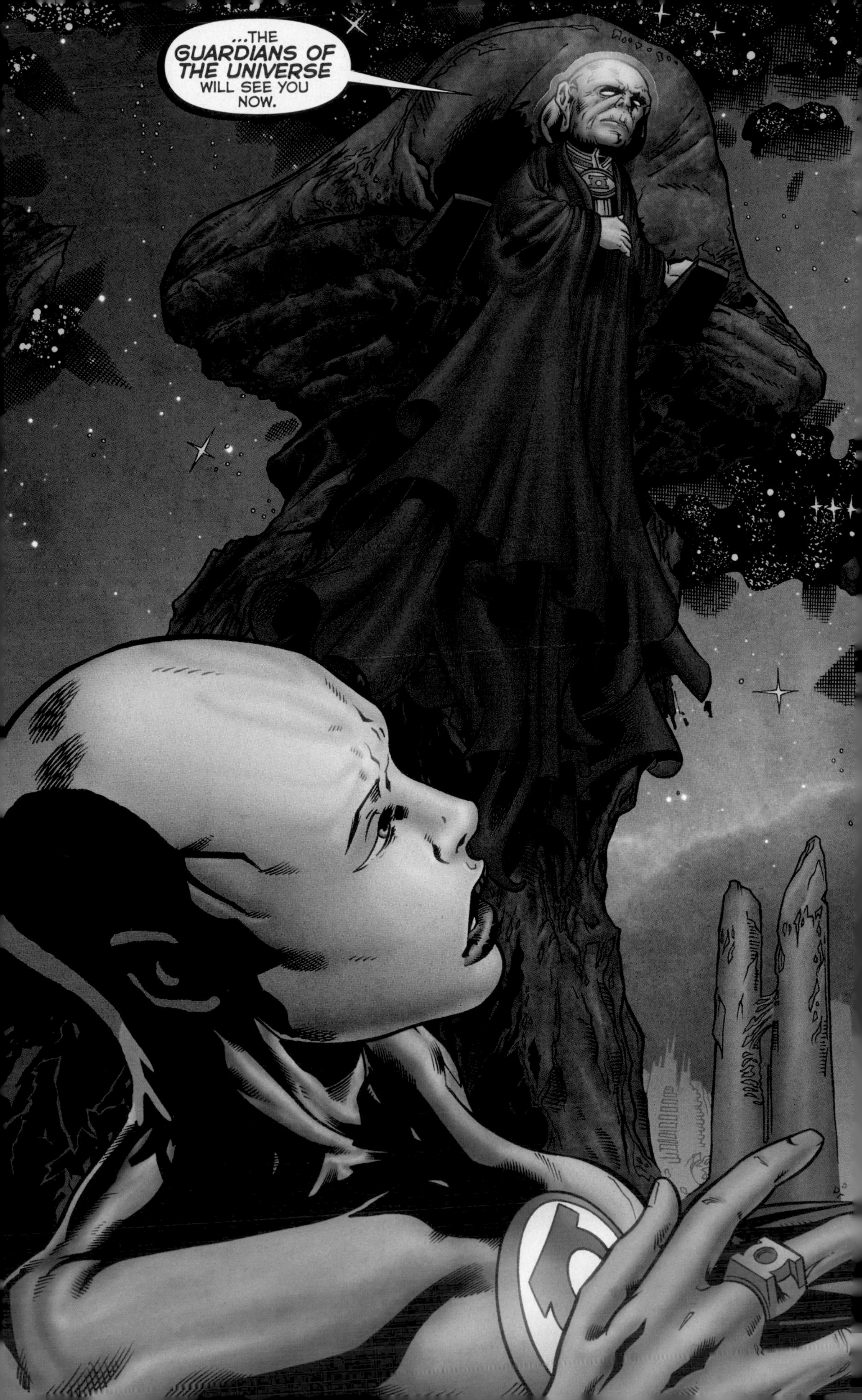
...THE GUARDIANS OF THE UNIVERSE WILL SEE YOU NOW.

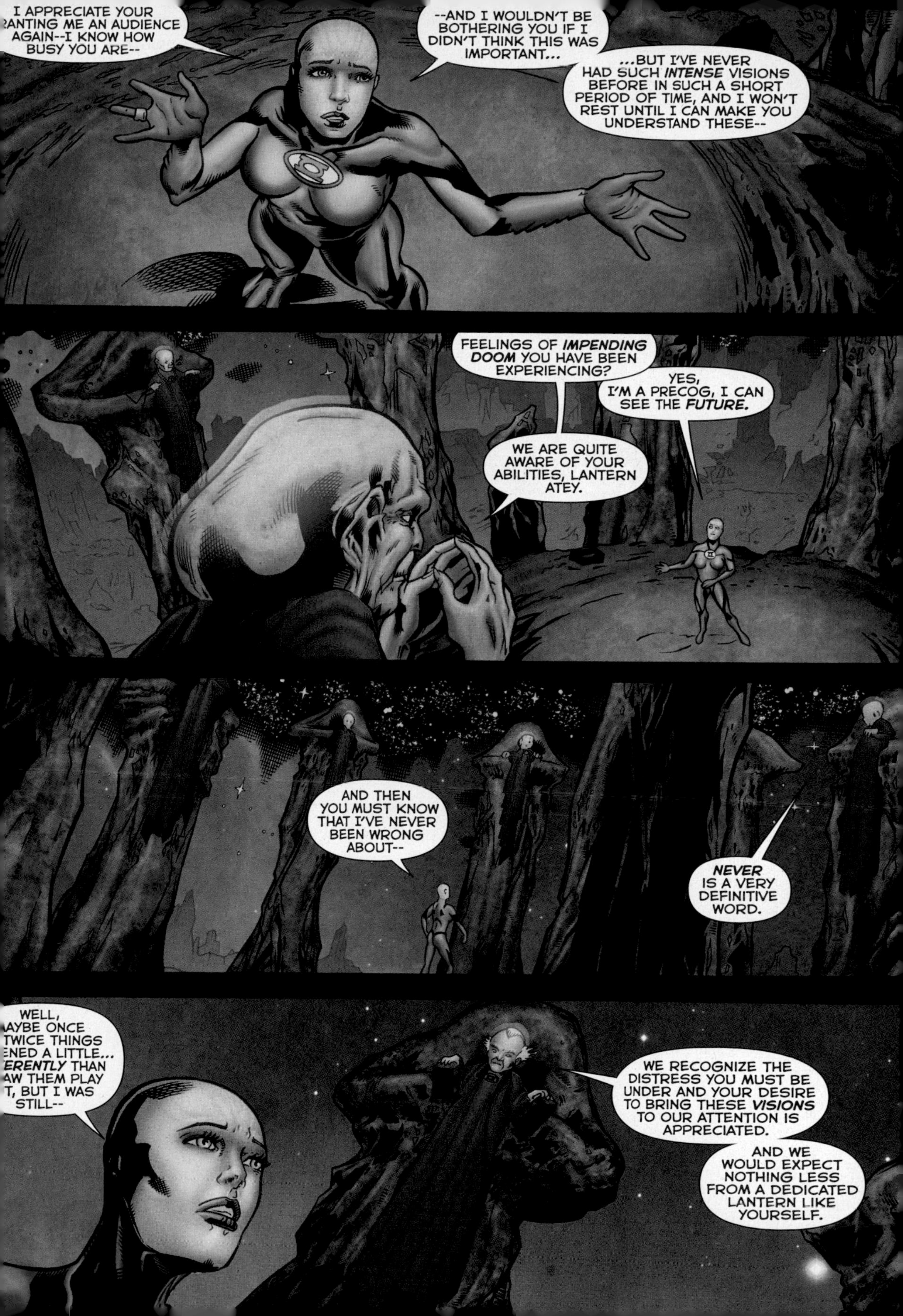

I APPRECIATE YOUR
RANTING ME AN AUDIENCE AGAIN--I KNOW HOW BUSY YOU ARE--
--AND I WOULDN'T BE BOTHERING YOU IF I DIDN'T THINK THIS WAS IMPORTANT...
...BUT I'VE NEVER HAD SUCH *INTENSE* VISIONS BEFORE IN SUCH A SHORT PERIOD OF TIME, AND I WON'T REST UNTIL I CAN MAKE YOU UNDERSTAND THESE--
FEELINGS OF *IMPENDING DOOM* YOU HAVE BEEN EXPERIENCING?
YES, I'M A PRECOG, I CAN SEE THE *FUTURE.*
WE ARE QUITE AWARE OF YOUR ABILITIES, LANTERN ATEY.
AND THEN YOU MUST KNOW THAT I'VE NEVER BEEN WRONG ABOUT--
NEVER IS A VERY DEFINITIVE WORD.
WELL, AYBE ONCE TWICE THINGS ENED A LITTLE... *ERENTLY* THAN AW THEM PLAY T, BUT I WAS STILL--
WE RECOGNIZE THE DISTRESS YOU MUST BE UNDER AND YOUR DESIRE TO BRING THESE *VISIONS* TO OUR ATTENTION IS APPRECIATED.
AND WE WOULD EXPECT NOTHING LESS FROM A DEDICATED LANTERN LIKE YOURSELF.

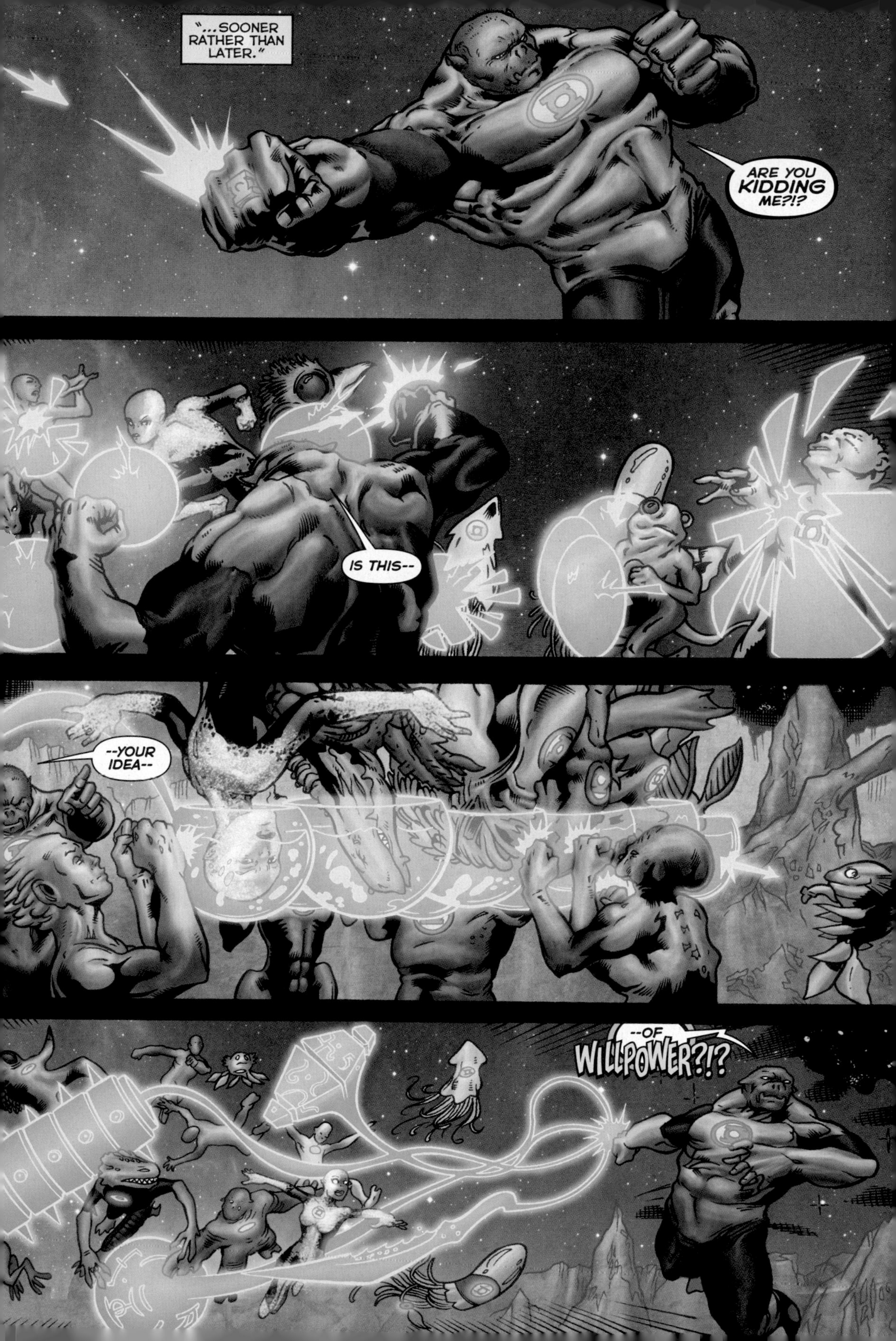
"...SOONER RATHER THAN LATER."
ARE YOU KIDDING ME?!?
IS THIS--
--YOUR IDEA--
--OF
WILLPOWER?!?

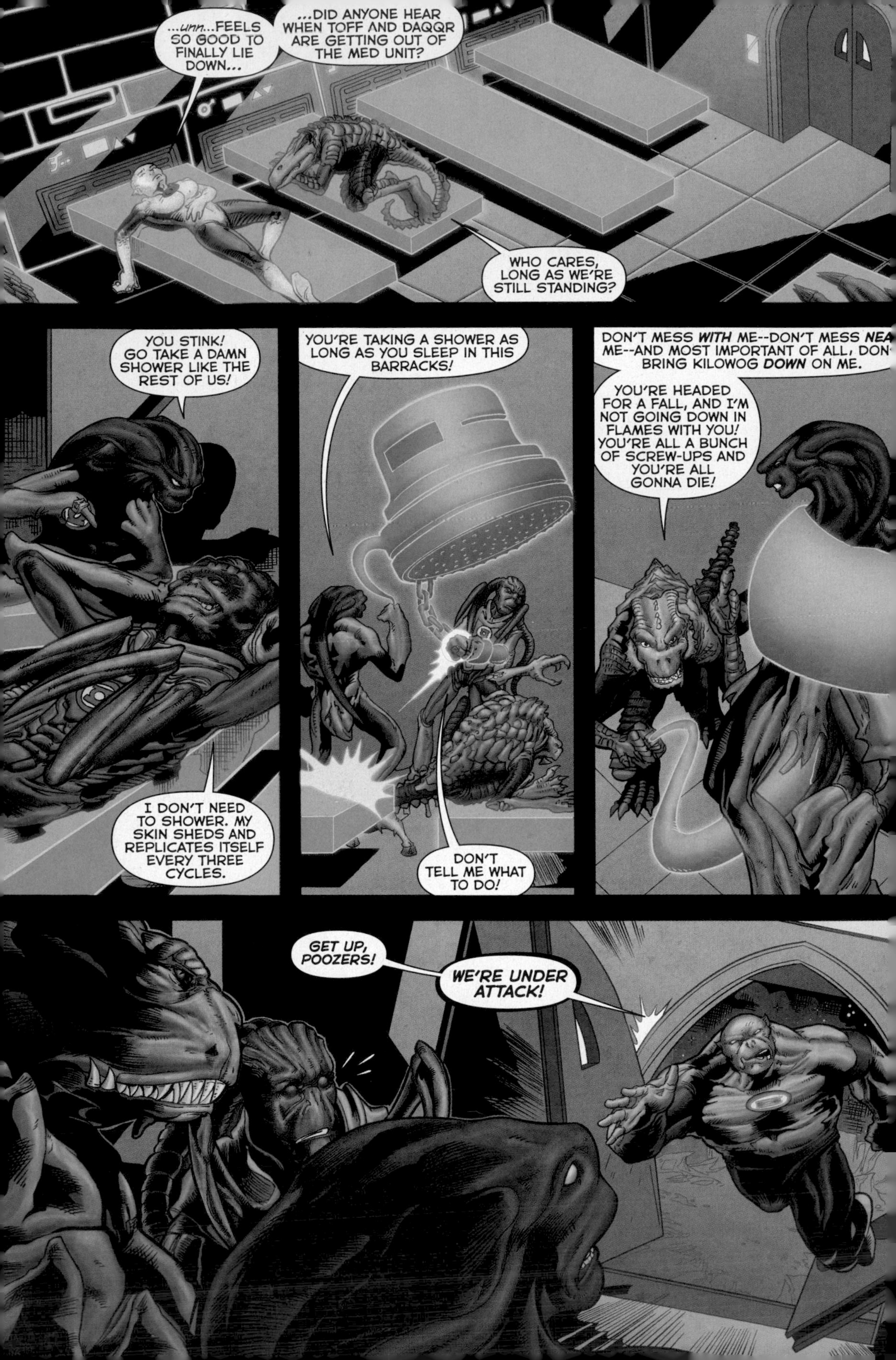

...unn...FEELS SO GOOD TO FINALLY LIE DOWN...
...DID ANYONE HEAR WHEN TOFF AND DAQQR ARE GETTING OUT OF THE MED UNIT?
WHO CARES, LONG AS WE'RE STILL STANDING?
YOU STINK! GO TAKE A DAMN SHOWER LIKE THE REST OF US!
I DON'T NEED TO SHOWER. MY SKIN SHEDS AND REPLICATES ITSELF EVERY THREE CYCLES.
YOU'RE TAKING A SHOWER AS LONG AS YOU SLEEP IN THIS BARRACKS!
DON'T TELL ME WHAT TO DO!
DON'T MESS WITH ME--DON'T MESS NEA ME--AND MOST IMPORTANT OF ALL, DON BRING KILOWOG DOWN ON ME.
YOU'RE HEADED FOR A FALL, AND I'M NOT GOING DOWN IN FLAMES WITH YOU! YOU'RE ALL A BUNCH OF SCREW-UPS AND YOU'RE ALL GONNA DIE!
GET UP, POOZERS!
WE'RE UNDER ATTACK!

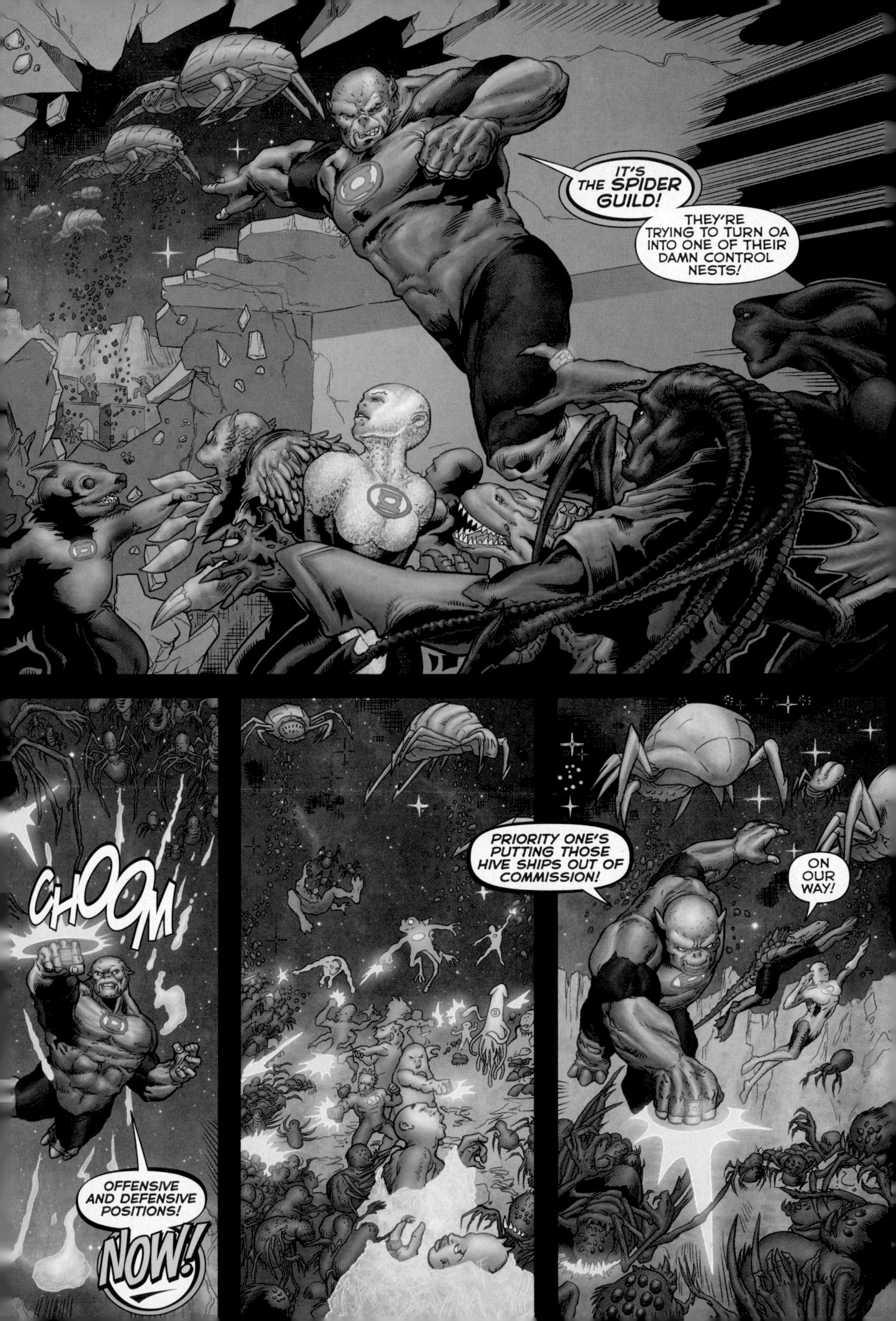
IT'S THE SPIDER GUILD!
THEY'RE TRYING TO TURN OA INTO ONE OF THEIR DAMN CONTROL NESTS!
CHOOM
OFFENSIVE AND DEFENSIVE POSITIONS!
NOW!
PRIORITY ONE'S PUTTING THOSE HIVE SHIPS OUT OF COMMISSION!
ON OUR WAY!

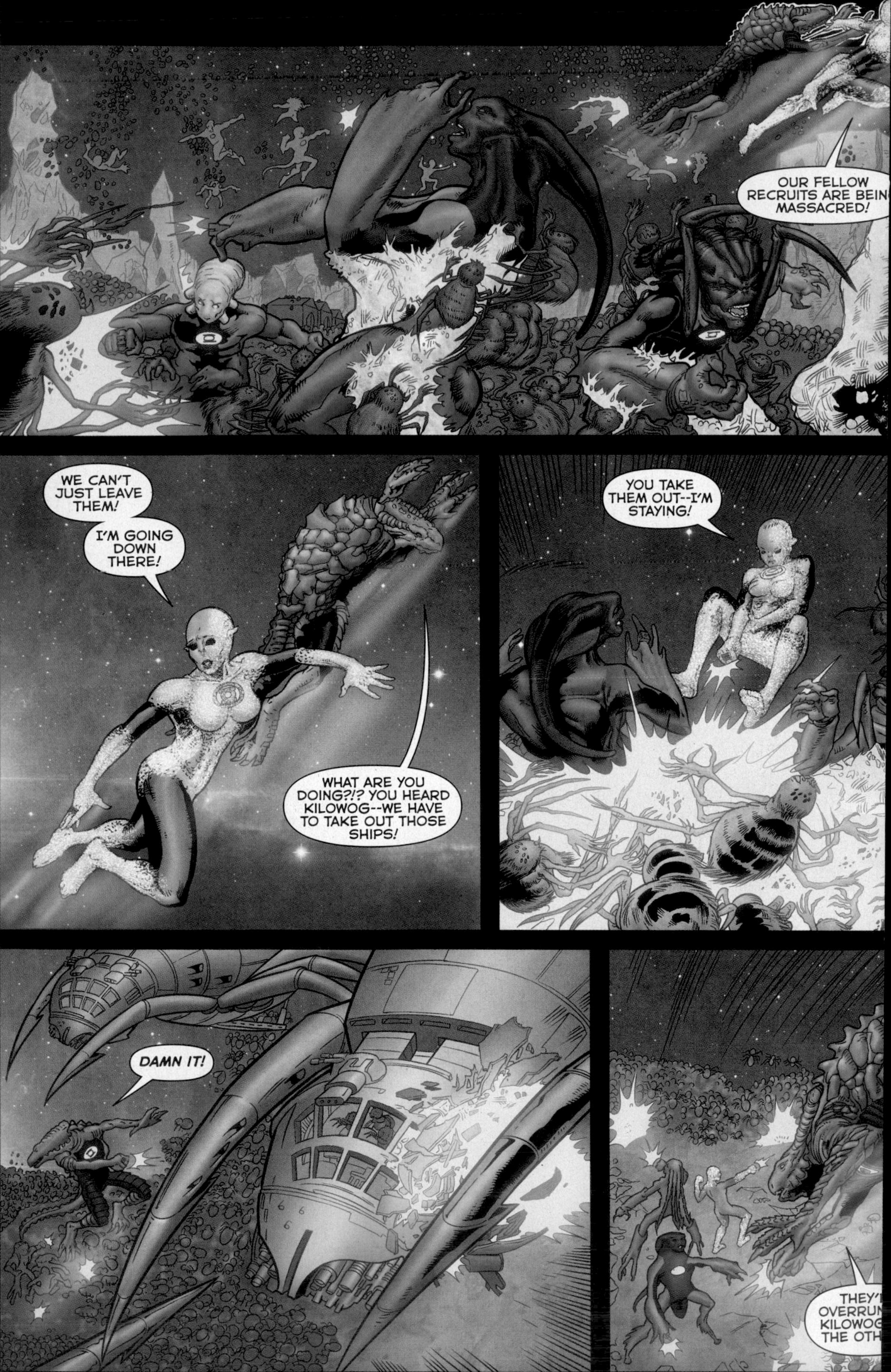
OUR FELLOW RECRUITS ARE BEIN
MASSACRED!
WE CAN'T JUST LEAVE THEM!
I'M GOING DOWN THERE!
WHAT ARE YOU DOING?!? YOU HEARD KILOWOG--WE HAVE TO TAKE OUT THOSE SHIPS!
YOU TAKE THEM OUT--I'M STAYING!
DAMN IT!
THEY'I OVERRUN KILOWOG THE OTH

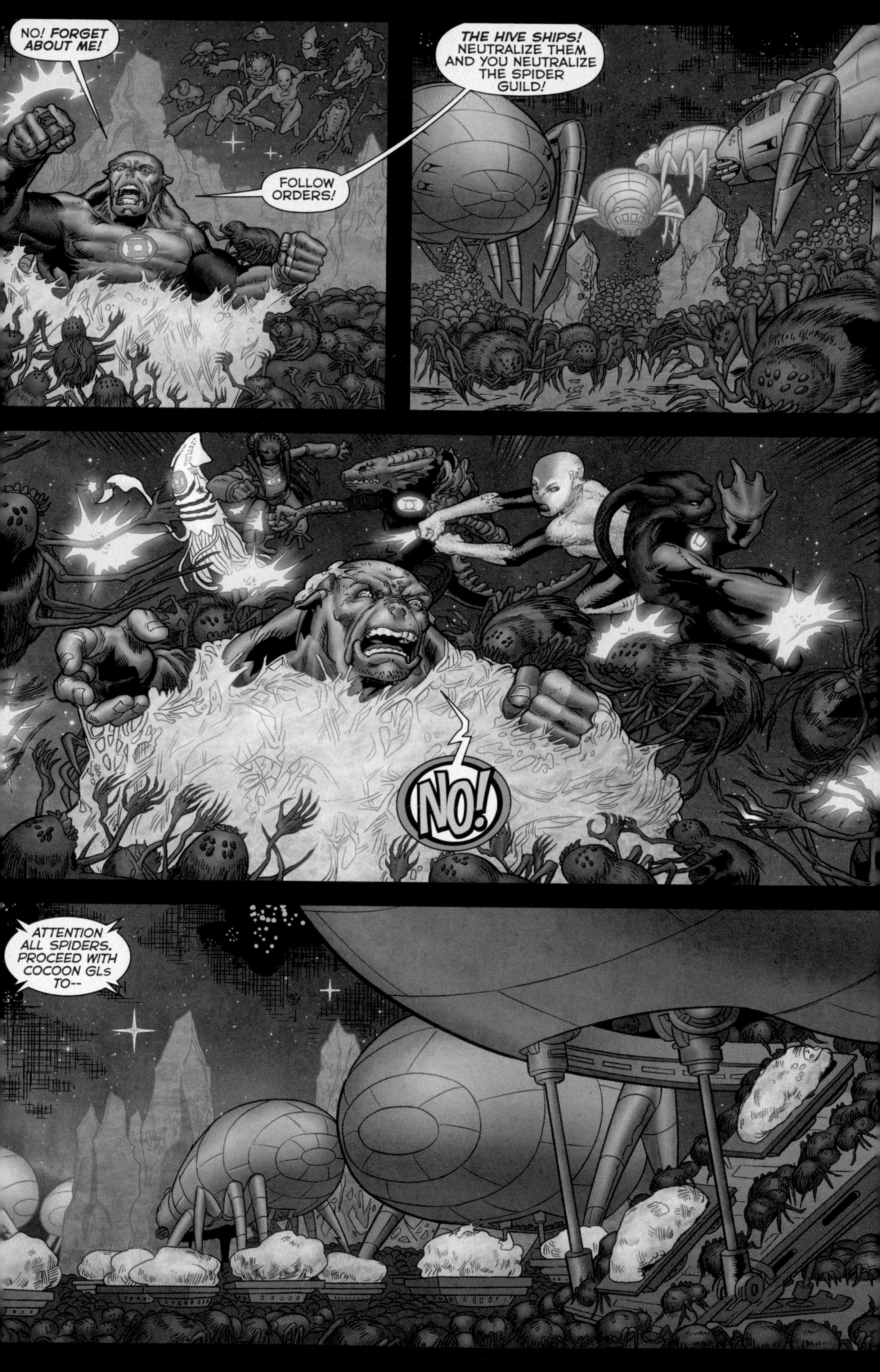
NO! FORGET ABOUT ME!
FOLLOW ORDERS!
THE HIVE SHIPS! NEUTRALIZE THEM AND YOU NEUTRALIZE THE SPIDER GUILD!
NO!
ATTENTION ALL SPIDERS. PROCEED WITH COCOON GLs TO--

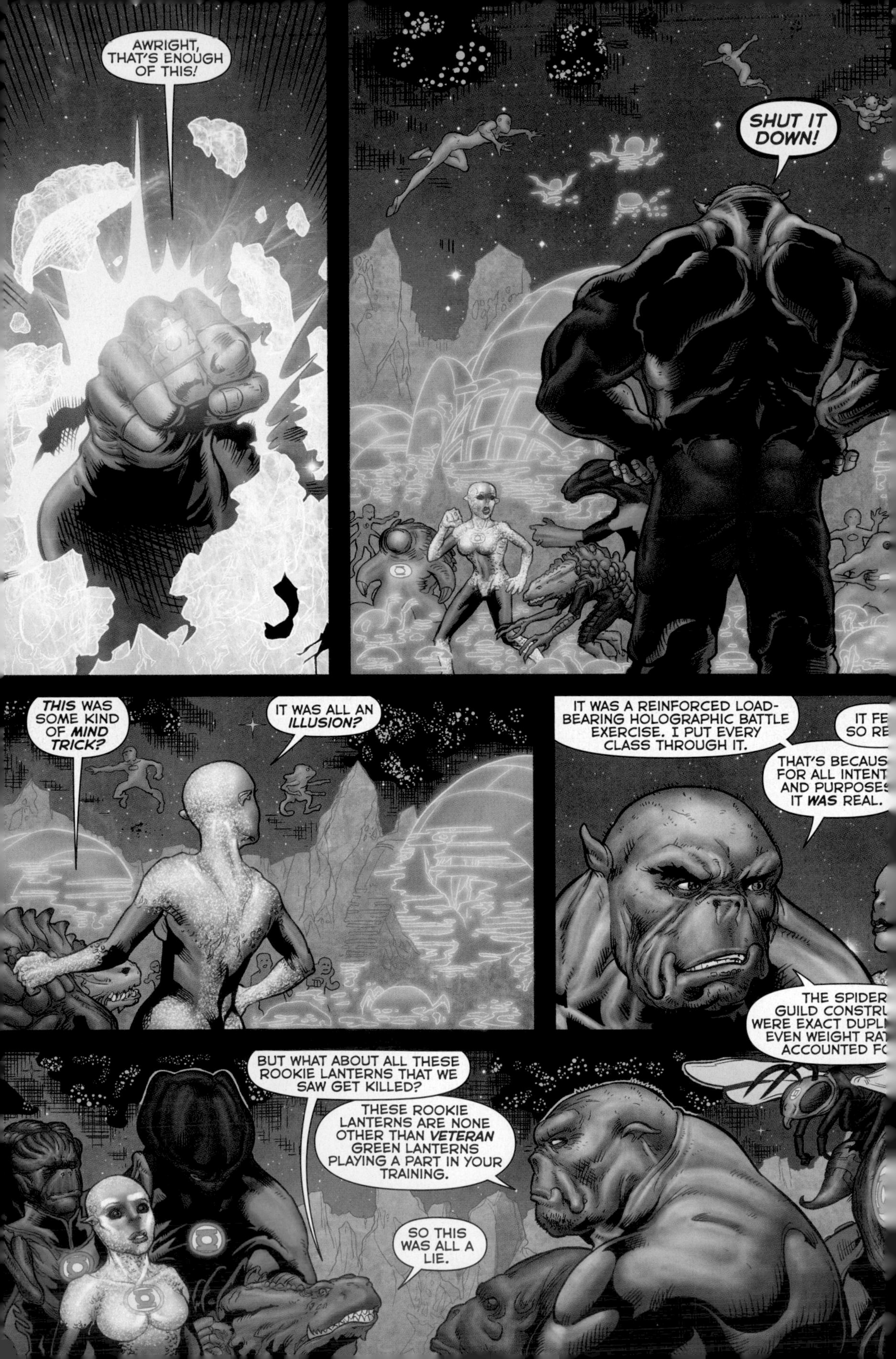
AWRIGHT, THAT'S ENOUGH OF THIS!
SHUT IT DOWN!
THIS WAS SOME KIND OF MIND TRICK?
IT WAS ALL AN ILLUSION?
IT WAS A REINFORCED LOAD-BEARING HOLOGRAPHIC BATTLE EXERCISE. I PUT EVERY CLASS THROUGH IT.
IT FE SO RE
THAT'S BECAUS FOR ALL INTENT AND PURPOSES IT WAS REAL.
THE SPIDER GUILD CONSTRU WERE EXACT DUPL EVEN WEIGHT RA ACCOUNTED FO
BUT WHAT ABOUT ALL THESE ROOKIE LANTERNS THAT WE SAW GET KILLED?
THESE ROOKIE LANTERNS ARE NONE OTHER THAN VETERAN GREEN LANTERNS PLAYING A PART IN YOUR TRAINING.
SO THIS WAS ALL A LIE.

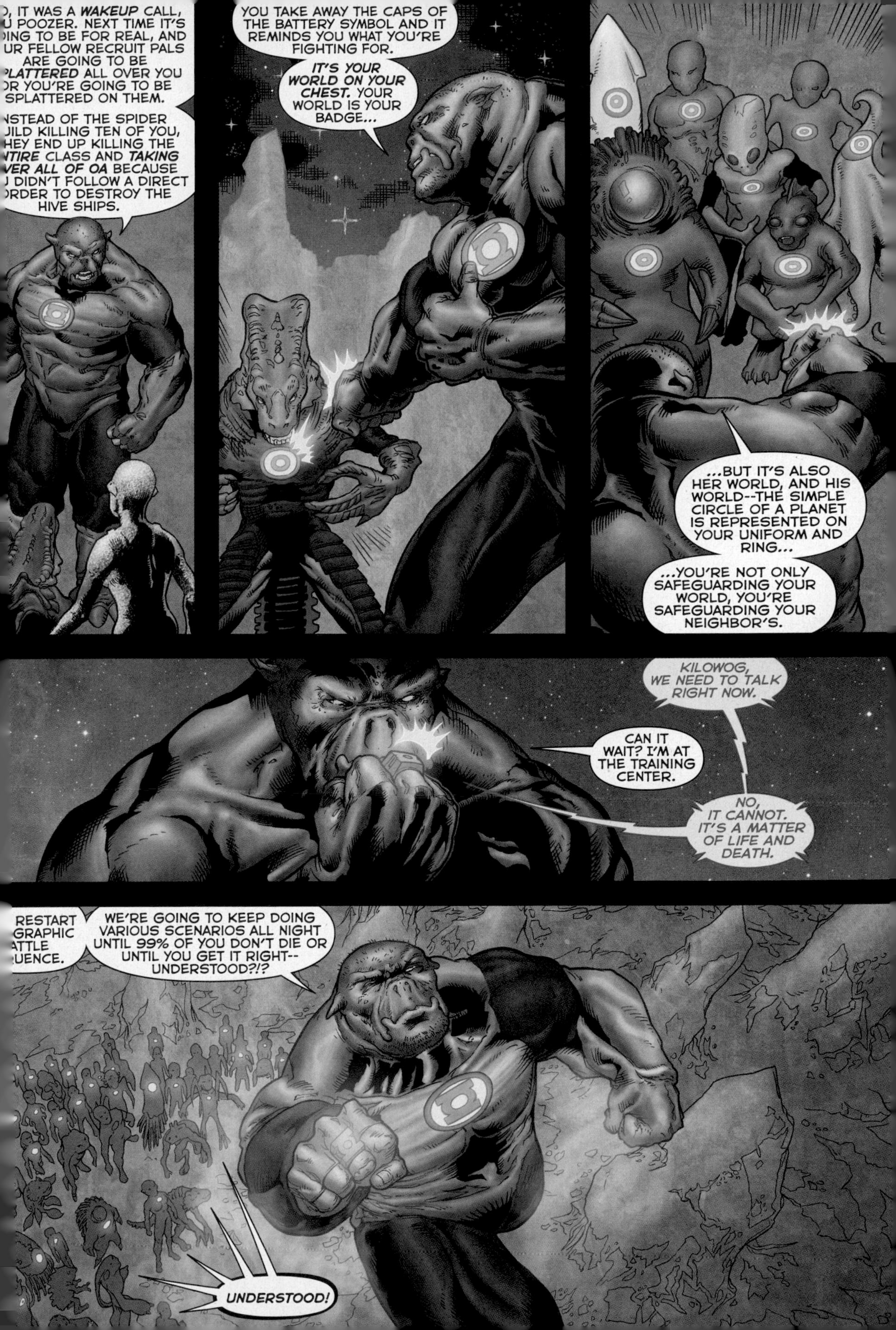

O, IT WAS A *WAKEUP* CALL, U POOZER. NEXT TIME IT'S OING TO BE FOR REAL, AND UR FELLOW RECRUIT PALS ARE GOING TO BE *PLATTERED* ALL OVER YOU OR YOU'RE GOING TO BE SPLATTERED ON THEM.
NSTEAD OF THE SPIDER UILD KILLING TEN OF YOU, HEY END UP KILLING THE *NTIRE* CLASS AND *TAKING VER ALL OF OA* BECAUSE U DIDN'T FOLLOW A DIRECT ORDER TO DESTROY THE HIVE SHIPS.
YOU TAKE AWAY THE CAPS OF THE BATTERY SYMBOL AND IT REMINDS YOU WHAT YOU'RE FIGHTING FOR.
IT'S YOUR WORLD ON YOUR CHEST. YOUR WORLD IS YOUR BADGE...
...BUT IT'S ALSO HER WORLD, AND HIS WORLD--THE SIMPLE CIRCLE OF A PLANET IS REPRESENTED ON YOUR UNIFORM AND RING...
...YOU'RE NOT ONLY SAFEGUARDING YOUR WORLD, YOU'RE SAFEGUARDING YOUR NEIGHBOR'S.
KILOWOG, WE NEED TO TALK RIGHT NOW.
CAN IT WAIT? I'M AT THE TRAINING CENTER.
NO, IT CANNOT. IT'S A MATTER OF LIFE AND DEATH.
RESTART GRAPHIC ATTLE UENCE.
WE'RE GOING TO KEEP DOING VARIOUS SCENARIOS ALL NIGHT UNTIL 99% OF YOU DON'T DIE OR UNTIL YOU GET IT RIGHT-- UNDERSTOOD?!?
UNDERSTOOD!

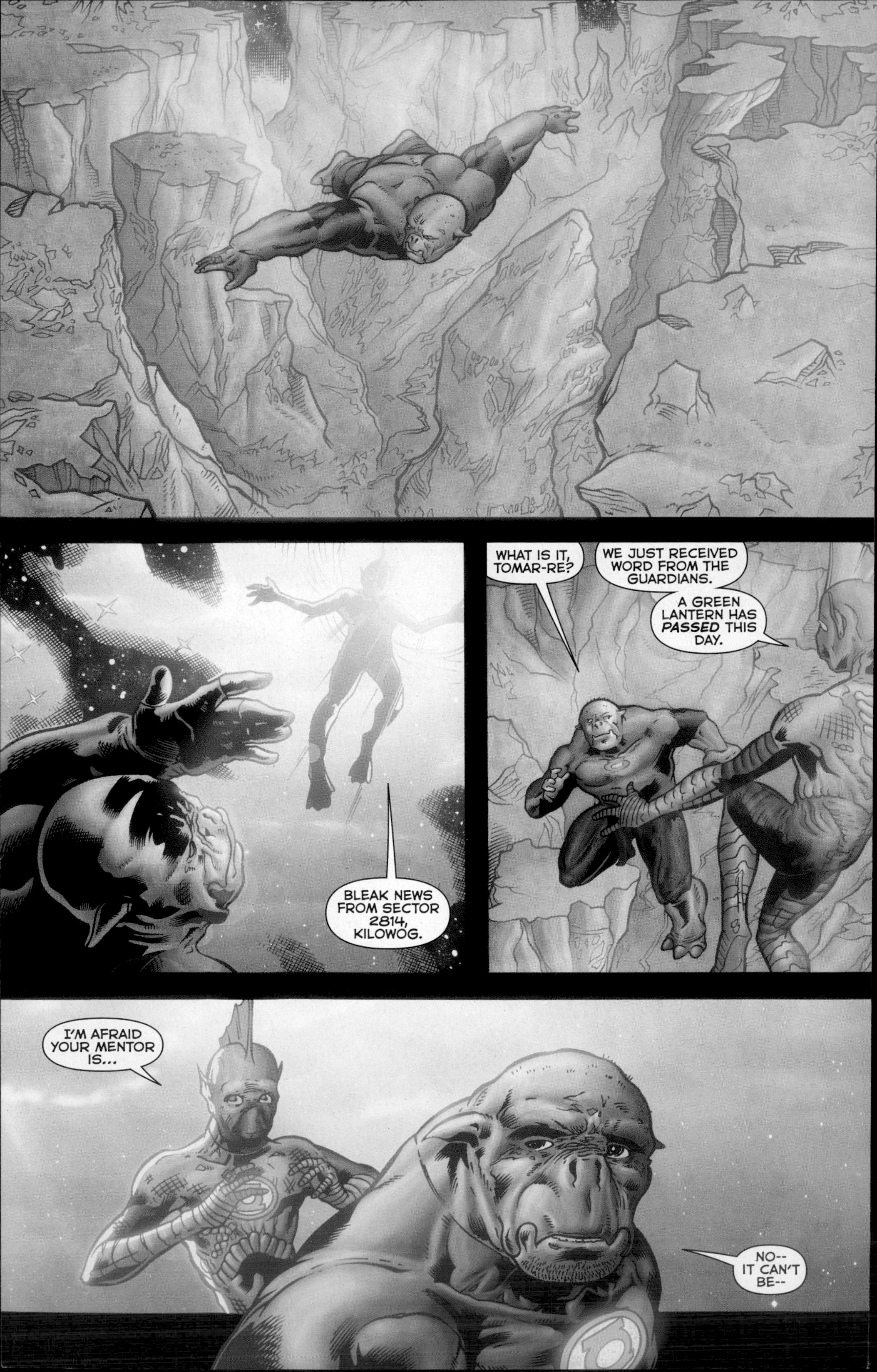
BLEAK NEWS FROM SECTOR 2814, KILOWOG.
WHAT IS IT, TOMAR-RE?
WE JUST RECEIVED WORD FROM THE GUARDIANS.
A GREEN LANTERN HAS PASSED THIS DAY.
I'M AFRAID YOUR MENTOR IS...
NO-- IT CAN'T BE--

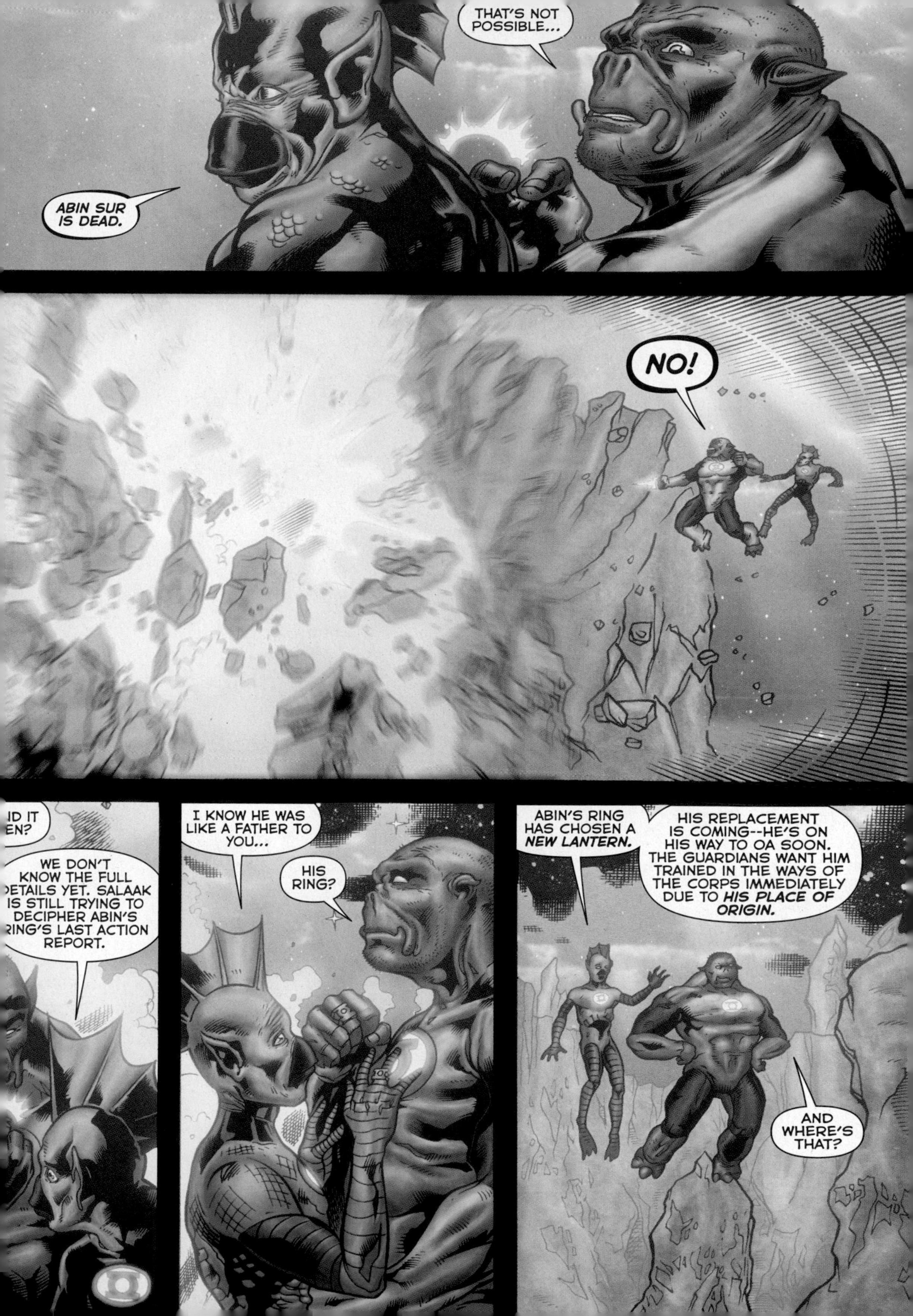
THAT'S NOT POSSIBLE...
ABIN SUR IS DEAD.
NO!
WE DON'T KNOW THE FULL DETAILS YET. SALAAK IS STILL TRYING TO DECIPHER ABIN'S RING'S LAST ACTION REPORT.
I KNOW HE WAS LIKE A FATHER TO YOU...
HIS RING?
ABIN'S RING HAS CHOSEN A NEW LANTERN.
HIS REPLACEMENT IS COMING--HE'S ON HIS WAY TO OA SOON. THE GUARDIANS WANT HIM TRAINED IN THE WAYS OF THE CORPS IMMEDIATELY DUE TO HIS PLACE OF ORIGIN.
AND WHERE'S THAT?

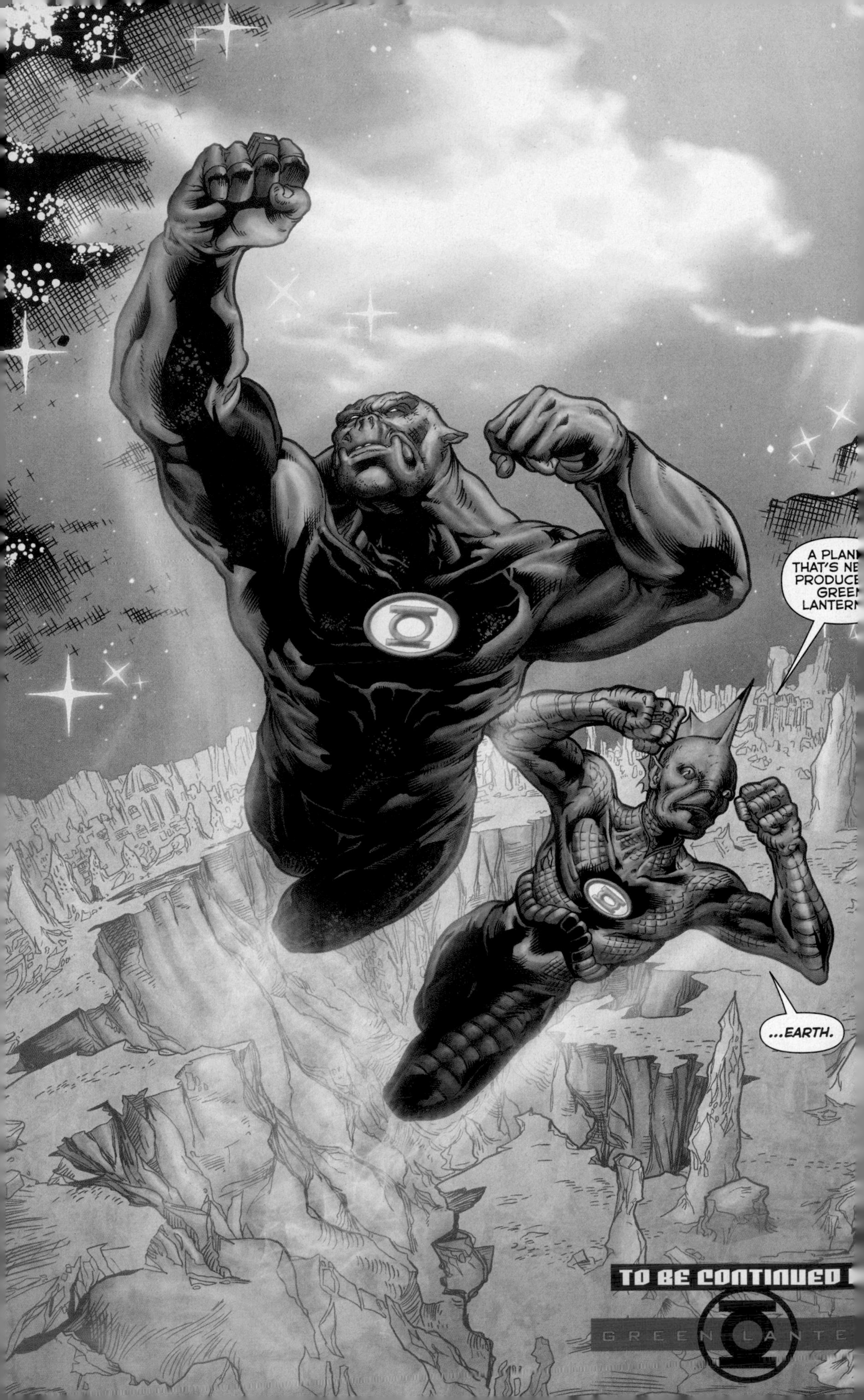
A PLAN
THAT'S NE
PRODUCE
GREEN
LANTERN
...EARTH.
TO BE CONTINUED
GREEN LANTE

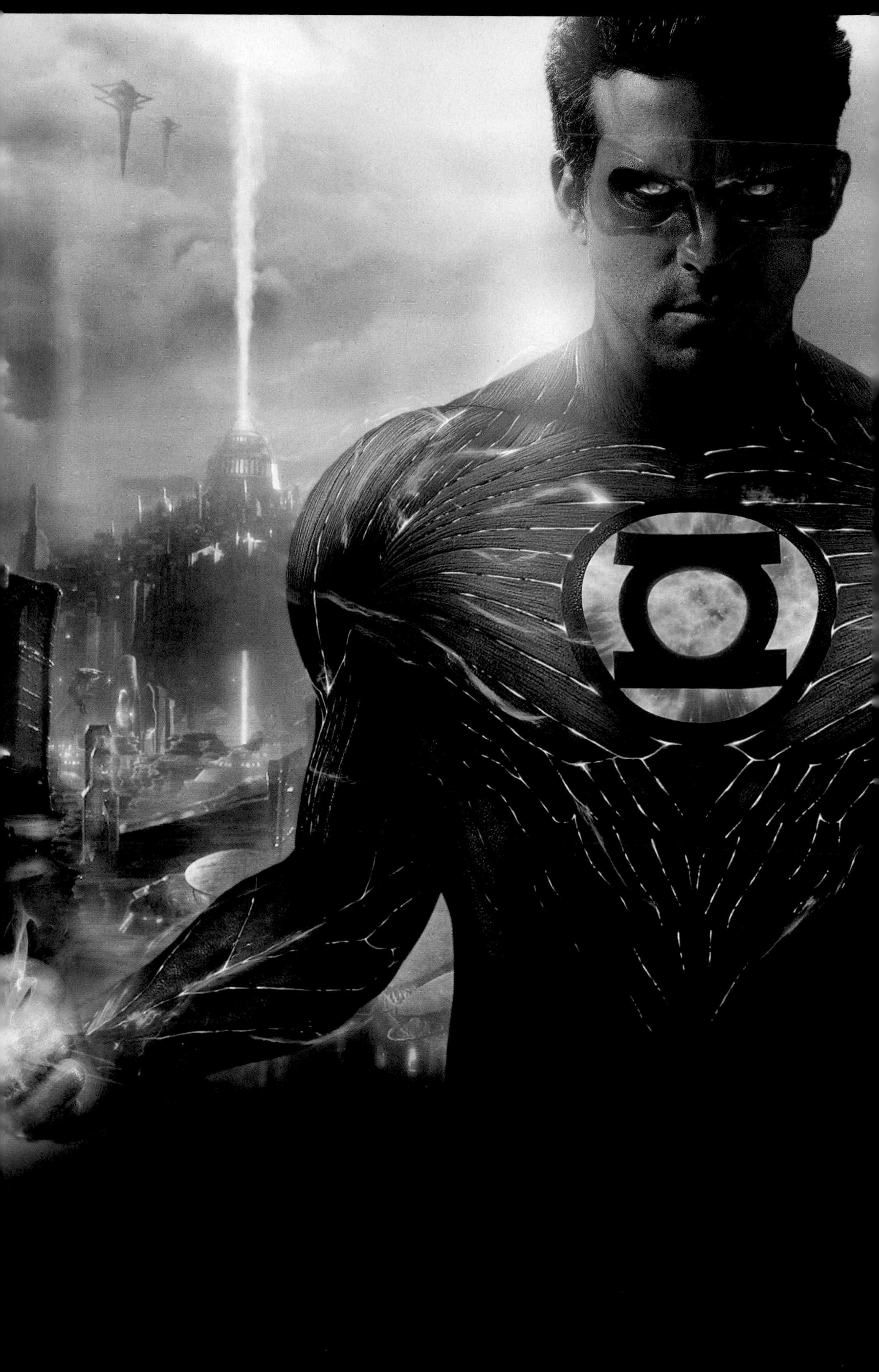

BEING HUMAN

GEOFF **JOHNS** & GREG **BERLANTI** writers

JERRY **ORDWAY** artist

EMERALD CITY

DONALD **DE LINE** & ADAM **SCHLAGMAN** writers

TYLER **KIRKHAM** penciller

BATT inker

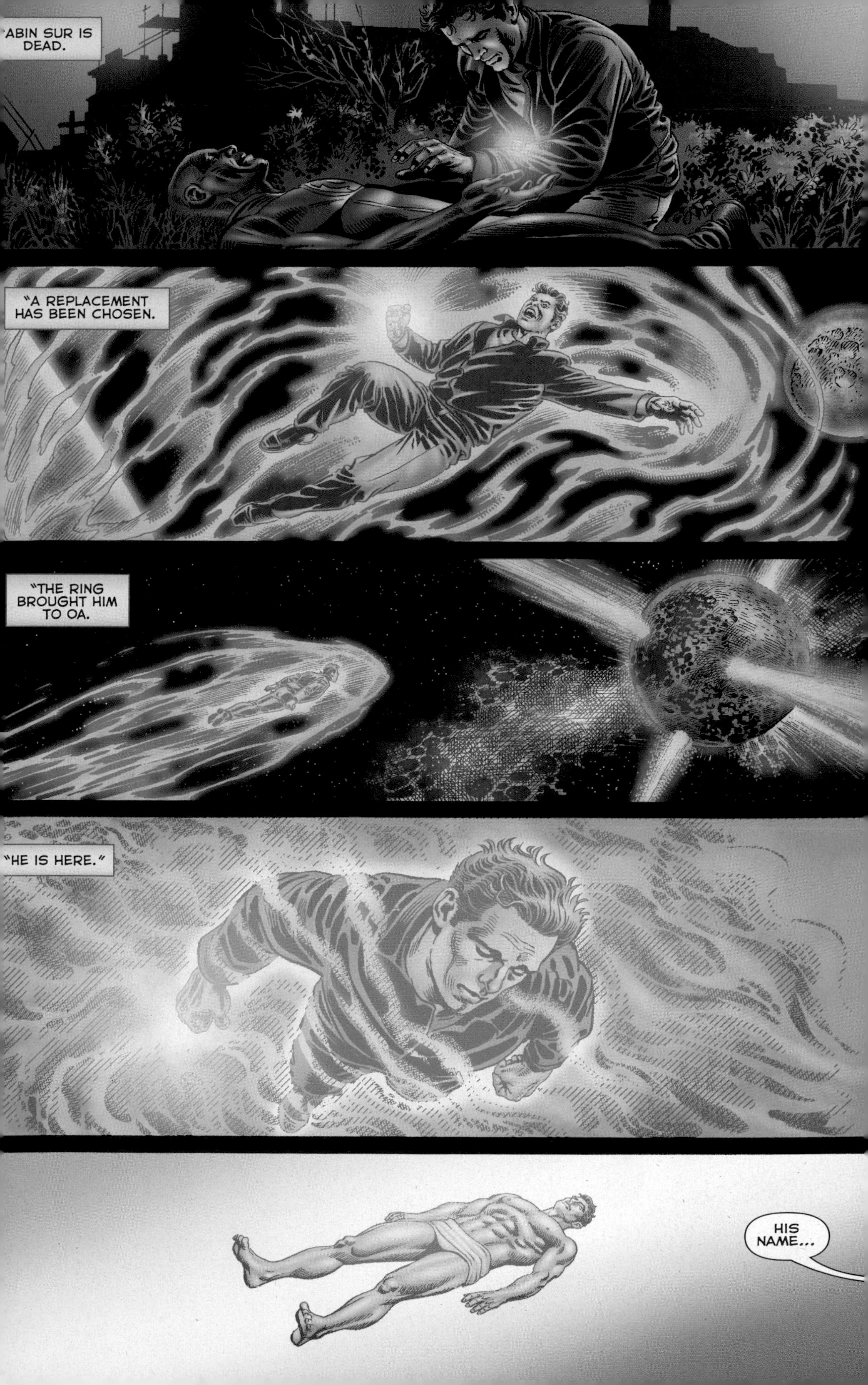
ABIN SUR IS DEAD.
"A REPLACEMENT HAS BEEN CHOSEN.
"THE RING BROUGHT HIM TO OA.
"HE IS HERE."
HIS NAME...

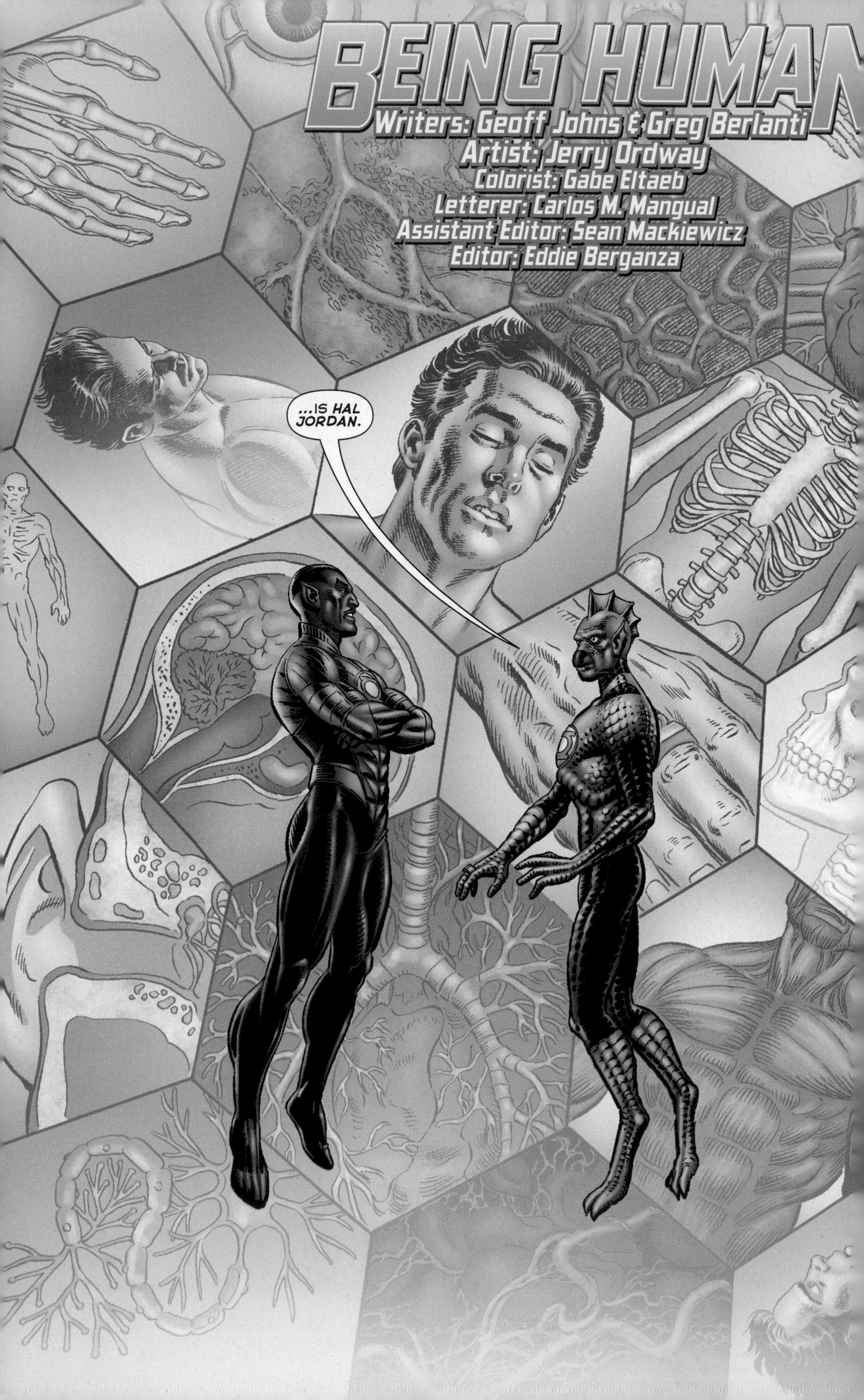
BEING HUMAN
Writers: Geoff Johns & Greg Berlanti
Artist: Jerry Ordway
Colorist: Gabe Eltaeb
Letterer: Carlos M. Mangual
Assistant Editor: Sean Mackiewicz
Editor: Eddie Berganza
...IS HAL JORDAN.

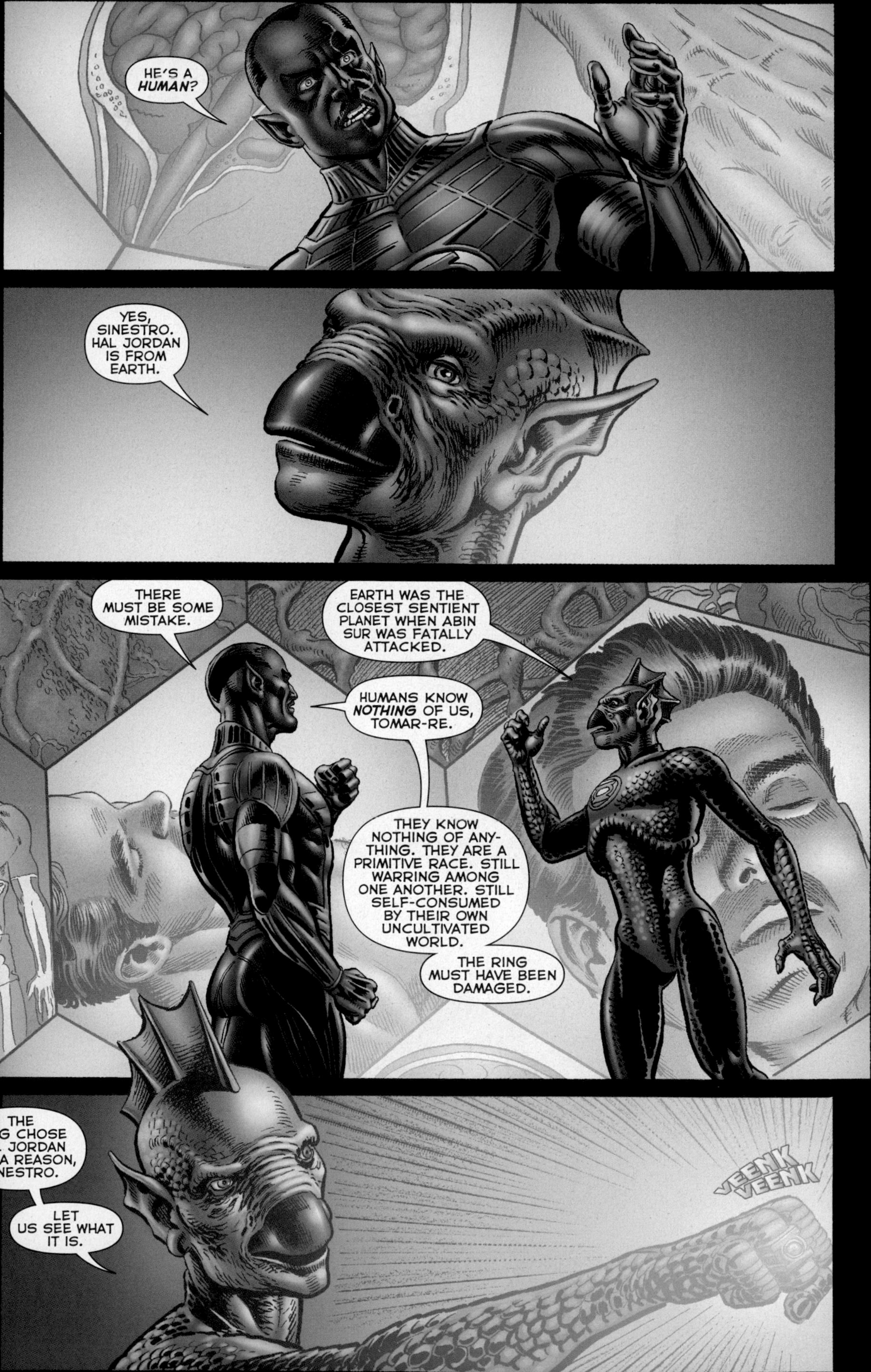
HE'S A HUMAN?
YES, SINESTRO. HAL JORDAN IS FROM EARTH.
THERE MUST BE SOME MISTAKE.
EARTH WAS THE CLOSEST SENTIENT PLANET WHEN ABIN SUR WAS FATALLY ATTACKED.
HUMANS KNOW NOTHING OF US, TOMAR-RE.
THEY KNOW NOTHING OF ANY-THING. THEY ARE A PRIMITIVE RACE. STILL WARRING AMONG ONE ANOTHER. STILL SELF-CONSUMED BY THEIR OWN UNCULTIVATED WORLD.
THE RING MUST HAVE BEEN DAMAGED.
THE G CHOSE . JORDAN A REASON, NESTRO.
LET US SEE WHAT IT IS.
VEENK VEENK

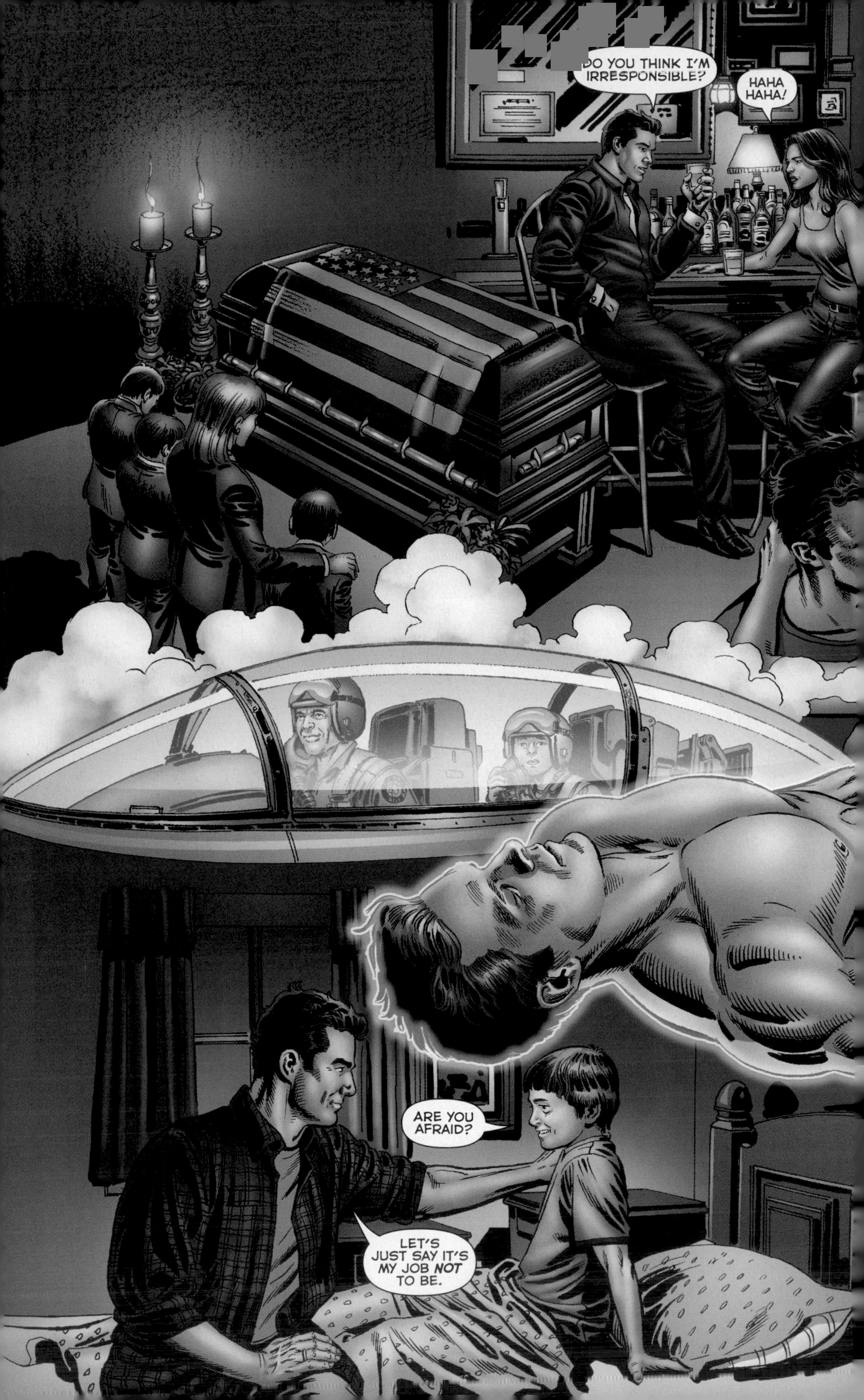
DO YOU THINK I'M IRRESPONSIBLE?
HAHA HAHA!
ARE YOU AFRAID?
LET'S JUST SAY IT'S MY JOB *NOT* TO BE.

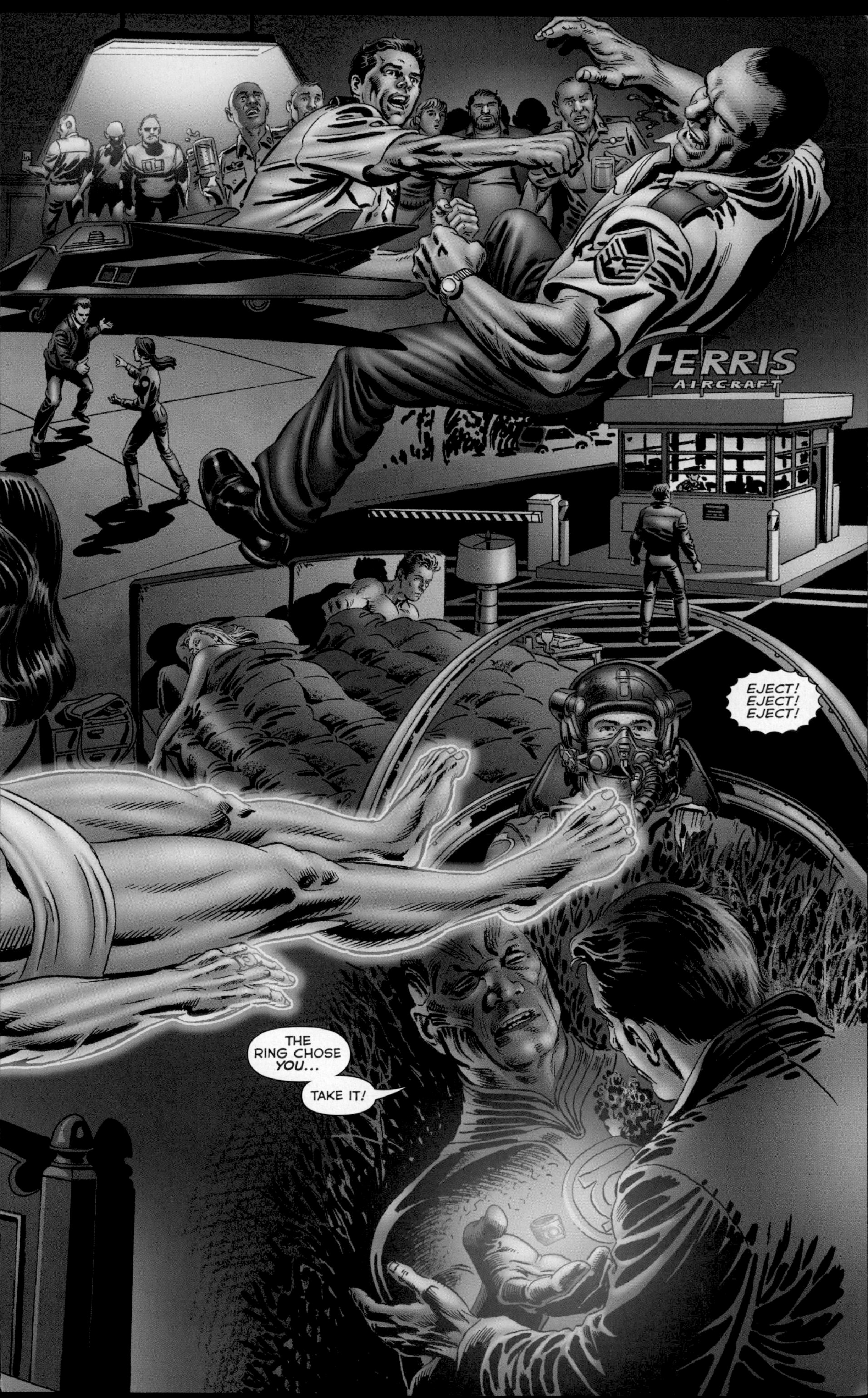
FERRIS
AIRCRAFT
EJECT! EJECT! EJECT!
THE RING CHOSE YOU...
TAKE IT!

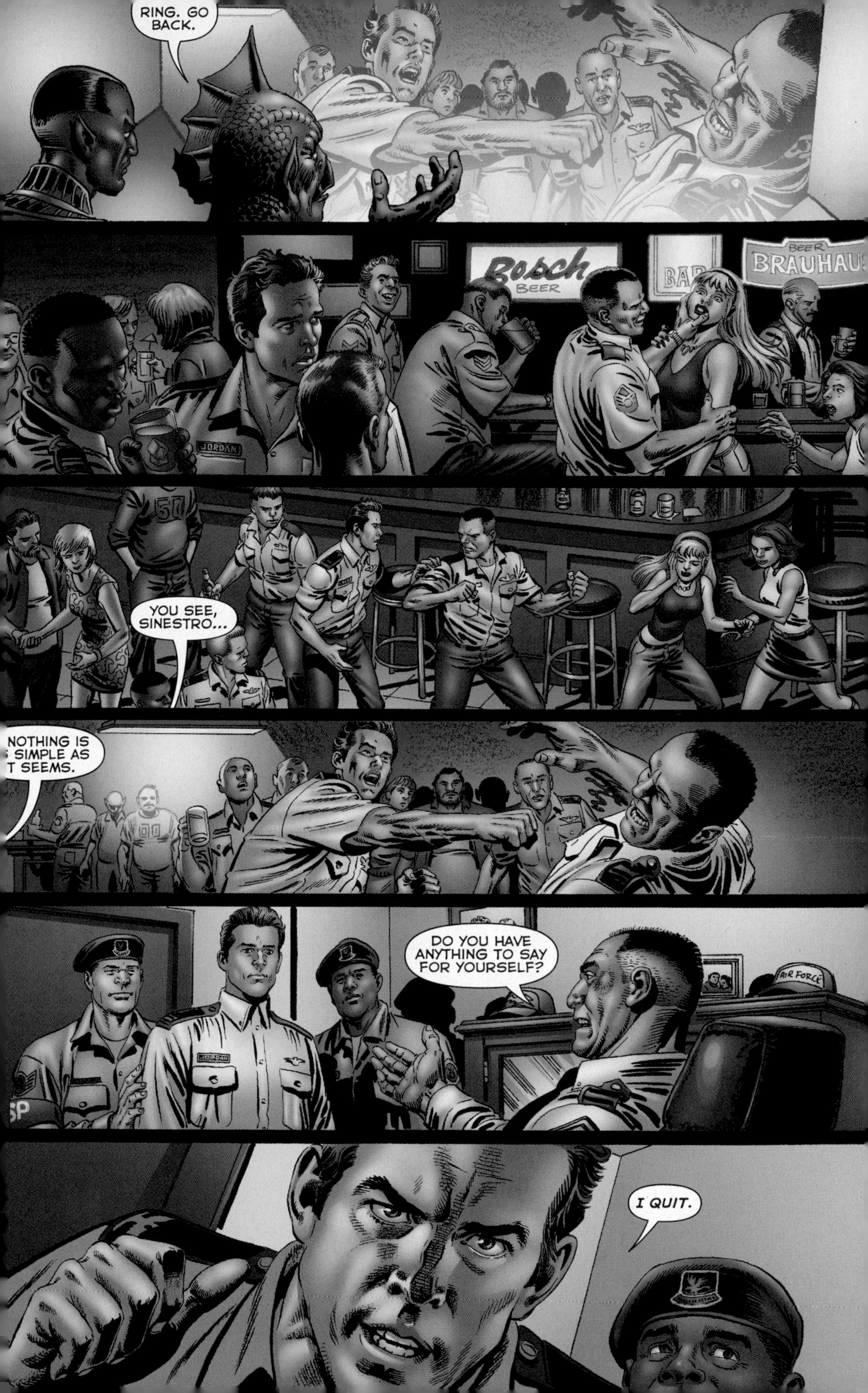
RING. GO BACK.
Bosch BEER
BAR
BEER BRAUHAUS
JORDAN
YOU SEE, SINESTRO...
NOTHING IS SIMPLE AS T SEEMS.
JORDAN
SP
DO YOU HAVE ANYTHING TO SAY FOR YOURSELF?
AIR FORCE
I QUIT.

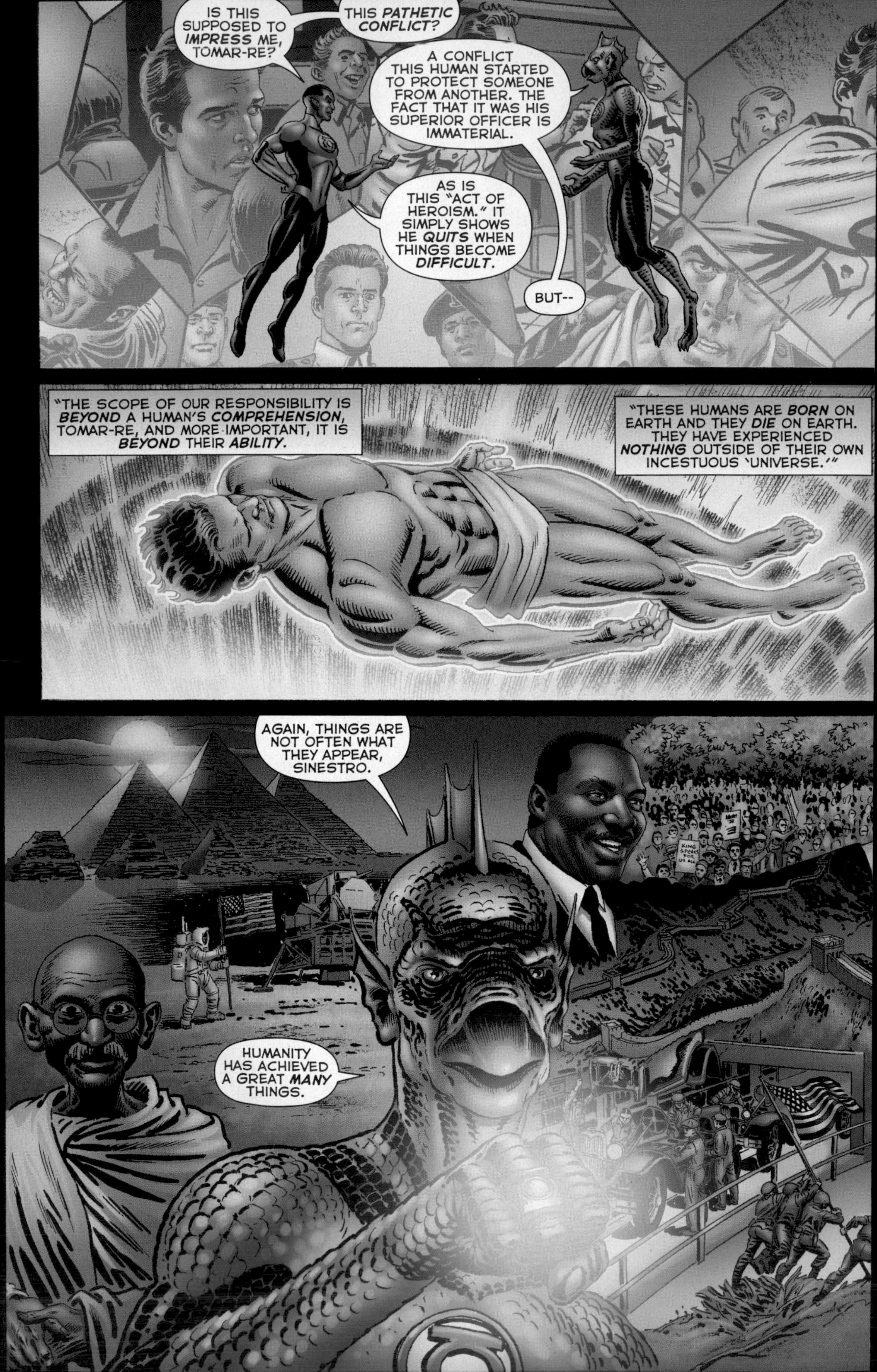
IS THIS SUPPOSED TO IMPRESS ME, TOMAR-RE?
THIS PATHETIC CONFLICT?
A CONFLICT THIS HUMAN STARTED TO PROTECT SOMEONE FROM ANOTHER. THE FACT THAT IT WAS HIS SUPERIOR OFFICER IS IMMATERIAL.
AS IS THIS "ACT OF HEROISM." IT SIMPLY SHOWS HE QUITS WHEN THINGS BECOME DIFFICULT.
BUT--
"THE SCOPE OF OUR RESPONSIBILITY IS BEYOND A HUMAN'S COMPREHENSION, TOMAR-RE, AND MORE IMPORTANT, IT IS BEYOND THEIR ABILITY.
"THESE HUMANS ARE BORN ON EARTH AND THEY DIE ON EARTH. THEY HAVE EXPERIENCED NOTHING OUTSIDE OF THEIR OWN INCESTUOUS 'UNIVERSE.'"
AGAIN, THINGS ARE NOT OFTEN WHAT THEY APPEAR, SINESTRO.
HUMANITY HAS ACHIEVED A GREAT MANY THINGS.

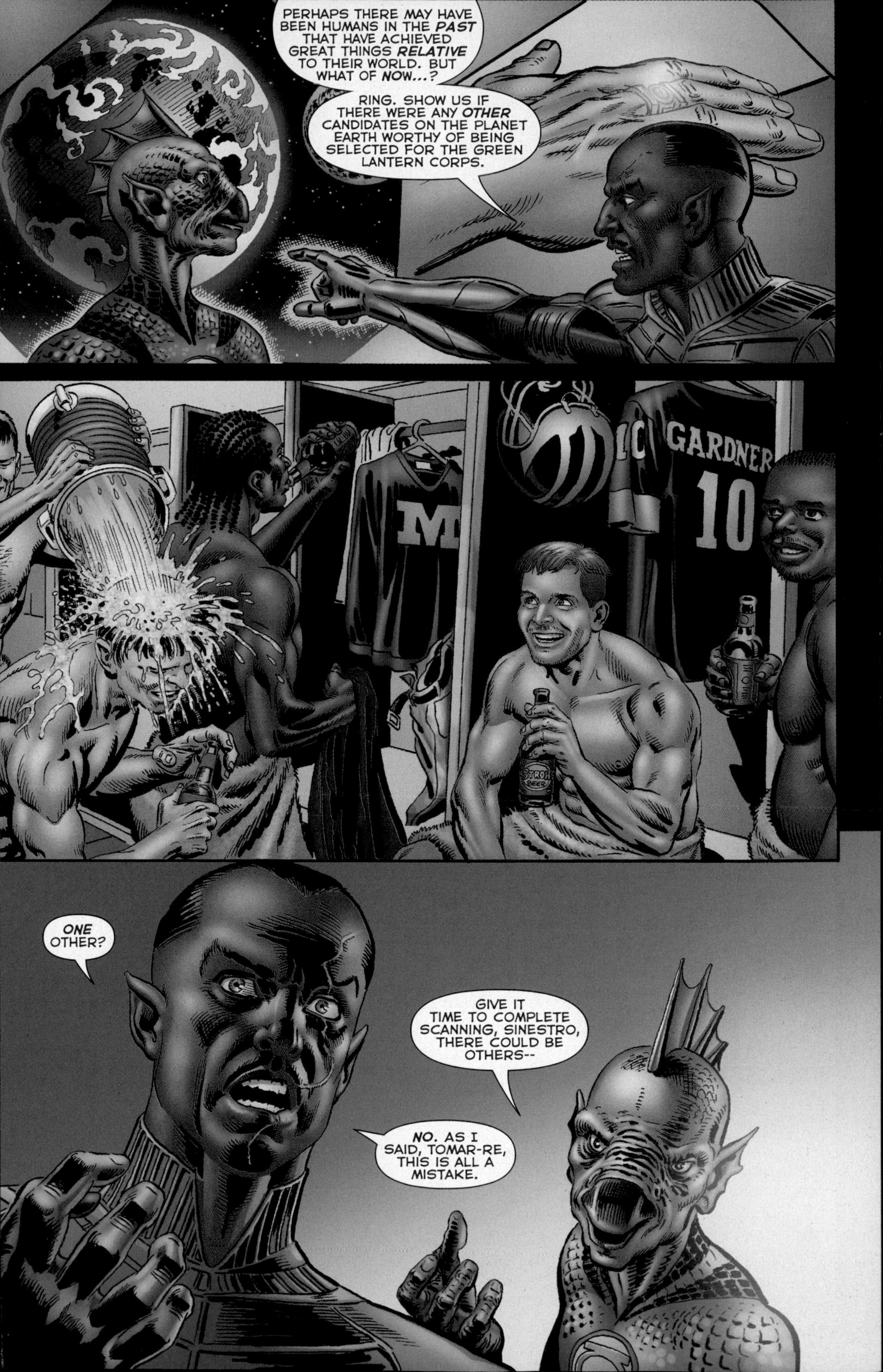
PERHAPS THERE MAY HAVE BEEN HUMANS IN THE PAST THAT HAVE ACHIEVED GREAT THINGS RELATIVE TO THEIR WORLD. BUT WHAT OF NOW...?
RING. SHOW US IF THERE WERE ANY OTHER CANDIDATES ON THE PLANET EARTH WORTHY OF BEING SELECTED FOR THE GREEN LANTERN CORPS.
GARDNER
10
M
STROH BEER
ONE OTHER?
GIVE IT TIME TO COMPLETE SCANNING, SINESTRO, THERE COULD BE OTHERS--
NO. AS I SAID, TOMAR-RE, THIS IS ALL A MISTAKE.

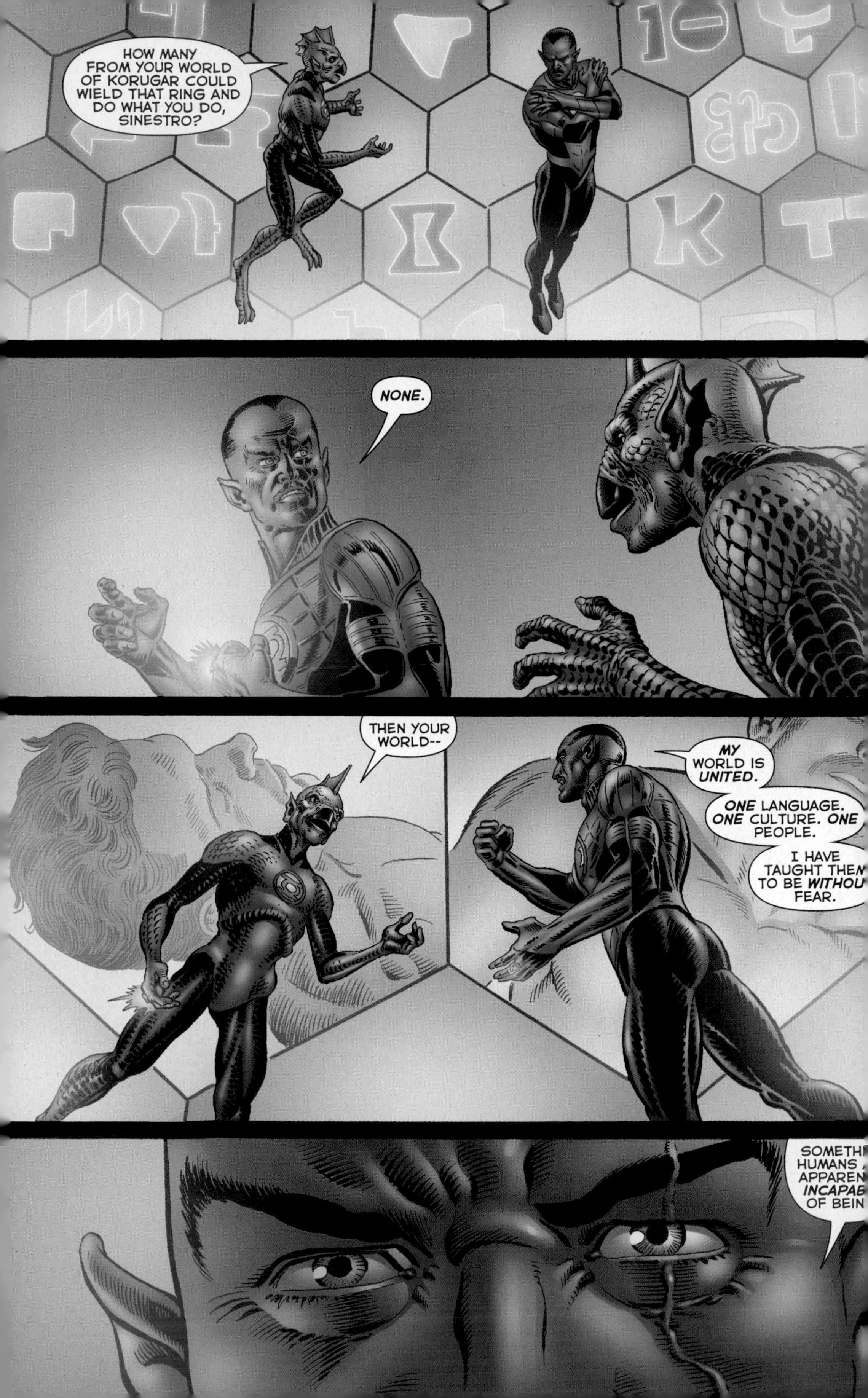
HOW MANY FROM YOUR WORLD OF KORUGAR COULD WIELD THAT RING AND DO WHAT YOU DO, SINESTRO?
NONE.
THEN YOUR WORLD--
MY WORLD IS UNITED.
ONE LANGUAGE. ONE CULTURE. ONE PEOPLE.
I HAVE TAUGHT THEM TO BE WITHOU FEAR.
SOMETH HUMANS APPAREN INCAPAB OF BEIN

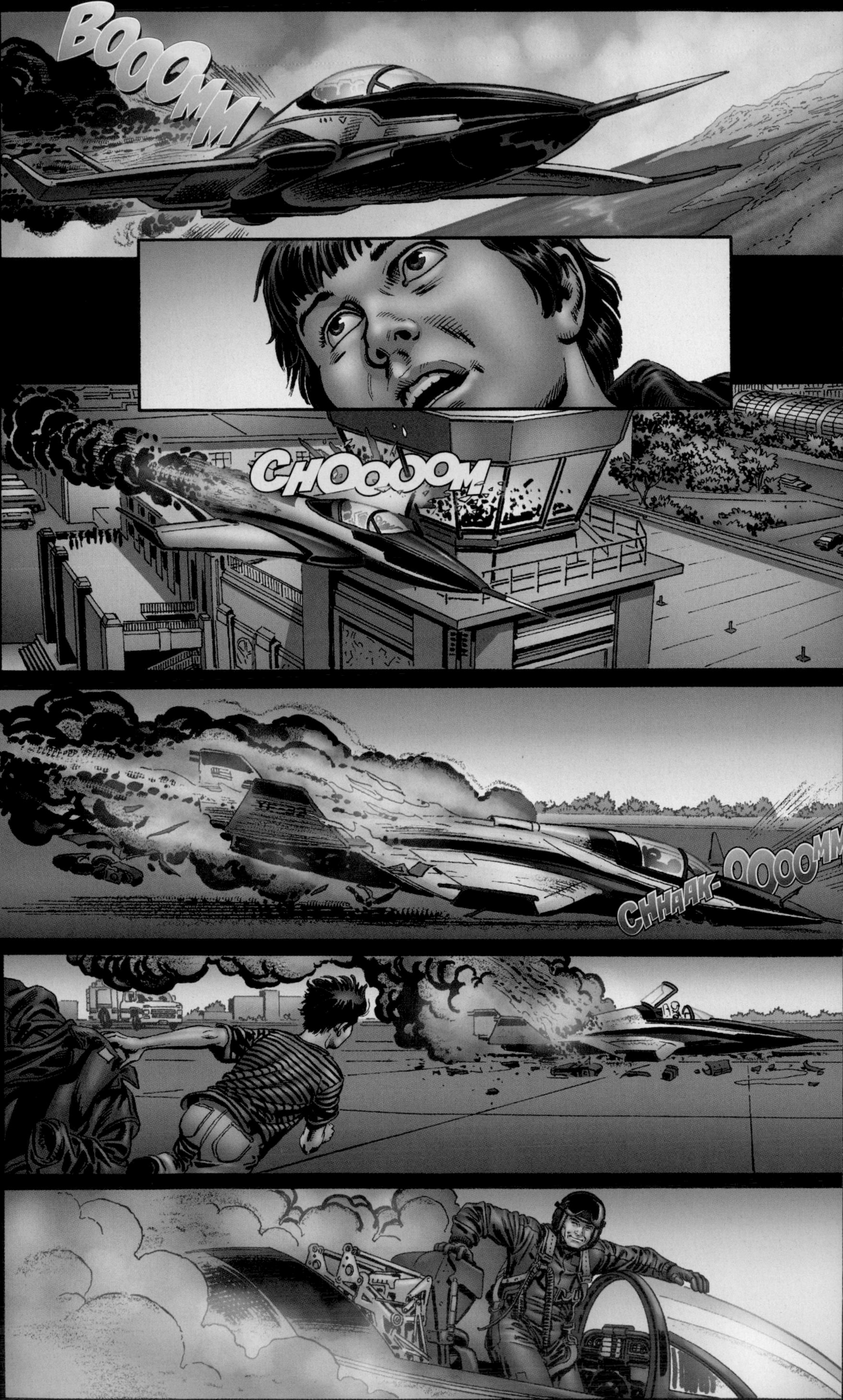
BOOOMM
CHOOOOM
CHHAAK-OOOOMM

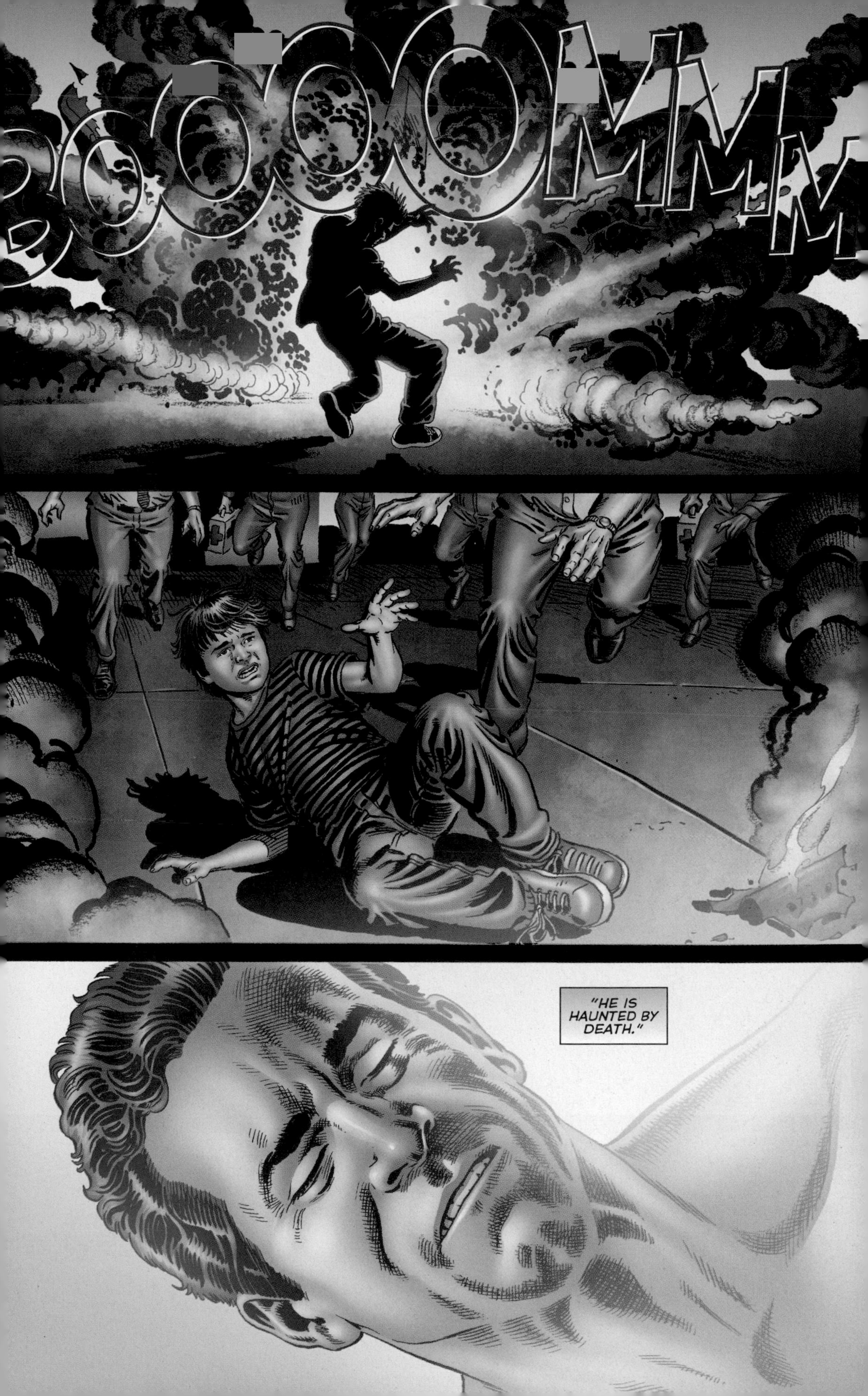
BOOOOMMM
"HE IS HAUNTED BY DEATH."

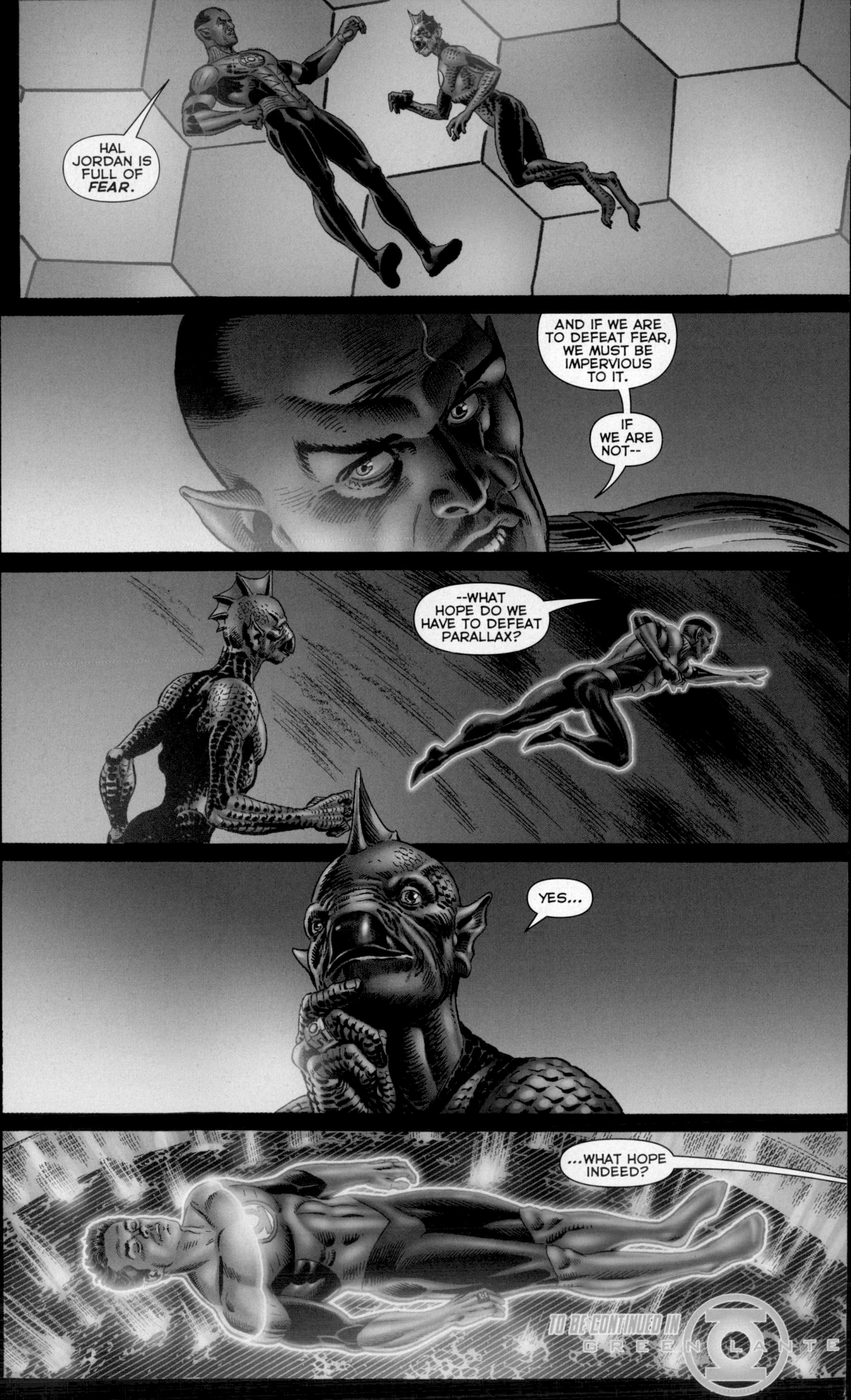
HAL JORDAN IS FULL OF *FEAR*.
AND IF WE ARE TO DEFEAT FEAR, WE MUST BE IMPERVIOUS TO IT.
IF WE ARE NOT--
--WHAT HOPE DO WE HAVE TO DEFEAT PARALLAX?
YES...
...WHAT HOPE INDEED?
TO BE CONTINUED IN
GREEN LANTERN

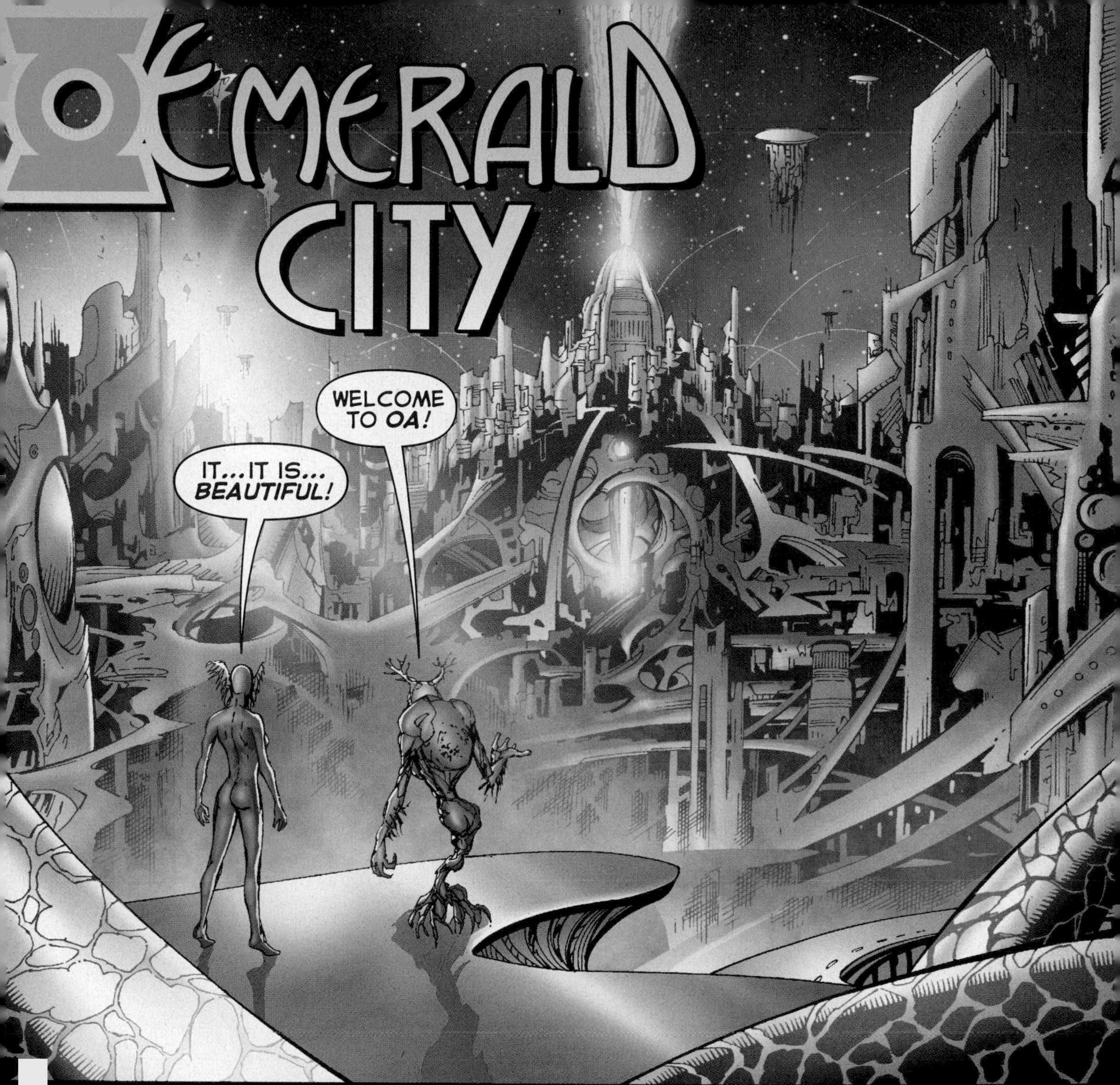
EMERALD CITY
WELCOME TO OA!
IT...IT IS... BEAUTIFUL!

TERS: DONALD De LINE AND ADAM SCHLAGMAN • PENCILLER: TYLER KIRKHAM
INKER: BATT • COLORS: RANDY MAYOR
LETTERS: CARLOS M. MANGUAL
ASSISTANT EDITOR: SEAN MACKIEWICZ
EDITOR: EDDIE BERGANZA

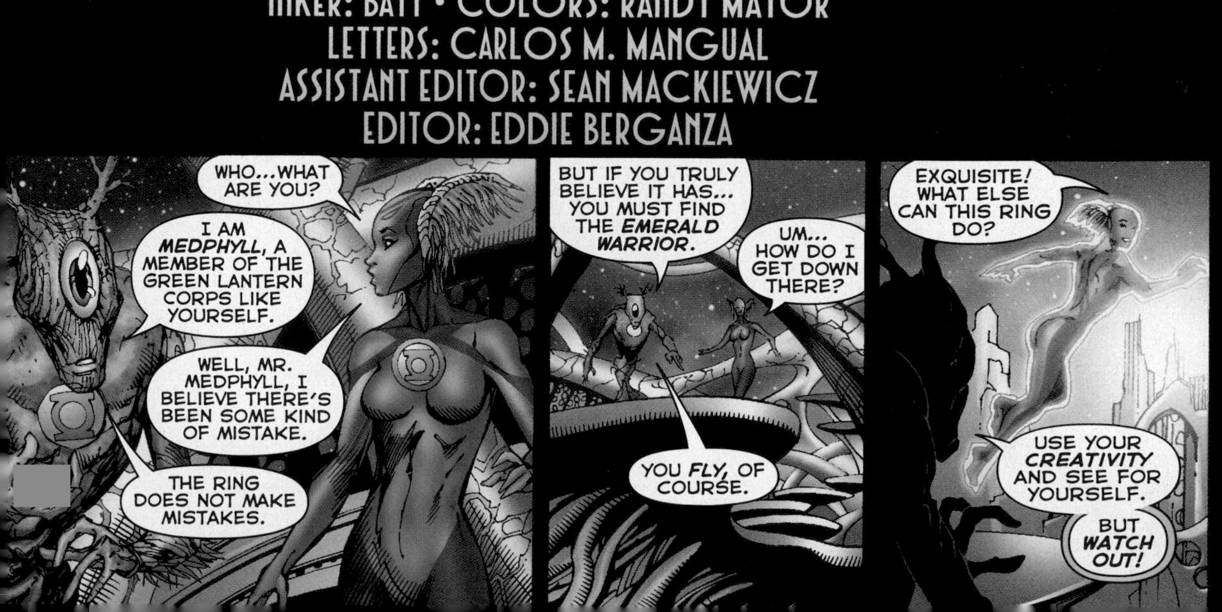
WHO...WHAT ARE YOU?
I AM MEDPHYLL, A MEMBER OF THE GREEN LANTERN CORPS LIKE YOURSELF.
WELL, MR. MEDPHYLL, I BELIEVE THERE'S BEEN SOME KIND OF MISTAKE.
THE RING DOES NOT MAKE MISTAKES.
BUT IF YOU TRULY BELIEVE IT HAS... YOU MUST FIND THE EMERALD WARRIOR.
UM... HOW DO I GET DOWN THERE?
YOU FLY, OF COURSE.
EXQUISITE! WHAT ELSE CAN THIS RING DO?
USE YOUR CREATIVITY AND SEE FOR YOURSELF.
BUT WATCH OUT!

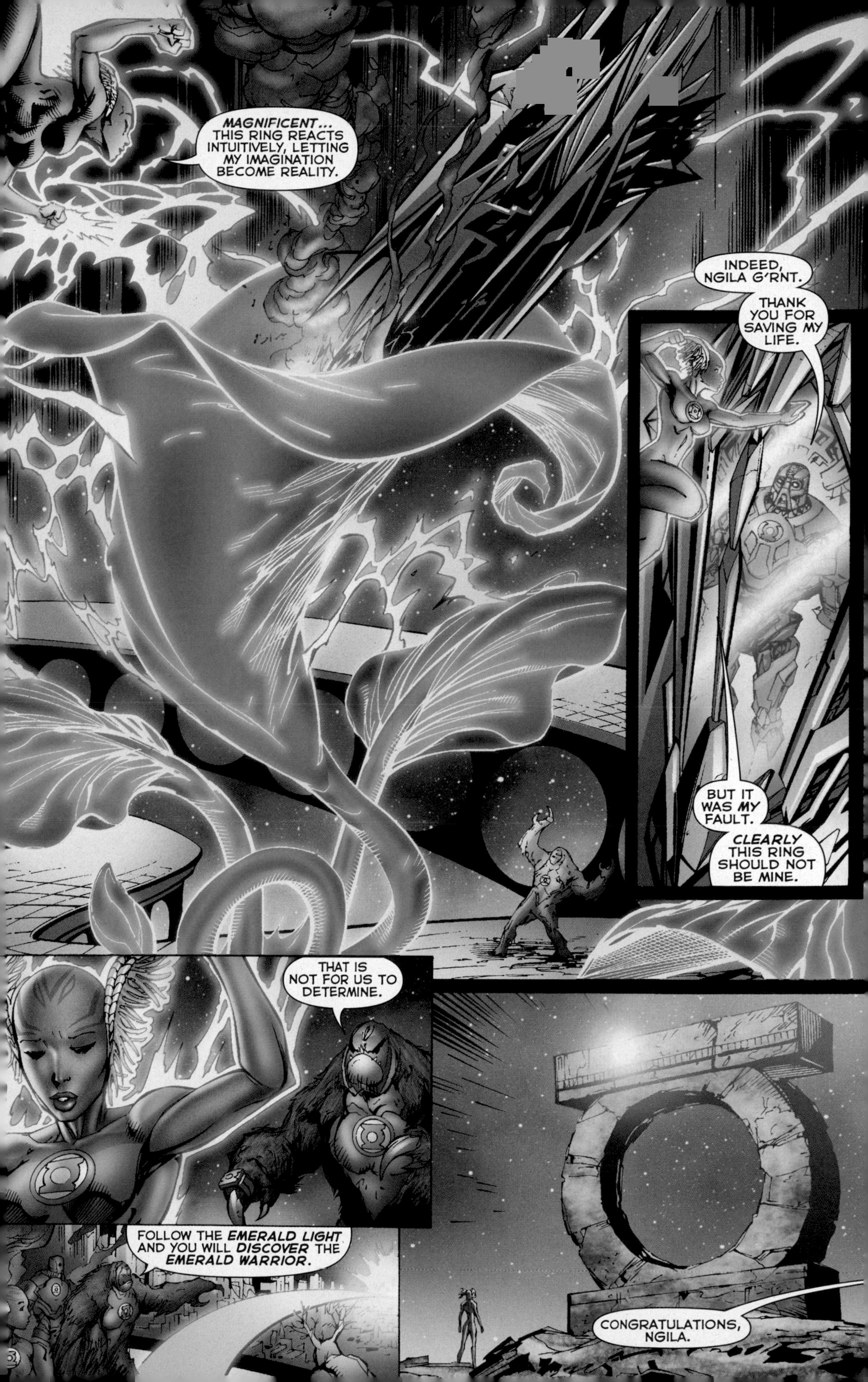
MAGNIFICENT... THIS RING REACTS INTUITIVELY, LETTING MY IMAGINATION BECOME REALITY.
INDEED, NGILA G'RNT.
THANK YOU FOR SAVING MY LIFE.
BUT IT WAS MY FAULT.
CLEARLY THIS RING SHOULD NOT BE MINE.
THAT IS NOT FOR US TO DETERMINE.
FOLLOW THE EMERALD LIGHT AND YOU WILL DISCOVER THE EMERALD WARRIOR.
CONGRATULATIONS, NGILA.

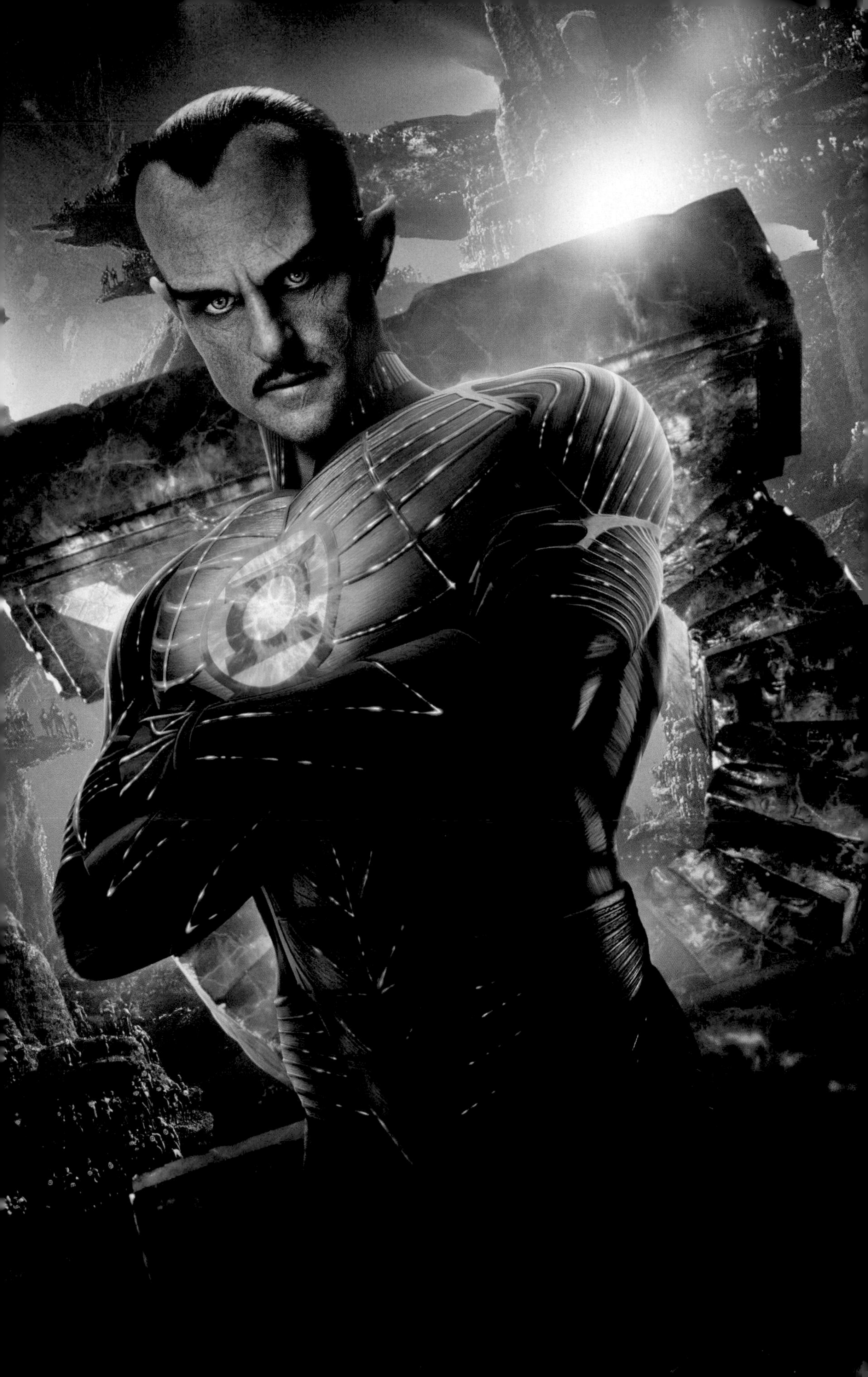

THE CHOSEN ONE

GEOFF **JOHNS** & MICHAEL **GOLDENBERG** writers

HARVEY **TOLIBAO**, CLIFF **RICHARDS** & JERRY **ORDWAY** artists

SECRET ORIGIN OF
THE GREEN LANTERN CORPS

GEOFF **JOHNS** & ADAM **SCHLAGMAN** writers

FERNANDO **DAGNINO** penciller

RAUL **FERNANDEZ** inker

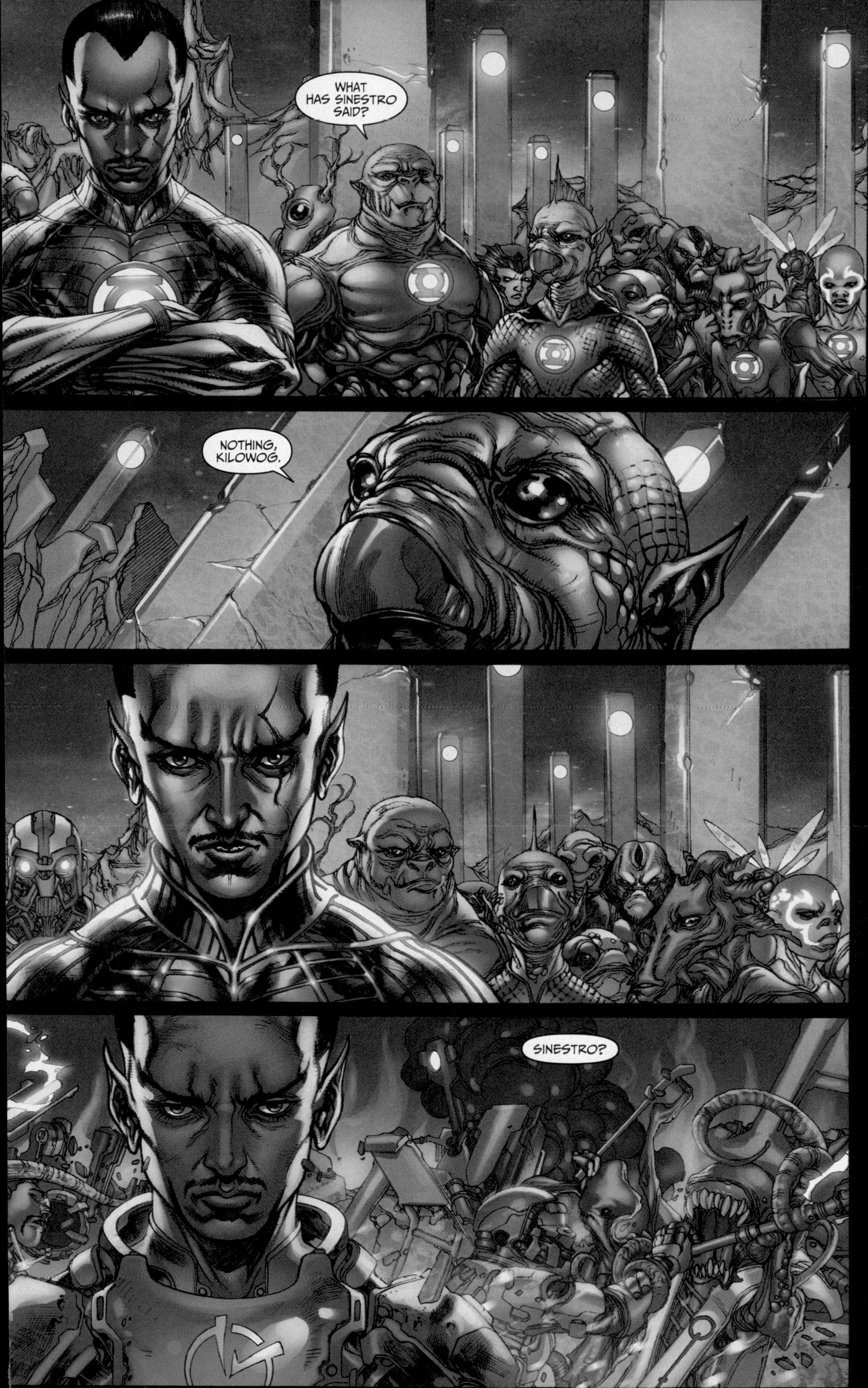
WHAT HAS SINESTRO SAID?
NOTHING, KILOWOG.
SINESTRO?

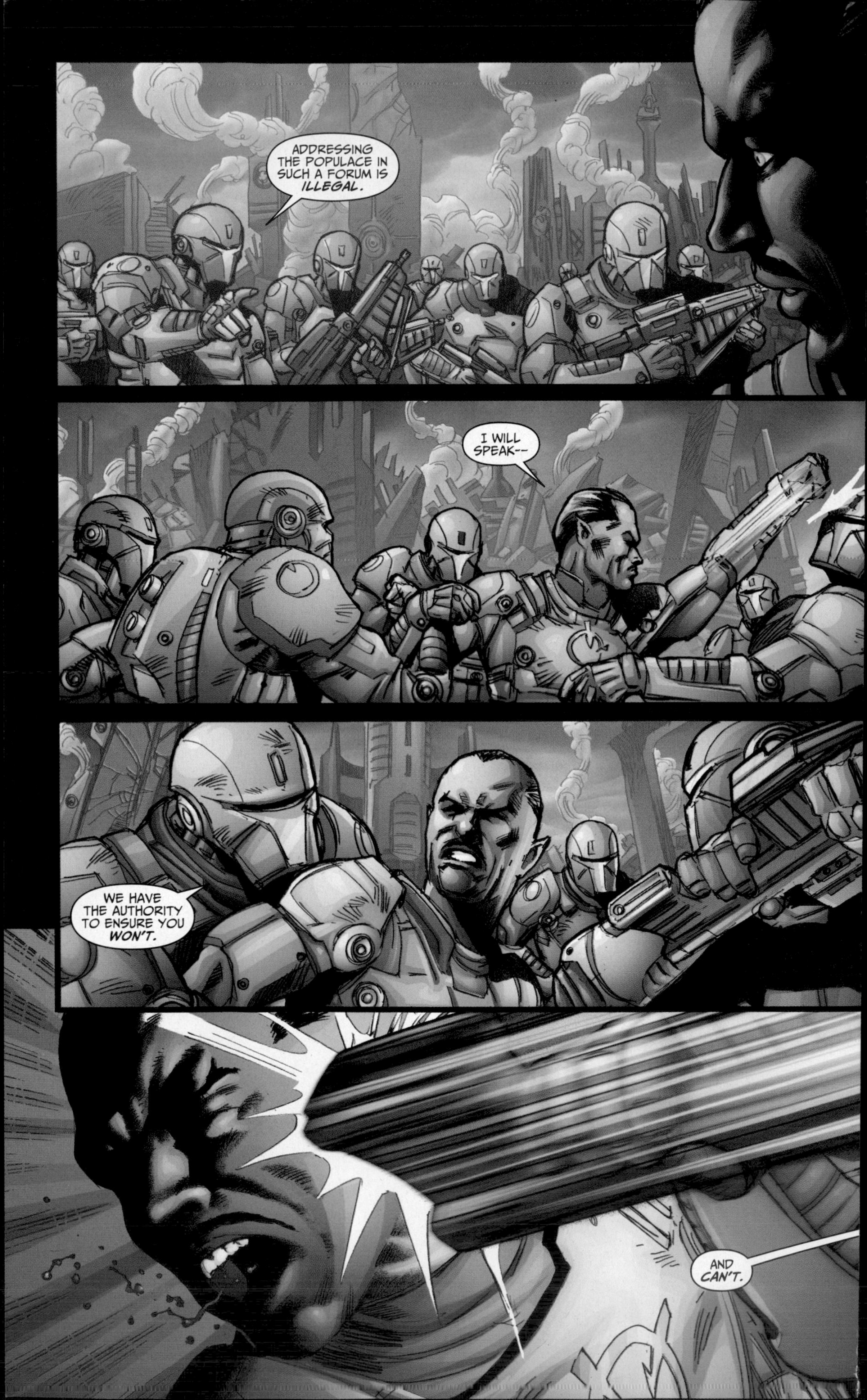
ADDRESSING THE POPULACE IN SUCH A FORUM IS ILLEGAL.
I WILL SPEAK--
WE HAVE THE AUTHORITY TO ENSURE YOU WON'T.
AND CAN'T.

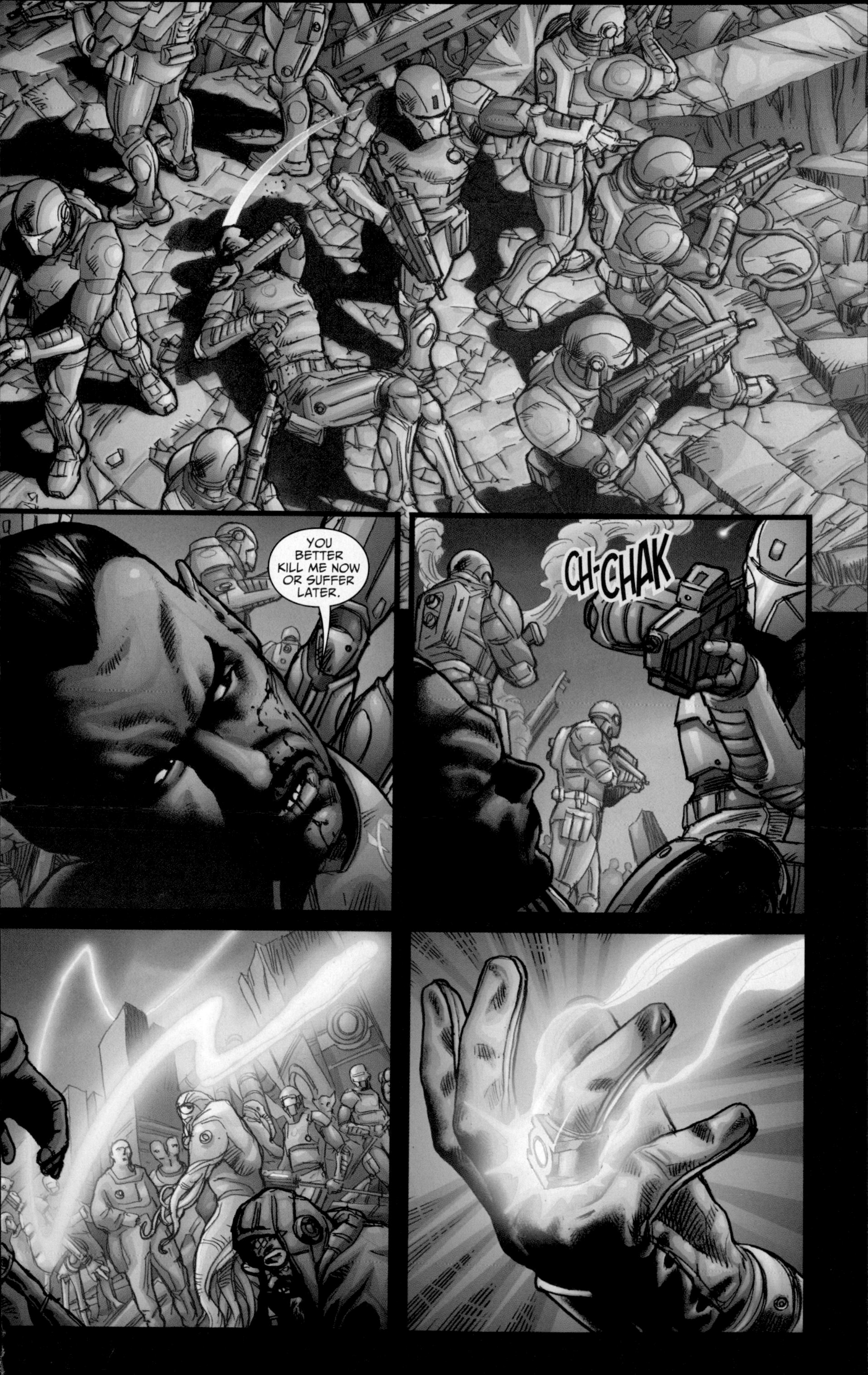
YOU BETTER KILL ME NOW OR SUFFER LATER.
CH-CHAK

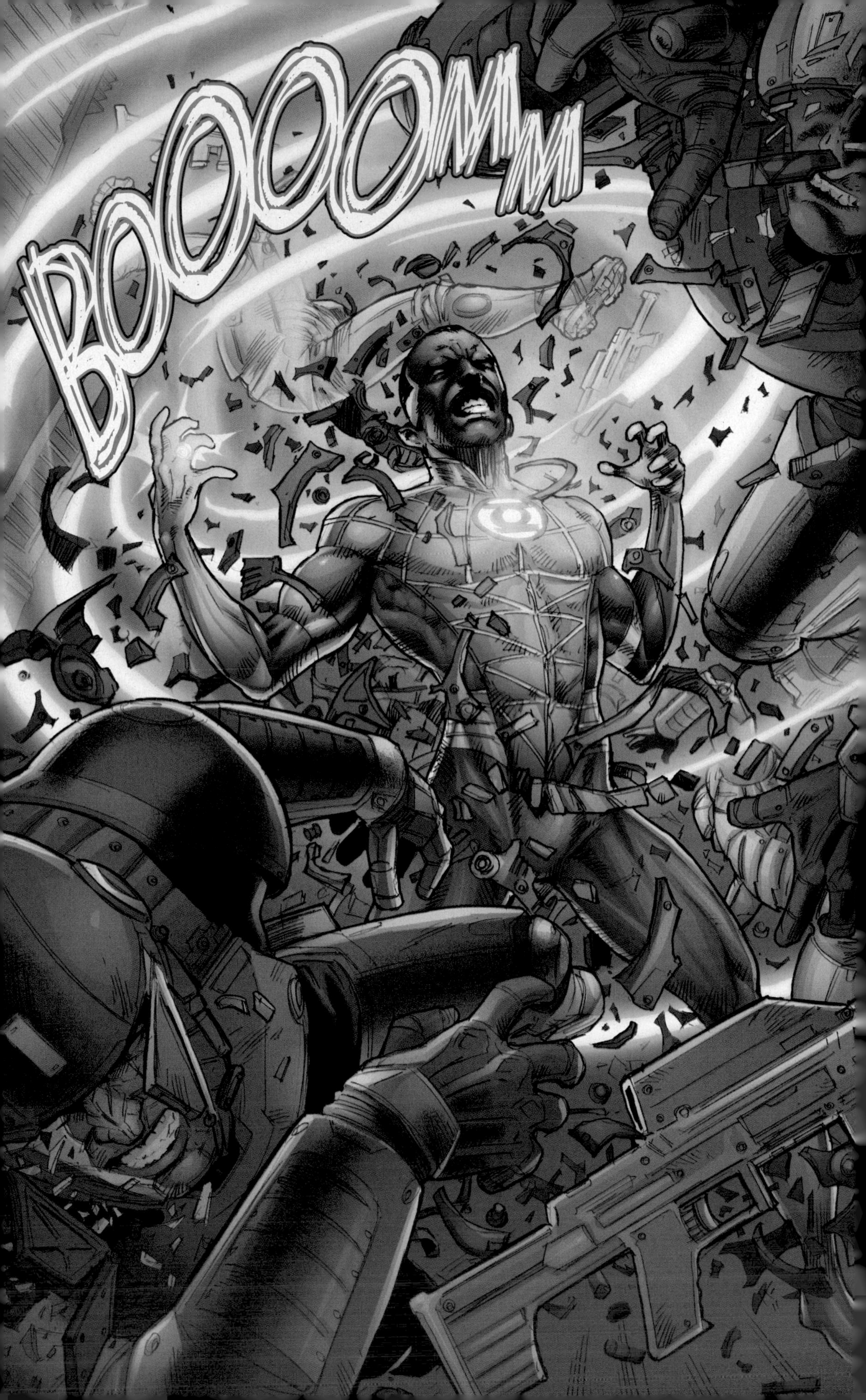
BOOOOOMMM

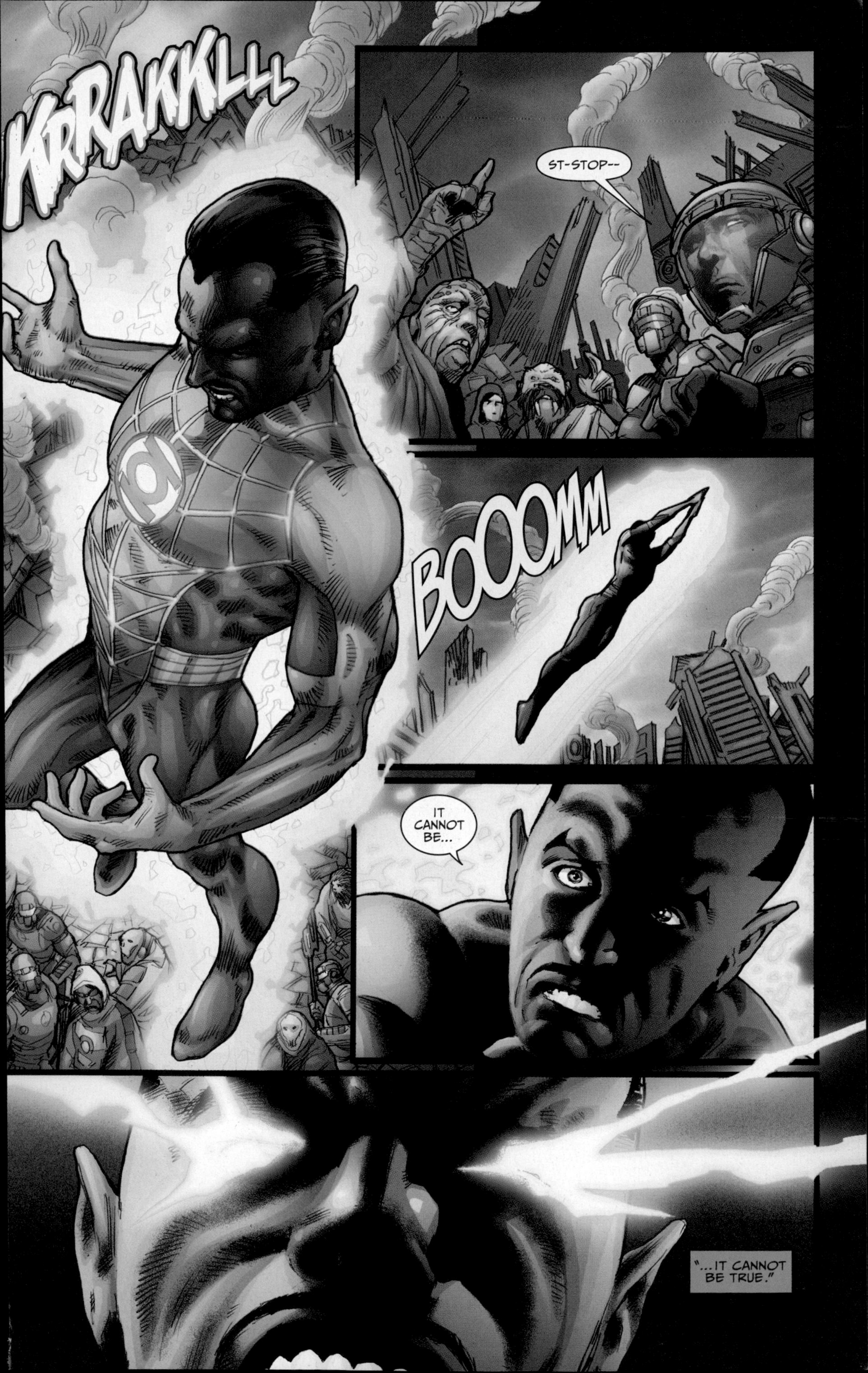
KRRAKKLLL
ST-STOP--
BOOOMM
IT CANNOT BE...
"...IT CANNOT BE TRUE."

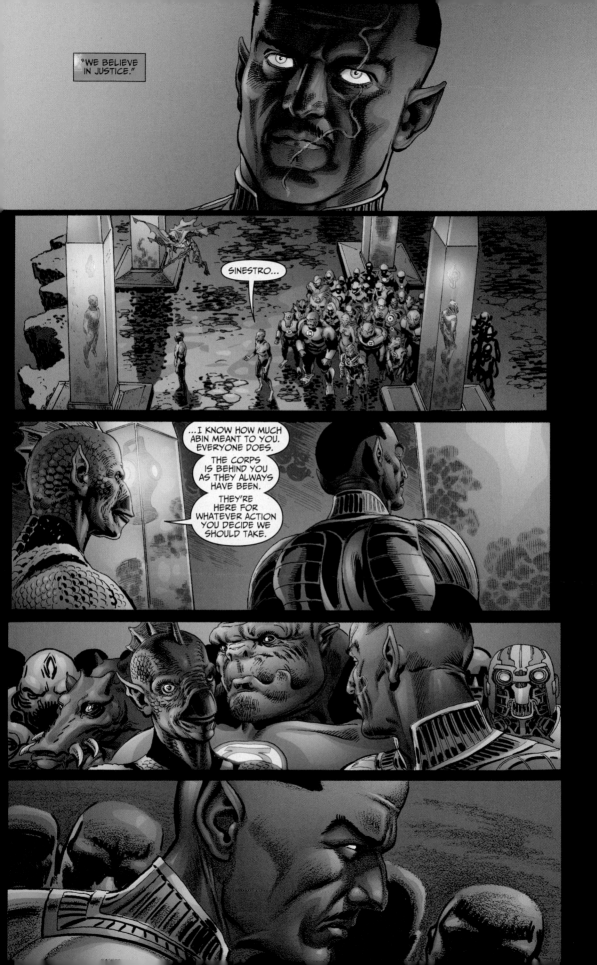

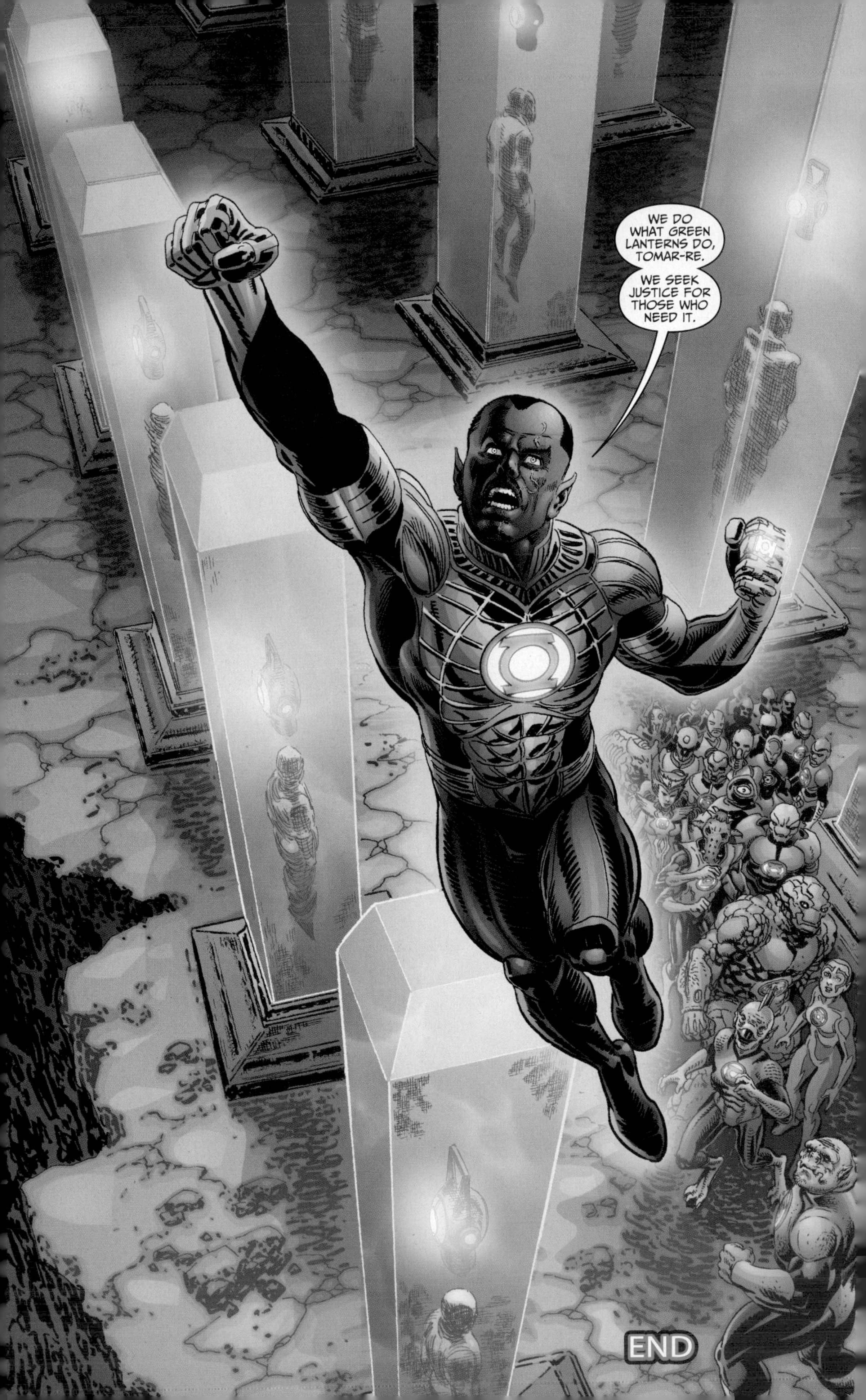
WE DO WHAT GREEN LANTERNS DO, TOMAR-RE.
WE SEEK JUSTICE FOR THOSE WHO NEED IT.
END

WITH THIS NEW POWER, THE GUARDIANS BUILT A WORLD FROM WHERE THEY COULD WATCH OVER THE UNIVERSE-- *THE PLANET OA.*

STORING THE ENERGY IN A *CENTRAL POWER BATTERY,* THE GUARDIANS *FORGED RINGS* CAPABLE OF CHANNELING IT.

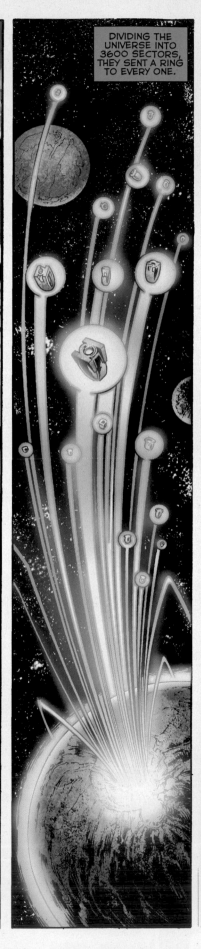

DIVIDING THE UNIVERSE INTO 3600 SECTORS, THEY SENT A RING TO EVERY ONE.

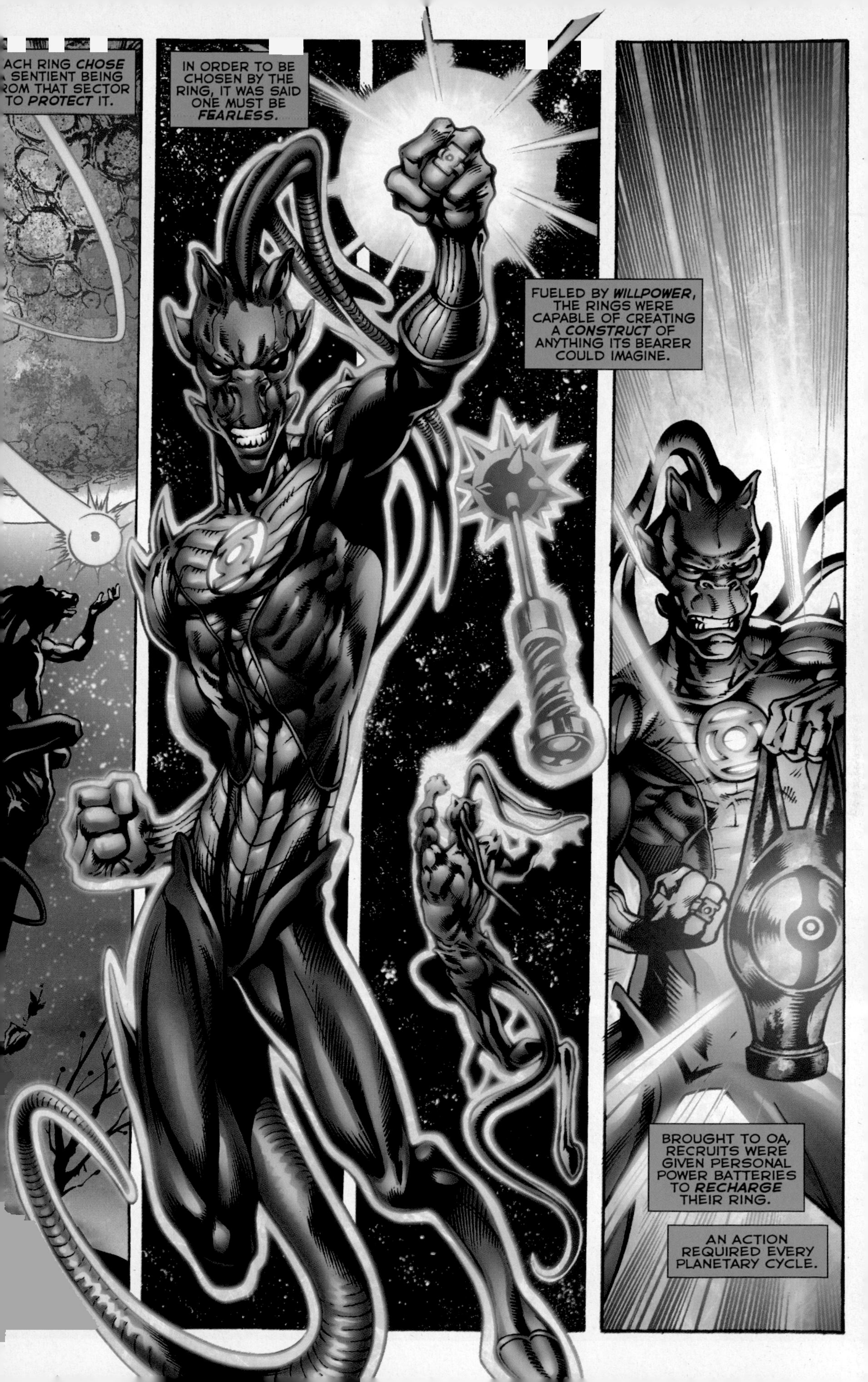
ACH RING *CHOSE* SENTIENT BEING ROM THAT SECTOR TO *PROTECT* IT.
IN ORDER TO BE CHOSEN BY THE RING, IT WAS SAID ONE MUST BE *FEARLESS*.
FUELED BY *WILLPOWER*, THE RINGS WERE CAPABLE OF CREATING A *CONSTRUCT* OF ANYTHING ITS BEARER COULD IMAGINE.
BROUGHT TO OA, RECRUITS WERE GIVEN PERSONAL POWER BATTERIES TO *RECHARGE* THEIR RING.
AN ACTION REQUIRED EVERY PLANETARY CYCLE.

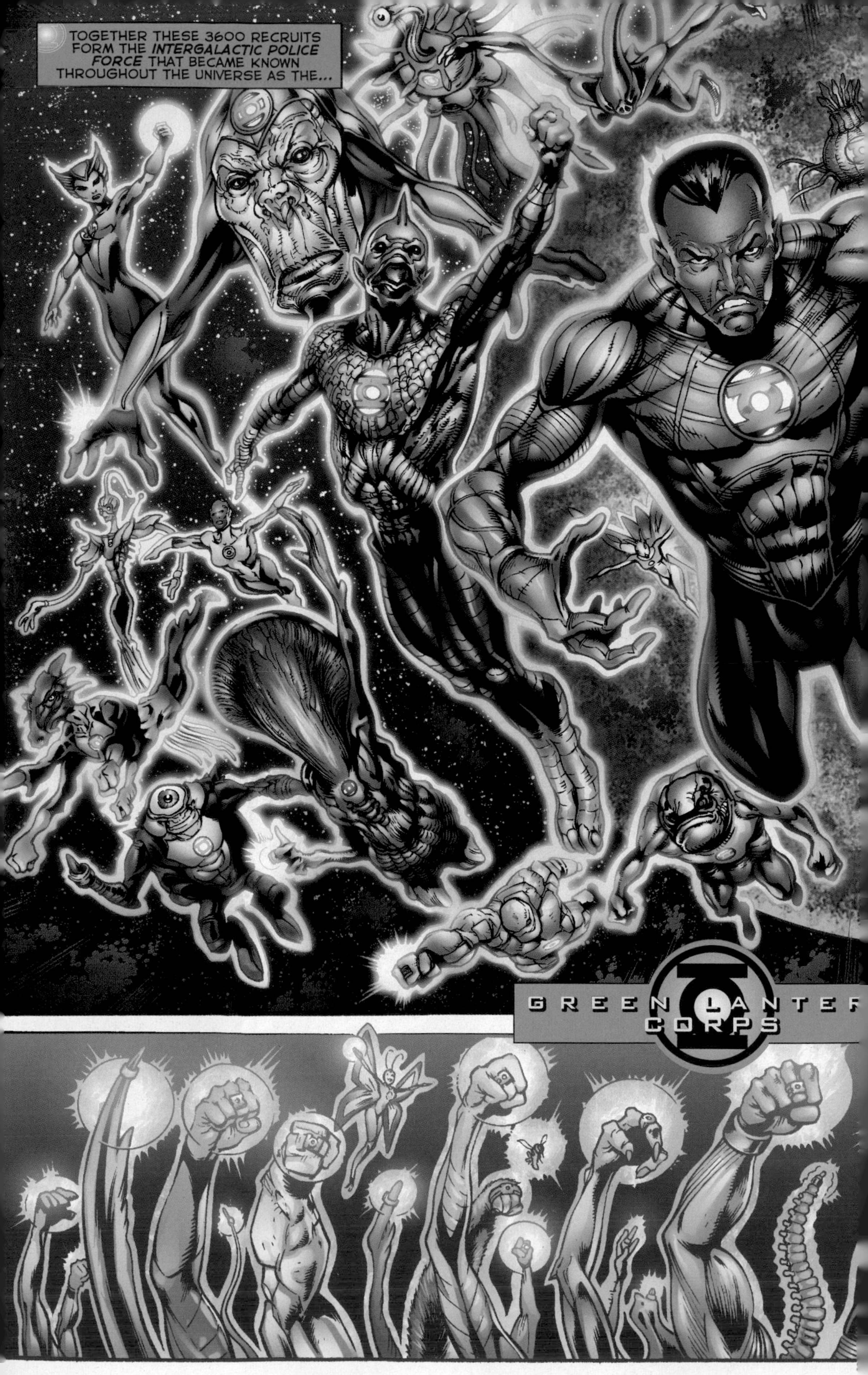
TOGETHER THESE 3600 RECRUITS FORM THE *INTERGALACTIC POLICE FORCE* THAT BECAME KNOWN THROUGHOUT THE UNIVERSE AS THE...
GREEN LANTERN CORPS

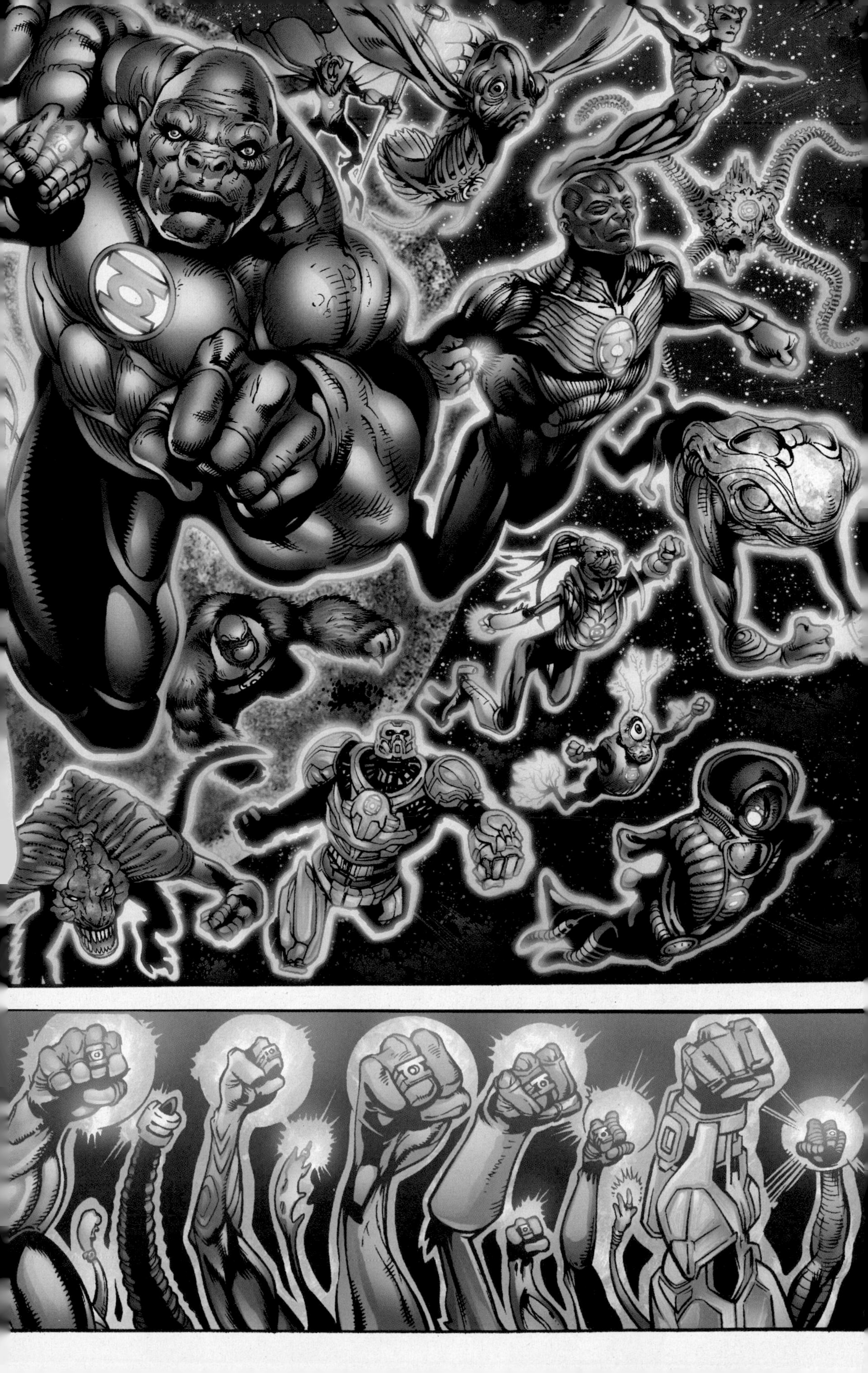

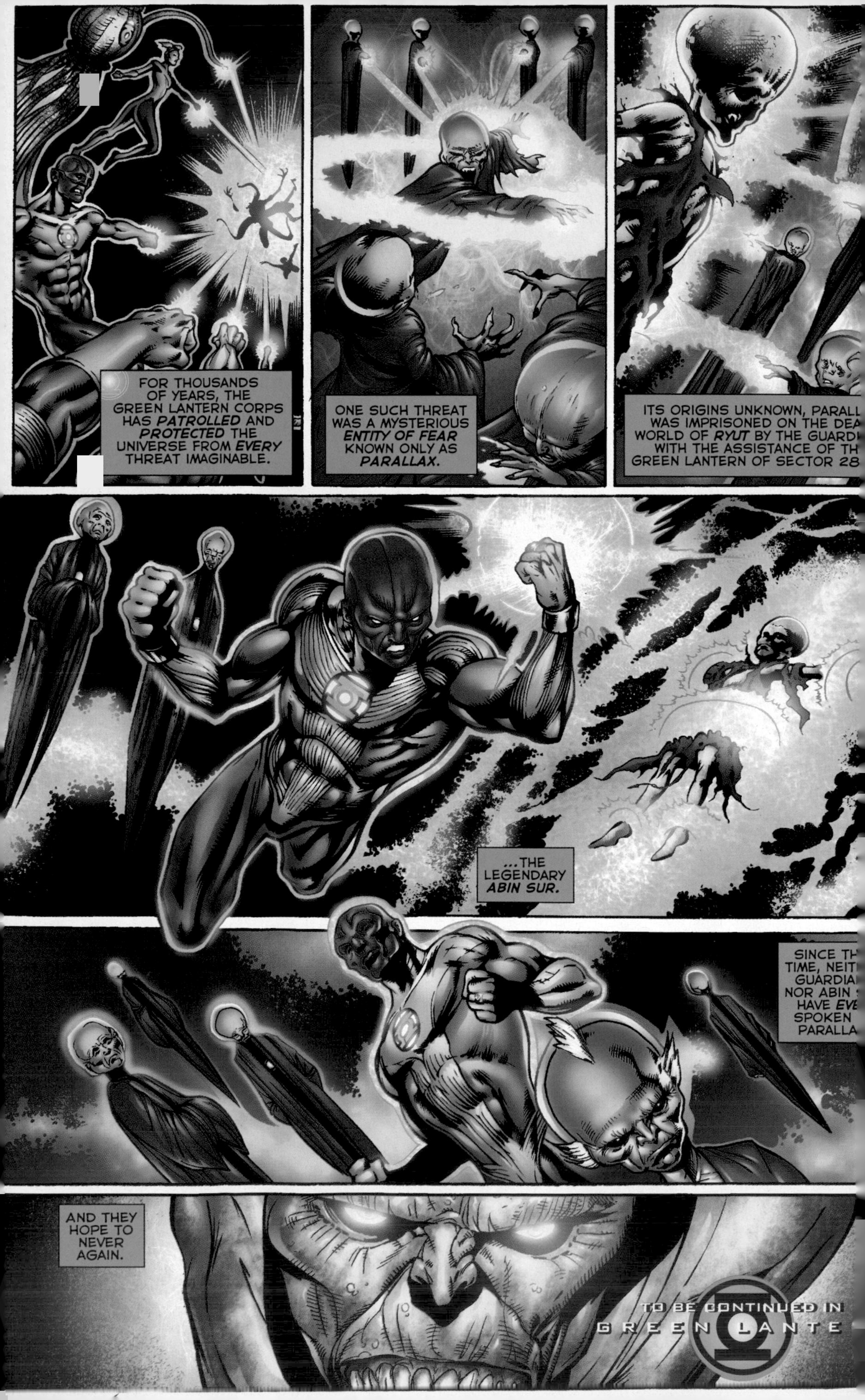
FOR THOUSANDS OF YEARS, THE GREEN LANTERN CORPS HAS PATROLLED AND PROTECTED THE UNIVERSE FROM EVERY THREAT IMAGINABLE.
ONE SUCH THREAT WAS A MYSTERIOUS ENTITY OF FEAR KNOWN ONLY AS PARALLAX.
ITS ORIGINS UNKNOWN, PARALL
WAS IMPRISONED ON THE DEA
WORLD OF RYUT BY THE GUARDI
WITH THE ASSISTANCE OF TH
GREEN LANTERN OF SECTOR 28
...THE LEGENDARY ABIN SUR.
SINCE TH
TIME, NEIT
GUARDIA
NOR ABIN
HAVE EVE
SPOKEN
PARALLA
AND THEY HOPE TO NEVER AGAIN.
TO BE CONTINUED IN
GREEN LANTE

MOVIE EXCLUSIVE

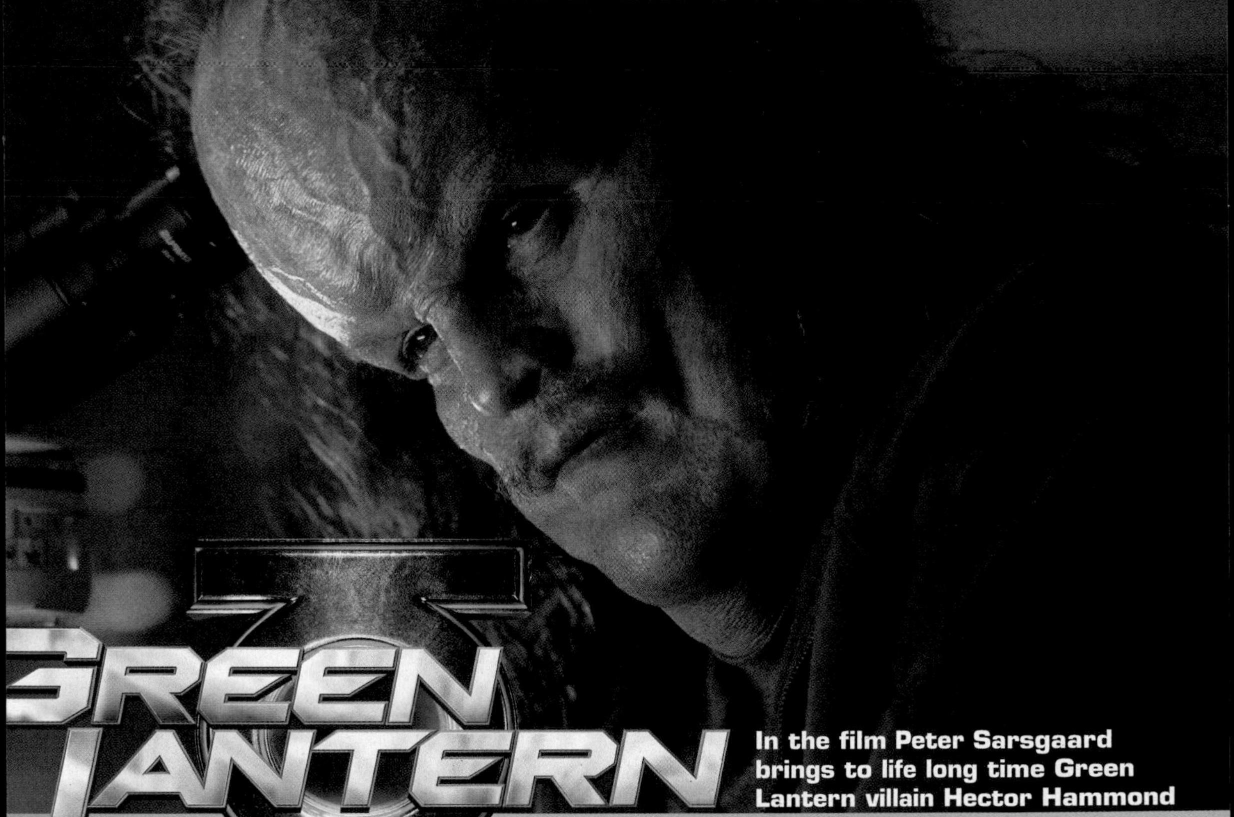
GREEN LANTERN

In the film Peter Sarsgaard brings to life long time Green Lantern villain Hector Hammond

ver let fear overcome you.

e we reintroduced Hal Jordan and the Green Lantern ps in 2004's GREEN LANTERN: REBIRTH, fear has been e center of our stories. In our world, fear is a force in our that we can't touch or quantify, but it is very real. It's ething that can keep us from following our dreams, it can te hate and it can paralyze us from living our lives with reedom we all deserve. I wanted to make fear very real e world of GREEN LANTERN, and I think that's part of uccess of the characters. It's not that Green Lanterns are en because they have no fear, it's because they have the y to overcome fear.

ot everyone does.

e people give in to fear and live a life surrounded by his is exactly what happens to Doctor Hector Hammond e GREEN LANTERN film. But before I briefly talk about or Hammond, let me back up and acknowledge that bi- ly cool still up there.

u're reading this, chances are you already know of the se of the first-ever live-action GREEN LANTERN movie ng Ryan Reynolds as the quintessential Hal Jordan, the derful Blake Lively as Carol Ferris, Mark Strong as the ct Sinestro and the unbelievable Peter Sarsgaard as or Hammond. If you didn't know we're that close to seeing Kilowog, Oa, Ferris Air and the Guardians of the Universe up on the big screen, now you do.

Last summer, I was on set down in smoldering New Orleans with producer Donald De Line during one of the scenes with Hal and Hector. (And to give you an idea of how into it Donald is, he was wearing his Green Lantern ring.) When Peter Sarsgaard walked on stage in full makeup it was scary. Hector Hammond has been a longtime character in the comics, someone I've enjoyed writing myself, but this scientist turned highly evolved telepath was never portrayed as frightening or as human as this. I was captivated watching director Martin Campbell (Casino Royale, The Mask of Zorro) work with Peter on getting a performance that, for me, elevated Hector Hammond to an entirely new level. Peter took the air out of the room. We were all speechless, mesmerized not only by the makeup that turned this grotesque longtime enemy of Green Lantern into a reality, but more important, by each and every word coming out of Peter's mouth. Hector Hammond has become a formidable and very real force for fear.

Coming up in the following pages you'll get looks at Hal's power battery and ring, the aliens of the Green Lantern Corps, Oa, the Guardians of the Universe and even the greatest Green Lantern that's ever lived…Sinestro!

All will be well,

Geoff Johns

Mark Strong IS Sinestro!

GREEN LANTERN

THE GREATEST GREEN LANTERN!

Before Sinestro fell from grace, becoming the ultimate Green Lantern villain and one of the greatest foes in history… he was the finest Green Lantern ever.

Respected by his Corpsmen and trusted by the immortal Guardians of the Universe, Sinestro is considered the greatest Green Lantern, having preserved definitive order in his sector. This regal Korugarian commands attention and needed an actor that could portray the same. Could anyone live up to the perfection of Sinestro?

Have No Fear, for Mark Strong IS Sinestro!

When Mark Strong *(Sherlock Holmes, Robin Hood, Kick Ass)* arrived on the set decked out in make-up and prosthetics, I thought Sinestro had walked right off the comics page. Take a look at that still… just incredible!

Back in August, I visited the Green Lantern movie set with Blackest Night and Sinestro Corps masterminds Geoff Johns and Ivan Reis – and what a trip it was. My mind is still blown from the experience. I was given the opportunity to hold the actual Power Battery and was able to wear the

Green Lantern ring… *In B…est Day, In Blackest* – sorry carried away. I could go o… pages about the amazing duction designs, how surreal Ryan Reynolds looke… Hal Jordan's flight suit, or how awestruck I wa… early CG tests of Oa and the different Green Lanterns, but instead let me focus the supreme highlight.

Sinestro.

I witnessed scenes of Sinestro in action, addressing entire Corps, and speaking with the Guardians. The … time I was glued to my seat, unable to turn away. Mark … it all. The voice – the demeanor – everything! Mark much of the film, has taken his inspiration from Geoff J… extraordinary run on GREEN LANTERN.

The same care and enthusiasm is being brought t… Green Lantern movie by visionary director Martin Can… *(Casino Royale)*, producer Donald De Line and the rest … cast and crew. I am beyond excited!

Long Live the Corps!!!!

Adam Schlagman

Tomar-Re brought to life by Sony Imageworks.

GREEN LANTERN

ALL IN THE DETAILS…

...a mantra Tomar-Re lives by which has aided him in ...ming an honored and highly respected Green Lantern. ...also a mantra that the filmmakers, like production ...ner Grant Major, costume designer Ngila Dickson and ...l effects supervisor Jim Berny have taken as their own. ...ucer Donald De Line and director Martin Campbell have ...nbled an amazing corps.

...ving up on the planet Xudar, Tomar-Re comes from a ...eful avian race that focuses their efforts on the arts and ...ces instead of war. His nature to examine everything has ...e Guardians of the Universe to appoint him the archivist ...protector of the sacred Book of Oa. When not studying ...ature of the Corps, Tomar-Re patrols sector 2813 where ...eveloped a close friendship with neighboring sector ...'s Green Lantern, Abin Sur. Tomar has taken an interest ...in's replacement Hal Jordan. Though Hal is *not* one ...etails, Tomar hopes to teach Hal what it means to be a ...n Lantern.

...the same thoughtfulness that Tomar-Re believes in is ...utilized to bring him and the rest of the Green Lantern ...s to life on the big screen.

We've watched test after test supervised by digital effects master Jim Berney based on the amazing design work by Grant and Ngila. Their passion for detail is much like Tomar-Re's. Something I found extremely interesting was the mix of motion capture and straight-up animation they used in creating the Green Lantern Corps. Some of the more humanoid Corps members like Tomar-Re and Kilowog started with motion capture, but most of their flying and movement beyond simple interaction was animated, some based on the movement of insects or animals and others created completely from scratch – giving them all a unique, and alien, feel. It's this attention to detail – from the scales on Tomar-Re's skin to the way he turns when he flies into the air – that will give the Green Lantern Corps more life than it's ever seen.

With talented people like Grant, Ngila and Jim and his team pouring their heart and soul into this, it makes you realize even more than you might already how truly amazing the Green Lantern universe is.

Let's follow the advice that Tomar-Re would give to Hal: Follow your heart, believe in your will and never, ever disrespect Sinestro!

Geoff Johns

GREEN LANTERN

KILOWOG - as brought to life by Sony Imageworks

One of the greatest challenges for the Green Lantern fi[...]
bringing the Green Lantern Corps to life. It falls to the [...]
of dozens of people overseen by director Martin Cam[...]
and led by production designer Grant Major and cos[...]
designer Ngila Dickson.

We've taken a look at the spiritual trainer of the Cor[...]
previous issues with Tomar-Re, but this time the big guy t[...]
the stage. Perhaps the most popular alien Green Lante[...]
next to Sinestro, of course – is the one member of the G[...]
Lantern Corps that can whip any rookie Lantern into sh[...]
Even an Earthman named Hal Jordan.

If the saying "Beware my power" were true for any [...]
Corps member, it'd be the Green Lantern knowr[...]
KILOWOG.

Along with every other GL fan, my introduction to this [...]
of a GL was in 1986's *Green Lantern Corps #201*. Kilo[...]
looked among the most alien of the existing GLs o[...]
day. The lone survivor of his home world Bolovax Vik[...]
came from a society of decidedly Socialist views—idec[...]
a police force where there is no rank. Now, of course[...]
spends most of his time on the Corps' headquartered [...]
of Oa.

And yet, his tough exterior and demeanor belies a thoug[...]
soul, and one couldn't ask for a better ally in letting no[...]
escape your sight. Kilowog might be tough as a rhin[...]
his trainees, doing anything he can to motivate and ed[...]
them. Without a family to call his own, he embrace[...]
rookies as if they were, with a tough love designed to [...]
them alive and do right by the ideals of the Corps.

The filmmakers have captured the essence of Kilo[...]
perfectly in the film. And with film, there's an entirely [...]
dimension to Kilowog and the rest of the Corps mem[...]
You'll see them brought to life with detail and power[...]
could never imagine.

Beware his power!

Brian Cunningham
Green Lantern Editor

: Nation,

'ear, Green Lantern is primed to take the world by with WAR OF THE GREEN LANTERNS in the comics, REEN LANTERN: ANIMATED SERIES this fall, GREEN ERN: RISE OF THE MANHUNTERS videogame, an ng line of consumer products and of course the GREEN ERN film. Everyone will understand the mantra NO FEAR 'ill be reciting the sacred oath.

y first look at the beginning of August 2010 when I visited reen Lantern Movie Set with team GREEN LANTERN/ KEST NIGHT, Geoff Johns and Ivan Reis. And what a trip My mind is still blown from the experience, but read on ne of the highlights I'm allowed to spill.

we arrived on set, producer Donald De Line greeted us. d is working closely with Chief Creative Officer Geoff to ensure that the Green Lantern Feature Film stays true characters. Donald excitedly brought us to view some tronics; we were awestruck to see a flythrough of Oa G tests of the different alien Green Lanterns. Production er Grant Major and costume designer Ngila Dickson Academy Award winners!) have been working tirelessly g the world of Green Lantern to life.

ome items had already been created... the props. I was o clutch the Power Battery in my hand and wear the Lantern ring. Check out these photos of Ivan and me ng up.

ere's Geoff near Hal Jordan's cockpit.

n steering the film is visionary director Martin Campbell o *Royale*). He has embraced the intricacies of the ogy and is bringing the world of Green Lantern to the een in an immense way. After a nice conversation about book flicks, it was time for filming.

entering the stage, we found ourselves completely nded by blue screens. You may ask why blue and not screens? Well, that's because the green, in the Green n costumes and their constructs, would be difficult to uish from a green background.

; Ryan Reynolds, and he's wearing Hal Jordan's flight cool! Ryan even swung by to say hello. Geoff John's LANTERN: SECRET ORIGIN is Ryan's bible and tion.

nly Mark Strong, who plays Sinestro, arrived. Just jaw ng. It's like Sinestro literally walked right off the comic We were able to witness scenes of Sinestro in action, sing the entire Corps and speaking with the Guardians. ailed 'em all!

pleased and grateful to the cast, crew and staff for such edible time and for their amazing vision, dedication termination in making this movie as great as it can be. een Lantern Corps couldn't be in better hands.

ve the Corps!!!

Schlagman

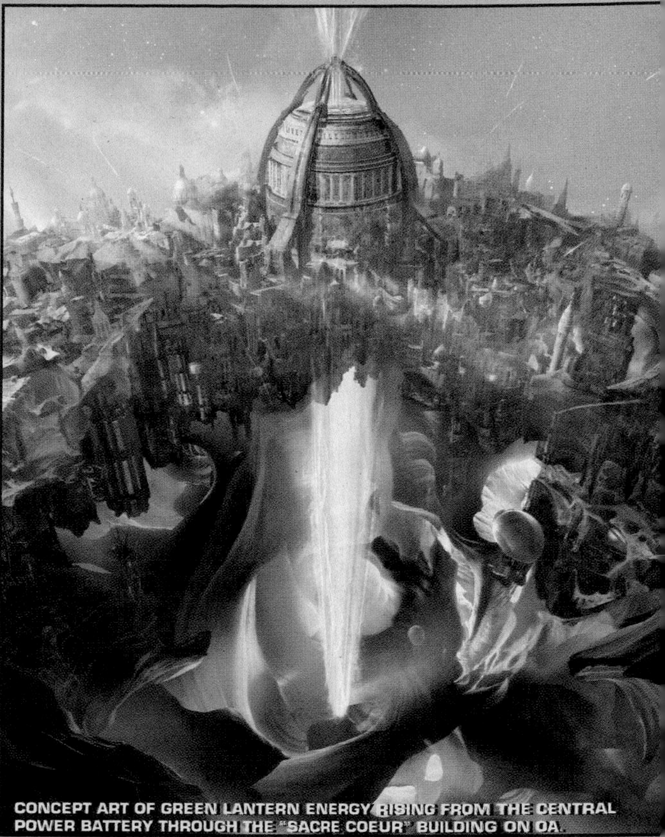

CONCEPT ART OF GREEN LANTERN ENERGY RISING FROM THE CENTRAL POWER BATTERY THROUGH THE "SACRE COEUR" BUILDING ON OA.

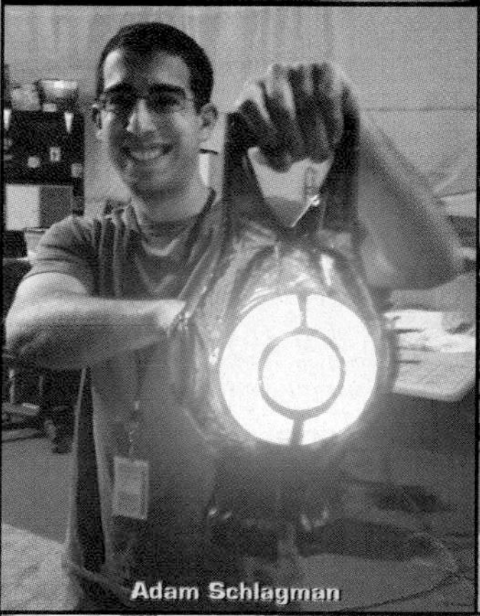

Adam Schlagman

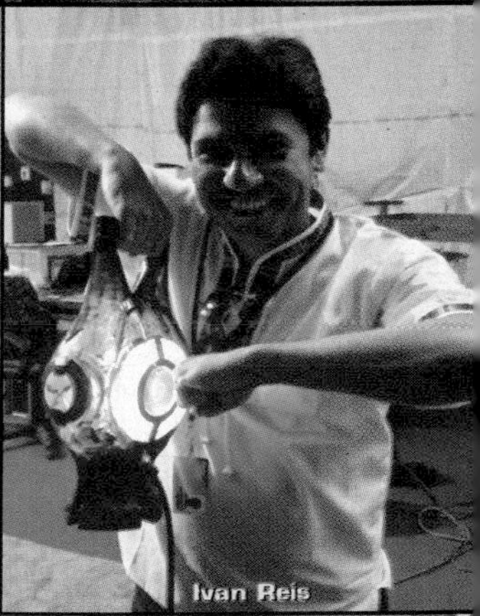

Ivan Reis

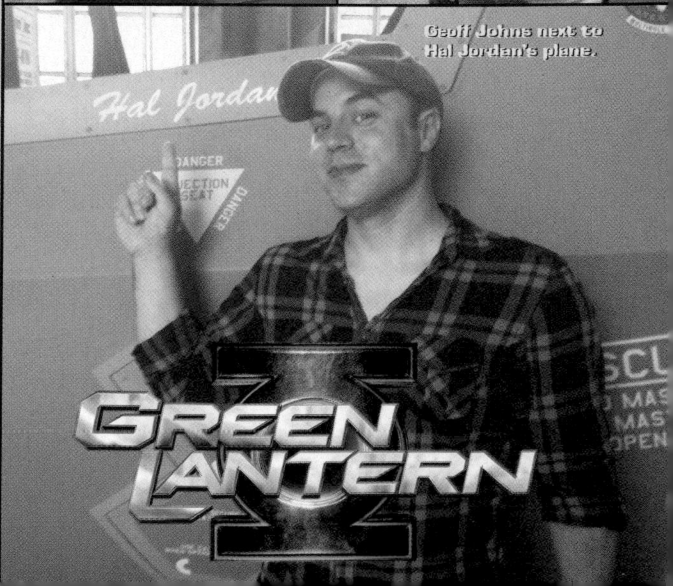
Hal Jordan
DANGER
EJECTION SEAT
GREEN LANTERN

Geoff Johns next to Hal Jordan's plane.

**Actor Temuera Morrison brings the doomed
Green Lantern officer to life on screen.**

Every story has a beginning.

So it's only fitting that in the ordered world the Guardians of the Universe seek that their mo
legendary Green Lantern starts with an "A."

Abin Sur, portrayed in the GREEN LANTERN film with pitch-perfect nuance by Temuer
Morrison (best known for his role as Jango Fett in *Star Wars: Episode II—Attack of th
Clones*).

A courageous alien from the planet Ungara, this Green Lantern was charged with protectir
sector 2814. His deeds were grand, but he gained true immortality with his actions in th
moment of his death. Having crashed to Earth in his vessel, he sent his power ring to see
out a successor – someone worthy to carry on the mantle. It selected a man capable o
overcoming great fear – test pilot Hal Jordan.

The rest is cosmic history told in the Book of Oa.

We saw the first glimpse of Abin at Comic Con as his dead body was placed on display. B
here we get to see how Abin is brought to life on screen – and how amazingly and vibrant
the emerald light flows off him.

It's clear that the movie team has taken great care to translate to the silver screen th
amazing artwork and designs of former GREEN LANTERN artist Ivan Reis concocted in th
"Secret Origin" arc that inspired the film.

Abin Sur, and the GREEN LANTERN feature film, has summoned movie audiences to witne
Abin's final instrumental act as Hal Jordan is chosen as the new Green Lantern of Sect
2814!

Eddie Berganza
DC Comics Executive Editor

The Great Hall of Oa

...EN LANTERN is an epic sci-fi adventure!

...feature film transports us on a journey through the stars to the alien planet Oa — the central ...inct of the Green Lantern Corps.

...h an abundance of futuristic spacecraft and ancient alien architecture and unique Green ...erns, Oa is a world like no other. Production Designer Grant Major and Sony Imageworks ...e put great effort into the creation of the planet, its detailed features and the Corps members ...inhabit it. On this very page you can catch a glimpse of the Great Hall featuring the Green ...ern Corps gathered together.

...Green Lantern Corps is composed of thousands of unique alien creatures spanning the ...erse from diverse worlds, extraterrestrial cultures and strange societies. Many of these ...erns are featured in the film. Playing key roles are the legendary Abin Sur, drill-sergeant ...uordinaire Kilowog, the detail-oriented Tomar-Re and of course the greatest of them all, ...stro.

...here are many other fan-favorite alien corpsmen sprinkled throughout. See if you can spot ...e of these fearless Lanterns in the film:

...odikka, one of the fiercest warriors
...zd, the smallest and boldest
...annu, the Lantern who would prefer to use his fists before his ring
...rvox, the friendly insectoid
...een Man, the most dedicated and loyal
...edphyll, the experienced veteran plant life-form
...orro, the caretaker of the Crypts
...amey Holl, the recent majestic recruit
...t Lop Fan, an enigma
...laak, the ultimate multitasker
...el, the battle-driven sentient robot
...z, the no-nonsense Warden of the Sciencells

...een Lantern, they are joined by
...ery first Earthman: Hal Jordan!

...m Schlagman
...tive Executive

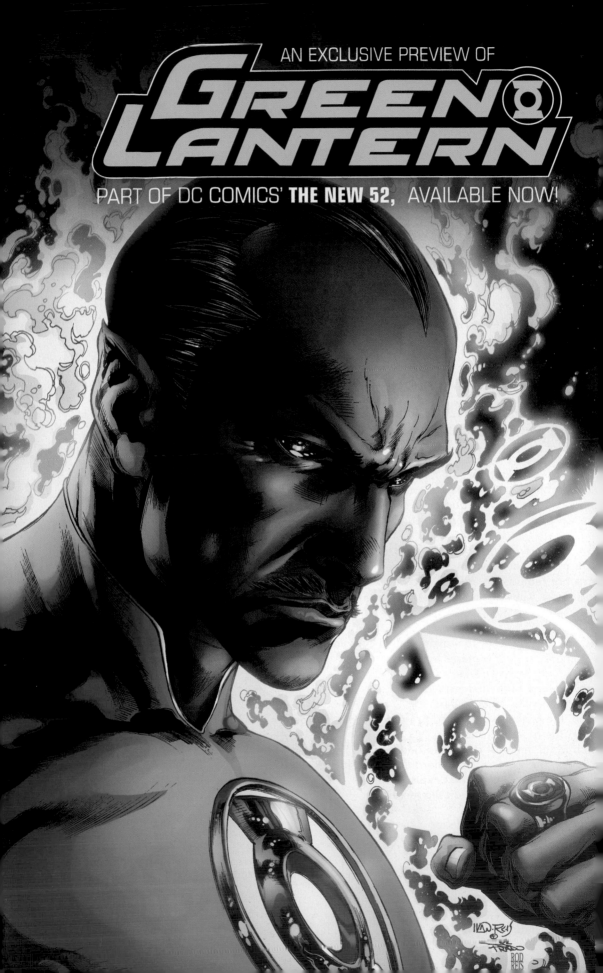

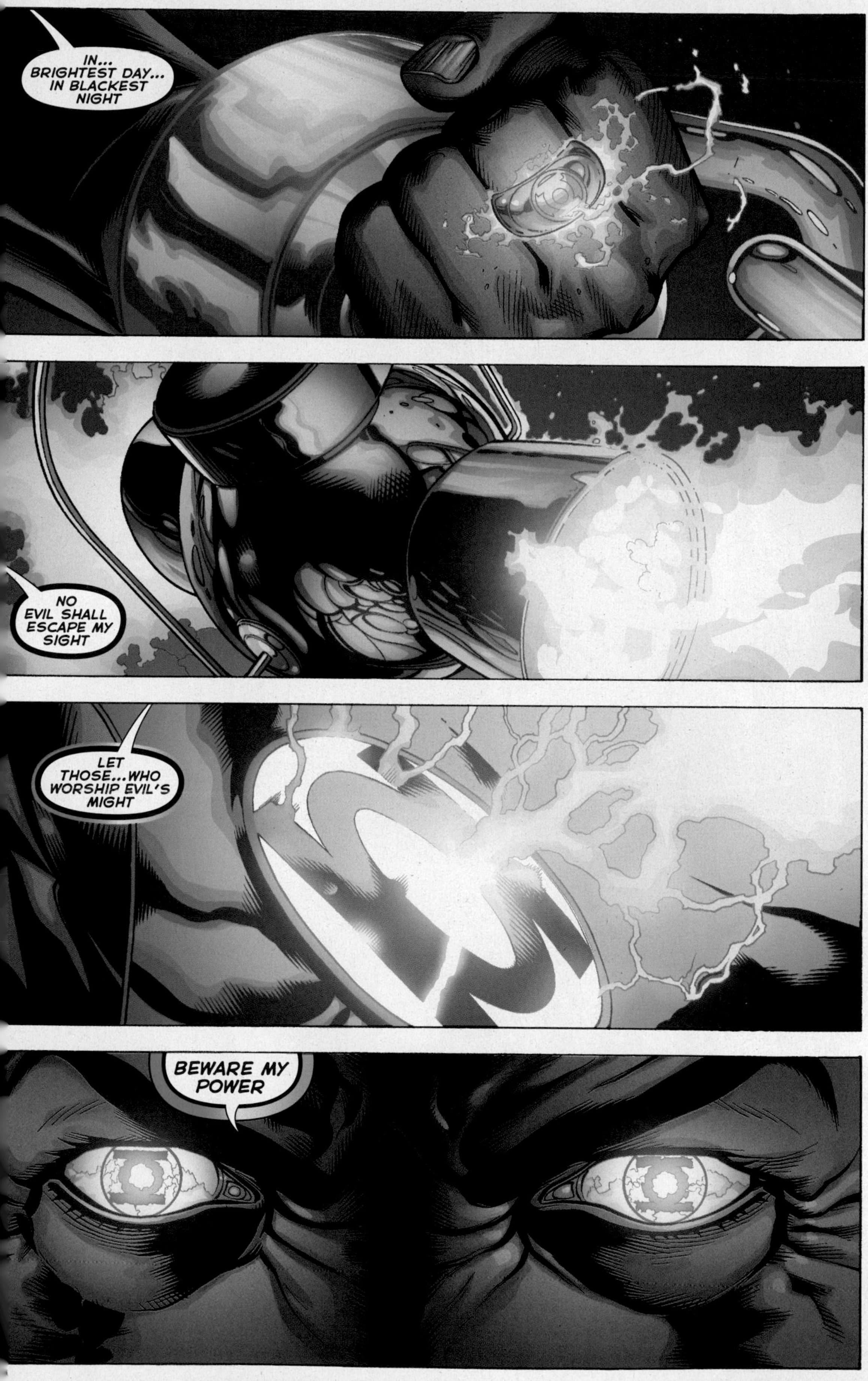
IN... BRIGHTEST DAY... IN BLACKEST NIGHT
NO EVIL SHALL ESCAPE MY SIGHT
LET THOSE...WHO WORSHIP EVIL'S MIGHT
BEWARE MY POWER

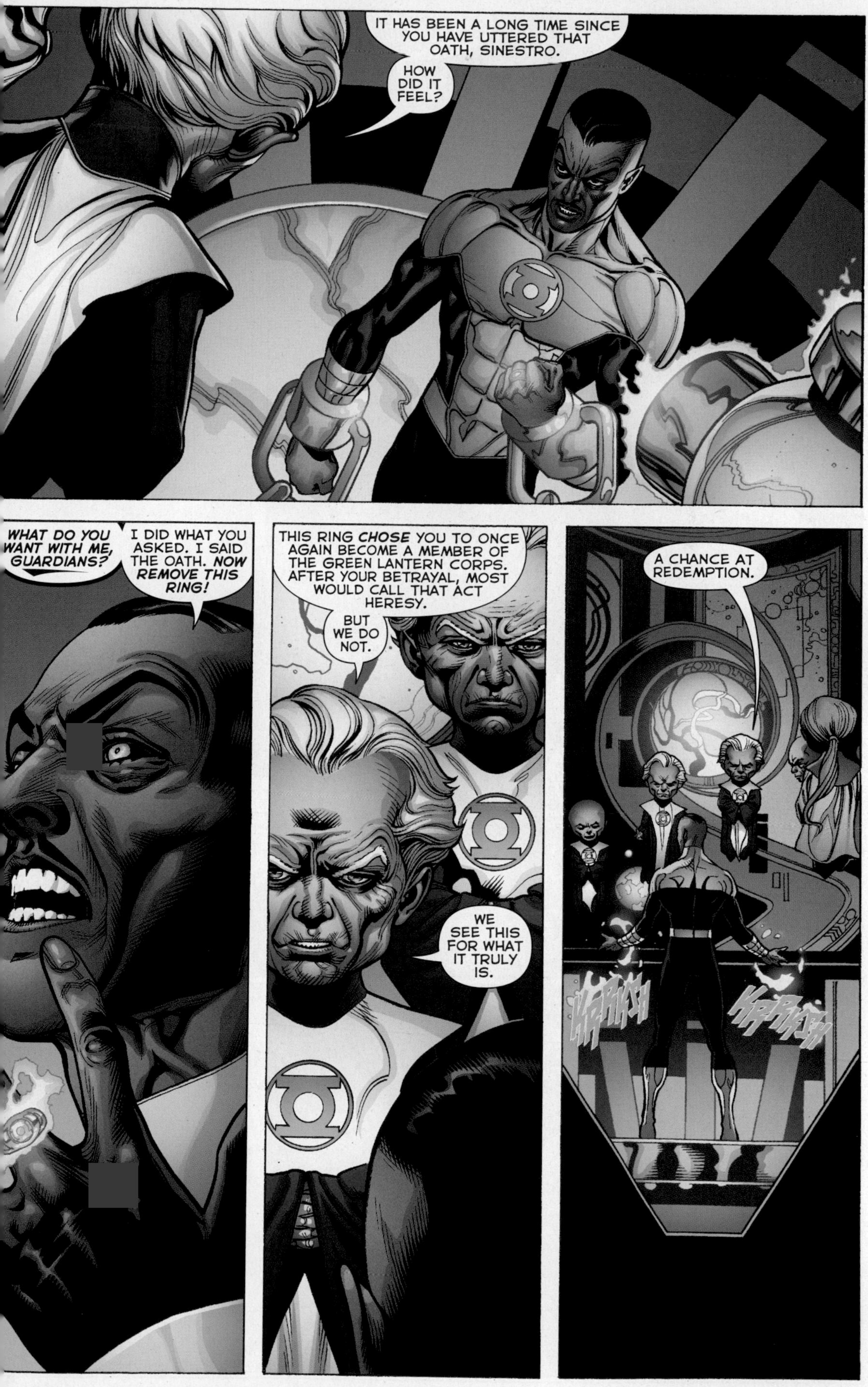
IT HAS BEEN A LONG TIME SINCE YOU HAVE UTTERED THAT OATH, SINESTRO.
HOW DID IT FEEL?
WHAT DO YOU WANT WITH ME, GUARDIANS?
I DID WHAT YOU ASKED. I SAID THE OATH. NOW REMOVE THIS RING!
THIS RING CHOSE YOU TO ONCE AGAIN BECOME A MEMBER OF THE GREEN LANTERN CORPS. AFTER YOUR BETRAYAL, MOST WOULD CALL THAT ACT HERESY.
BUT WE DO NOT.
WE SEE THIS FOR WHAT IT TRULY IS.
A CHANCE AT REDEMPTION.